Confrontation

CONFRONTATION
The Middle-East War and World Politics

Walter Laqueur

Wildwood House · Abacus

First published 1974 simultaneously by
Wildwood House and Sphere Books
© 1974 by Walter Laqueur

Hardback edition by Wildwood House Ltd,
1 Wardour Street, London W1V 3HE

ISBN 0 7045 0096 5

Paperback edition by Abacus, 30-32 Gray's Inn Road,
London WC1X 8JL

ISBN 0 349 12159 1

The author and publishers gratefully acknowledge permission
to reproduce extracts from copyright material which appear
on the following pages:
page 7 from *A Dictionary of Modern War* by Edward Luttwak
(Allen Lane, London, 1971), © Edward Luttwak 1971; also by permission
of Harper & Row, Publishers Inc., New York
page 35 from *Eretz Hazvi* by Arye Eliav (Am Oved, Tel Aviv, 1972)
pages 232-3 from *The Road to War* by Walter Laqueur (Weidenfeld
and Nicolson, London, 1968; Macmillan & Co., New York)

Printed and bound in Great Britain
by Butler and Tanner Ltd, Frome and London

Contents

Preface

The fourth Arab-Israeli war was nicknamed 'Operation Spark' by President Sadat. It sparked off a crisis in détente, the eclipse, temporary or permanent, of Western Europe, a world energy shortage and it also opened a new phase in the struggle for the Middle East. This multiple crisis is the subject of a book which starts with the pre-history of the war of Yom Kippur (or 10 Ramadan) and ends with the signing of a first accord between Israeli and Egyptian representatives on November 11th, 1973. It deals with both a local conflict and world politics, with military, political and economic warfare. It was easy to write the history of the Six Day War because it was in the last resort only a local war; in 1973 the whole world was affected, the scene constantly shifted and the end is not yet in sight.

The value of an account provided so soon after the events will be disputed by some but there are also advantages in writing with the atmosphere of the crisis fresh in mind, before myth-making takes over. I had no access to unpublished material but these documents will not be available anyway for many years. I would hazard the guess that about 90 per cent of the sources of interest to the historian are almost immediately available; one only has to know where to look for them, as the late Sir Lewis Namier used to say. There are some unsolved questions that I have tried to indicate in my account. I faced a similar problem in 1967 when I wrote *The Road to War* (*The Road to Jerusalem*, in the American edition); many new details have come to light since but I saw no necessity to revise my views as far as the broad outlines of the history of that war was concerned. The present study is to a certain, limited extent based on conversations with some of the *dramatis personae*. Though I refer in this study mainly to newspaper accounts I had the opportunity to discuss the events described with some of those who had taken part in the decisive meetings in Washington and Moscow, in Tel Aviv and Cairo. It was possible on occasion to lift slightly the veil of mystery, only to realize that there was no mystery.

The lack of historical perspective is a greater problem than the apparent lack of sources. But a definitive history of this crisis will be written only many years hence and the aim of this book is far more modest: to provide an anatomy of a local crisis which became a world conflict. The greatest difficulty was in keeping a certain detachment at a time when passions were running high. While there is no such thing as a history acceptable to both Israelis and Arabs, Russians and Americans, oil producers and oil consumers it is equally true that there is little value in a partisan account other than boosting the morale of one's side. Madelin once wrote that the historian ought to stand upon the wall of the besieged city and behold at the same time the besiegers and the besieged. Unfortunately this is easier said than done and it may also mean that one fails to get a good look at either side. I have tried hard not to ignore the aspirations and interests of all those involved, I have not attempted to write pseudo-objective history. It would be unreasonable to expect all critics and readers to share one's views; the only sensible course of action in this context (as in others) is Dante's: '*Segui il tuo corso, e lascia dir le genti*.' ('Do your own thing, and let people say what they will.')

In this book I have drawn on articles I published in *Commentary* ('On the Soviet departure from Egypt', December 1972; 'Oil', written with Edward Luttwak, September 1973, and 'Kissinger', December 1973). In writing the third chapter I was greatly helped by Major General (ret.) Dr Mattityahu Peled and Dr Martin van Creveld; as I have indicated in the text much of this chapter is their work rather than mine. I am greatly indebted to Henry Pavlovich for having helped me with the research on Chapter Five, Annabel Whittet and Bernard Krikler for having read the whole manuscript and, needless to say, improved it.

WALTER LAQUEUR

London/Washington
January 1974

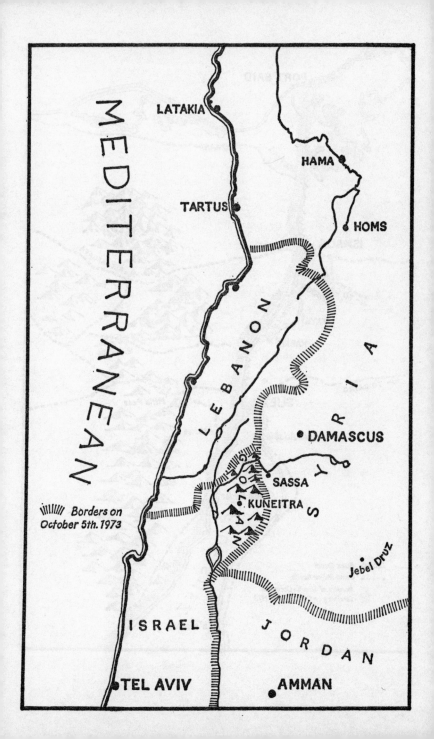

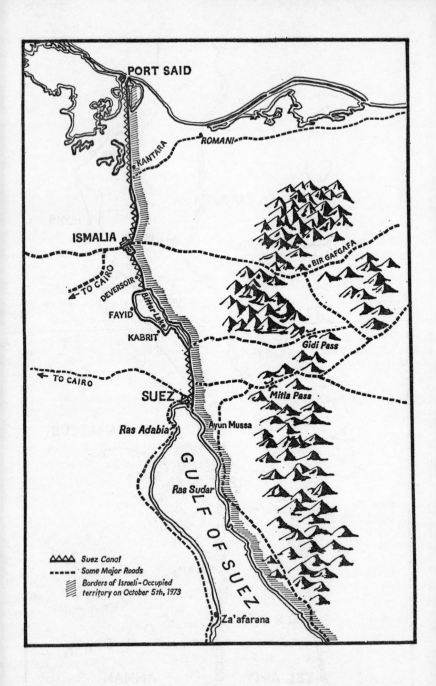

PORT SAID

KANTARA

ROMANI

ISMALIA

BIR GAFGAFA

TO CAIRO

DEVERSOIR

Bitter Lake

FAYID

KABRIT

Gidi Pass

TO CAIRO

Mitla Pass

SUEZ

Ras Adabia

Ayun Mussa

G U L F   O F   S U E Z

Ras Sudar

ΛΛΛΛ Suez Canal
------ Some Major Roads
        Borders of Israeli-Occupied
        territory on October 5th, 1973

Za'afarana

Chapter One   From War to War

The Six Day War ended on the Egyptian front on the morning of June 9th, 1967. On the Syrian front fighting slowly petered out the day after. In the course of the war 679 Israeli soldiers had been killed and 2,563 wounded. Eleven thousand and five hundred Egyptians were killed; 6,094 Jordanian soldiers were killed or missing; and the Syrians did not publish exact figures. The cost of the war to Israel was, according to its finance minister, $750 million; as for the Egyptians, President Nasser estimated that they had lost 80 per cent of their war material.

It was only when the guns fell silent that the Israelis realized the full magnitude of their victory. A week before the very survival of the state had been at stake; surrounded by enemies who had sworn to throw the Jewish intruders into the sea, militarily outnumbered by a wide margin, they had not expected in their wildest dreams that the formidable armies threatening them would be routed within a matter of days. True, in later years some Israeli generals and politicians would argue that the fears and apprehensions of the pre-war days had been unjustified, that the existence of the state was never really in danger. But this is arguing with the benefit of hindsight. The Israeli generals were confident on June 4th that quality would prevail over quantity, that the higher morale of their forces and their better training would be decisive in the end, despite the enemy's massive Soviet equipment of tanks, heavy guns and aircraft. There was confidence, but there was no certainty.

The shock in the Arab states was even greater. Only a few days earlier they had exchanged messages to the effect that they would soon meet again in Jerusalem and Tel Aviv, the only question being who would be there first. The hour of liberation of the Arab homeland had struck. Israel was doomed. Arab leaders found it impossible even to consider that Israel could successfully defend itself. True, it had resisted attack in 1948, but then it had faced small, unco-ordinated forces, the soldiers of King Faruq, King Abdullah, the Iraqi Hashemites and some bungling Syrian politicians. In 1956 the Israelis had reached the Suez Canal after a few days of fighting, but this campaign had been carried out in collusion with the British and the French. In 1967 Israel was alone, having to cope not with one Arab country but with several of them. Above all, the Arabs were fired by a new spirit of Arab revolutionary nationalism, there was a new breed of leaders, true patriots who had done away with the corruption and the incompetence of their predecessors.

Arab expectations were greater in 1967 and so was the shock of defeat. Nasser, as he later said, felt during the first weeks after the defeat 'like a man walking in a desert surrounded by moving sands, not knowing whether, if he moved, he would be swallowed up by the sands or would find the right path'.[1] Yet if the army had crumbled, the home front did not; when Nasser announced his resignation on the evening of June 9th, 1967, popular acclaim ('Nasser, Nasser, don't leave us, we need you') made him change his mind within a few hours. It is quite possible that Nasser had not really wanted to resign and that the demonstrations were stage-managed; but in any case he still had the support of the masses. The feeling among the people was that without Nasser they would be utterly helpless, like children without a father. The generals had failed and were disgraced, but there was little blame for Nasser.

The military losses were staggering. Egypt had lost two-thirds of its military aircraft – most of them on the very first day of fighting – 800 of its 1,000 tanks, and most of its guns. In these critical days the Soviet Union stepped in, the true friend of the Arab cause. An air bridge was established almost the moment the cease-fire went into force; several ships loaded with planes, tanks, and other war supplies appeared in Egyptian ports every week. These Soviet deliveries of modern war material worth billions of dollars were not only militarily significant, they were of great political importance. Egypt had lost a battle, but it was not to concede defeat in what was to be a long drawn-out war. At the Khartoum conference of the heads of Arab states, not long after the end of the war, Egypt was to declare defiantly, 'No recognition of Israel, no negotiations, no peace.' Not long after, the little Israeli destroyer *Eilat* was hit and sunk by an Egyptian rocket vessel of Soviet origin near Port Said, and the Egyptian forces on the west bank of the canal began shelling the Israeli positions on the other side. The Egyptians steadily massed their forces on the canal; they felt both strong and confident enough to escalate the fighting. Fifteen Israeli soldiers were killed and many more wounded in a massive artillery barrage in the space of a few hours. Eventually the Israelis were to lose almost as many men in the border war as during the six days of 1967.

A certain recurring pattern emerged: the Egyptians would intensify their shelling along a front line of more than a hundred miles, the Israelis would retaliate with commando raids deep into the Egyptian rear. In record time in January and February 1969 the Israelis built the Bar Lev line, a series of fortifications to replace the flimsy provisional constructions which had hitherto provided but little shelter for the thin line of Israelis holding the east bank. In an artillery duel in March 1969 the Egyptian chief of staff was killed; soon after a countrywide blackout was introduced. On April 1st, Nasser declared that the ceasefire was null and void; in June he announced that the war of attrition had begun. Fighting reached a new climax on July 20th, 1969, when Israeli air power was first thrown into battle on a massive scale to attack the Egyptian gun and missile positions. Three days later the Egyptian president declared that the third and final stage of liberation had been reached, which would lead to the crossing of the canal. But the effects of the Israeli air offensive were soon felt; it had succeeded in destroying many Egyptian anti-aircraft gun positions and SAM-2 missile sites. Israeli forces along the canal were heavily outnumbered in men and artillery; it was Dayan's strategy to relieve the pressure by means of a limited air offensive which, however, gradually crept closer to Cairo and other centres in the rear. The U.N. secretary general had reported in early July 1969 that the ceasefire had broken down and open warfare was being waged on the canal front, but the real escalation was yet to come.

If Nasser could not expect substantial help from the other Arab countries, how was he to cope with the exodus of half a million civilians from the Canal Zone? Morale in the Egyptian forces (in the words of one commentator) reached a new low: 'The U.A.R. had lost over one-third of its first-line combat aircraft and virtually all of its air defences in the Canal Zone at the cost of only a single Israeli aircraft – a Piper Cub.'[2] But Nasser was not shaken in his resolve to continue the struggle; he rejected the Rogers Plan which even pro-Egyptian observers regarded as 'not unfavourable to Egypt', inasmuch as it proposed that the Israelis should give up virtually all the territory they had seized during the war. Israel reacted with air strikes in depth. Beginning in January 1970, Israeli F-4 Phantoms struck at many targets inside Egypt, including the suburbs of Cairo. In the bombing of a factory at Abu Za'bal on February 12th, 1970, eighty-eight workers were killed. There were frantic calls for Soviet help, and on January 20th, 1970, Nasser went to the Soviet capital. Pointing to the gravity of the situation, he asked for Soviet intervention in the war. The Soviet leaders accepted the fact that the Egyptians needed help urgently; another collapse would have had fatal consequences for the Soviet prestige in the Middle East. But they also realized that a new air bridge and the delivery of more sophisticated equipment would not be sufficient by itself; except for the active participation of thousands of Soviet military experts on every level of the Egyptian defence system, there would be no quick results. And so the decision was taken to intervene in strength.

The *Strategic Survey* of the Institute of Strategic Studies says that 'the sheer volume of Soviet military support for the United Arab Republic during 1970 was without any precedent. Never before had the Soviet Union injected anything like the quantity of sophisticated military equipment into a non-communist country in such a short time.'[3] In fact, it would be difficult to think even of a Warsaw Pact country which received such quantities of arms. A few figures should suffice. At the beginning of 1970 there were no Soviet pilots or missile crews in Egypt. By the end of that year more than 200 Soviet pilots were flying MiG-21J interceptors, and 12-15,000 Soviet officers and soldiers were manning some 80 S A M missile sites. Six airfields were exclusively manned by Soviet personnel; and in addition there were some 4,000 Soviet instructors in the other branches of the Egyptian army.

Soviet intervention had immediate military and political results. The Israeli deep-penetration raids ceased both because they now became very costly – seven Israeli aircraft were destroyed between

June 30th and August 7th – and also because the Israeli Government grew more and more apprehensive of a head-on collision with Soviet forces. Nevertheless, they did clash occasionally. On July 30th five Soviet-piloted MiG-21Js were shot down by Israeli airmen. Most ominous from the Israeli point of view was the fact that the SAM missile sites were inching forwards towards the canal. Israeli air strikes slowed this process but could not halt it. Originally it may have been the Soviet intention merely to provide air cover for the Egyptian cities and thus to make Israeli deep penetration impossible. This eased Nasser's political position somewhat, but it had no effect on the military situation. The Egyptian troops in the front line were severely battered by heavy air strikes: in June alone some two thousand Egyptian casualties were reported. On June 29th Nasser again went to Moscow; that very same night Soviet forces succeeded in establishing a considerable number of SAM-2 and SAM-3 sites on the edges of the canal. As General Bar Lev, the Israeli chief of staff, admitted a few days later, the military balance had shifted seriously against Israel. On August 7th a ceasefire came into force, as part of the (second) Rogers Plan; in the first instance it was to last for ninety days, but in fact it remained in force up to the outbreak of war, more than three years later. By the time the ceasefire came into force a few Soviet missile sites were already within the ceasefire zone and the truce did not prevent the Russians and Egyptians from continuing to build many new sites after August 7th in violation of the terms of the truce.

According to an authoritative report, some 5-600 surface-to-air missile launchers now covered the western approaches to the canal. The forward sites in the system, spread $7\frac{1}{2}$ miles apart, protected not only the canal but also covered an area extending 12 miles beyond the Israeli front line. The Israeli Government protested, and, after checking the evidence, Washington reluctantly admitted that there had been a violation of the ceasefire terms. But in the American view there was nothing that could be done about it. An official government spokesman said that the U.S. administration was satisfied that the U.A.R. did not want to achieve a decisive military advantage with the help of the U.S.S.R. under cover of the ceasefire; the violation of the ceasefire did admittedly strengthen Egyptian defences but it was definitely not an offensive build-up. At the time, it appeared little more than a storm in a teacup; many observers in Washington were a little annoyed by what they regarded as Israeli pettiness. In the end the Israelis themselves, albeit reluctantly, accepted the *faits accomplis*. Only three years later would it appear that the building of a nearly impregnable anti-aircraft wall was of decisive importance, not only with regard to Egyptian air defences but in launching offensive action across the canal. If the canal were to become a battlefield again, Israeli air superiority would no longer be assured. Experience during the war of attrition had shown that Soviet missile sites could be destroyed only at a heavy price, and that it did not take long to make them operational again.

If the Israelis did not at the time insist on the removal of the missile sites, there were a number of reasons which made the S A M bases appear less formidable than they really were: one of them being that those in the armistice zone were within range of heavy Israeli artillery. Furthermore, it was widely assumed that defence (i.e. the S A M sites) in the air-electronics war had just about reached the limit of its effectiveness, whereas the offensive was about to make dramatic progress. This referred above all to certain new E.C.M. devices (electronic counter-measures). During the last months of the war of attrition the Israeli air force had just received the new electronic penetration aids which were quite heavy (about two tons, thus reducing the payload that could be carried by 40 per cent) and the technique of which the pilots had not yet mastered. There was every reason to assume that with the improvement of these devices, the Israeli planes would once again become more than a match for the Egyptian air-defence network. It was also argued that the Soviet-Egyptian air-defence system implied that no Soviet or Egyptian plane could operate within its area.[4]

All this was true, but it disregarded the fact that the Israelis needed air superiority far more than the Egyptians, precisely in view of their inferiority on the ground. Furthermore, the Israelis were not aware at the time that there was still plenty of room for improving anti-aircraft missiles; the Soviets had always invested much more in this field than the West. In addition to the existing surface-to-air missiles (SAM-2 and SAM-3)* even more advanced devices were to appear after the war of attrition: SAM-4 (designated 'Ganef' by NATO) and SAM-6 ('Gainful'). These were mobile missile-launchers and therefore difficult to locate and destroy. If the Israeli planes, such as the F-4 Phantom, out-performed most Soviet aircraft, Soviet-Egyptian air defence limited the Israeli air force's freedom of manoeuvre more and more. The full impact of these changes was to emerge in the first days of fighting in 1973.

The war of attrition had ended in a draw. Nasser had started it because he felt he had no alternative: something had to be done to compel the Israelis to give up the occupied territories. Since all-out war and an invasion of Sinai were thought impossible, the next best thing was to force the Israelis to keep a large part of their manpower under arms, thus weakening their economy. True, Egypt had to pay a heavy price: more than 10,000 casualties and the destruction of many factories and other installations. But there was always the hope that Egypt could afford such losses more easily than Israel. Israel's leaders were inclined to agree with this appraisal, hence their decision to escalate the war rather than play it by Nasser's rules. The decision to engage in deep-penetration raids was a fateful one because it caused massive Soviet intervention. The Israeli Government discussed the issue during the last weeks of 1969; according to some sources, it was widely believed that the deep-penetration raids could even bring about Nasser's fall.[5] The initiative for once did not come only from the right-wing Gahal ministers – among its advocates were 'doves', such as the foreign minister and the ambassador to Washington, who had been invited to Jerusalem to participate in consultation.

* The SAM-2 missile ('Guideline'), a two-stage anti-aircraft missile, first used in 1957, is 35 feet long and weighs 4,875 lb. Directed by a radar-computer unit and guided by radio command, the weight of its warhead is 288 lb. It can be detonated either by proximity fuse or by command. Its speed is Mach 3.5, its effective ceiling 60,000. It has been relatively ineffective below the range of 3,000 feet and against planes manoeuvring at high speed. SAM-3 ('Goa') is smaller and more mobile, with an overall length of 20 feet. It is similar in construction to the American Hawk missile, has an effective range of 10 miles but is primarily intended to be used against aircraft flying at low altitudes down to about 500 feet.
E. Luttwak, *A Dictionary of Modern War* (Allen Lane, London, 1971).

Dayan did not oppose the plan though he had no exaggerated political expectations with regard to the effects of the air offensive. Military experience in other parts of the world should have taught the ministers that political and military effects of saturation bombing are almost always well below expectations, but in Israel, as in Egypt, there was the feeling that something had to be done about the situation at Suez and quickly at that. The political risk was thought to be small, for Nasser was at his most intransigent and the Soviets were already in Egypt – several thousands of them – well before the first deep-penetration raid was carried out on January 7th, 1970. It is probably correct to state that Soviet military penetration in Egypt would have continued anyway, but it is doubtful whether there would have been such a sudden and massive influx of Soviet men and material. In other words, it is likely that the war of attrition would have lasted longer than it actually did if Israel had refrained from these raids, and if it had relied less on its air force in the struggle on the Suez front. This would have involved more victims and a greater strain on the country's economy, but, on the other hand, Nasser would probably not have obtained so many and such sophisticated weapons – including an effective anti-aircraft system. For the Israelis there were other ways and means of defending Suez. Generals Sharon and Tal had at various times suggested that no stationary defence was needed and that it would be sufficient if the east bank of the canal were controlled by patrols while it was within the reach of the Israeli guns. But they did not apparently press their views with great emphasis and conviction; those who favoured a static defence line prevailed. The use of the air force on a wide scale was no doubt the cheapest way to resist the Egyptian attacks, at least as far as the loss of human life was concerned. This had always been a consideration of paramount importance in Israeli strategic thought, both in view of the small size of the Jewish population in comparison with the Arabs, but also in view of the recent and most tragic chapter of Jewish history. Israel, it was thought, simply could not afford to lose many more of its young men, and this limited the military leaders' freedom of action: certain options were closed to them.

The ceasefire had come into force on August 7th; only a short while later, on September 28th, Nasser suddenly died. He had suffered a heart attack the year before, a fact that was however known only to a small circle of confidants. The last year of his life had on the whole not been a happy one. True, the Egyptian economy had recovered and the army was stronger and better equipped than ever before. But of his former comrades-in-arms no one of stature remained, he was surrounded by mediocrities; there were complaints about the constantly increasing number of Russians in Egypt. The Israelis were still in Sinai, and his prestige outside Egypt was not remotely what it had been before June 1967. In the words of a Palestinian intellectual, 'He is like a Chinese vase that has been cracked. He will never be the same again.'[6] True, in Libya and the Sudan nationalist officers had come to power who looked up to him as their idol, but the new Iraqi rulers were hostile and Jordan was in the throes of a civil war. The Arab world, in brief, was no more united at the time of Nasser's death than it had been before the Six Day War, and the liberation of the Palestinian homeland seemed as remote as ever.

The Struggle for the Succession

There was no obvious successor to Nasser, and it was widely assumed at the time that a group of people ('collective leadership') rather than one individual would replace the leader who had ruled the country single-handed for a decade and a half. The decisive political roles during the period immediately after Nasser's death were indeed played by the men of Nasser's inner circle, a group of officials linked to one another by ties of family or friendship, or mutually beholden in other ways. Leading members of this group were Ali Sabri (the head of the 'Russian Party'), Mohammed Fayek (minister of information), Sami Sharaf (minister of presidential affairs), Mahmud Fawzi (minister of defence), Sharawi Guma (minister of interior) as well as several secret-service chiefs (Ahmed Kamel, Amin Huweidi, Fathi Deeb) and some officials of the state party including Abdel Muhsin Abul Nur. Since all the members of this group were subsequently arrested and brought to trial for plotting to overthrow the government, and since the proceedings of the trial have been published, it is possible to retrace fairly accurately the steps taken by them in the search for a front man to act as president in the early weeks after Nasser's death.[7] Right from the beginning, it appears, Anwar Sadat was the proposed candidate: a 'stupid' man, he was thought to be easily manipulable. Other names were discussed and dismissed. The group had great respect for Ali Sabri, but he was 'hated by the masses'. They objected to Zakariya Mohieddin because he was 'a strong personality and it would be very difficult to control him'. Hussein Shafei, Nasser's old friend and comrade-in-arms, was thought to be not equal to the job. Finally, only Sadat remained; his election was all the more convenient since he was already vice-president of the republic.

It took a mere six months for the Egyptian 'Mafia', as its critics called the inner circle, to discover that Sadat was not at all easy to manipulate; on the contrary, he was 'cagey, unpredictable, and wished to follow his own line in domestic matters and external policies'. In drawing up a brief against Sadat, the group focused on two matters in particular: first, the proposed federation with Libya and Syria – which, the members insisted, had to gain the consent of the peoples concerned and which they maintained would be meaningless anyway without the participation of the Sudan. Secondly, according to the evidence given later by Ahmed Kamel, chief of intelligence, the group wanted to resume the war against Israel and to implicate the Soviet Union in the actual fighting: 'they [the Russians] could not possibly abandon the Egyptians to their fate. Partial victory would confirm the group in power, defeat would be blamed on Sadat.' (These were not central to the conspirators' concerns – they would have been willing, if necessary, to take exactly the opposite line; as Ahmed Kamel said, 'The principal aim for them was to remain in control of authority...') The subsequent course of the plot is fascinating material for the student of conspiracies, but of limited interest in the present context. As is well known, it failed utterly, partly because too many persons and factions were involved and also because the conspirators disagreed among themselves on many issues. On May 13th, 1971, the members of the group handed in their collective resignation; this was to be in preparation for a coup designed to remove Sadat, yet it was a curiously passive approach and one that involved many risks. The Voice of the Arabs radio station, temporarily in the group's hands, broadcast news of the resignations, and a few stage-managed demonstrations followed. But no public outcry was heard, no overwhelming demand that the men be restored to office. Sadat weathered the storm with surprising ease. The plotters were arrested, subsequently brought to trial, and sentenced to long prison terms. No one in Egypt, with the exception of a few of the 'Mafia's' fellow-travellers, was sad to see them go. A new government under Aziz Sidqi was appointed and the Arab Socialist Union, which had been the conspirators' main bulwark, underwent a massive purge.

Sadat and the Russians

The events of May 1971 left Sadat with far greater freedom of movement, but still insecure in his position. He had decapitated the old intelligence service and weakened other pillars of the regime, but had no new power base with which to replace them. He enjoyed the support of a few friends and well-wishers, and, since the conspirators were so thoroughly disliked, he more or less automatically received some public credit for having ousted them. But that was all.

As for the Soviets, they must have watched the course of events with some dismay. Many Western commentators said at the time that the May purges were directed specifically against the leaders of the 'Russian Party', but this was an exaggeration. In all probability, the plotters had acted on their own; there is no evidence that they informed Moscow of their intentions beforehand, and it is unlikely that the Russians would have given their blessing to such an amateurish enterprise. The Egyptian communists were certainly not involved; on the contrary, one of them was co-opted into the government by Sadat after the coup failed. A leading communist literary figure, Abder Rahman el Sharqawi, later wrote that 'they [the Mafia] had established a kingdom of vampires'. Even the Soviet press eventually condemned the conspirators.

Still, in the final analysis, though the Russians distrusted all Egyptians, they distrusted some more than others. The fact is that they had established a working relationship with Nasser and his inner circle whereas Sadat was unpredictable and the possibility even existed of his making a deal with the United States. President Podgorny was therefore dispatched to Cairo with unseemly haste within two weeks of the attempted coup. He returned to Moscow with Sadat's signature on a fifteen-year 'Treaty of Friendship and Co-operation'. The treaty, which was given much publicity at the time, pledged Soviet support for the U.A.R. in its struggle to become a socialist society, and bound each of the two parties not to enter any alliance or take any action directed against the other party or to conclude any other international agreement at variance with the terms of the treaty.

Taken at face value, the treaty seemed to represent a grave setback for Egypt because its stipulations were so patently one-sided and appeared to reflect a growing dependence on the Soviet Union. No one in his right mind would have assumed that the Russians would ever consult Sadat on vital questions of foreign policy and defence. The only justification for the treaty from the Egyptian point of view was the secret military clauses, which (as Sadat said in his speech before the National Assembly on June 2nd, 1971) 'added new guarantees which had not been defined previously'. Yet it is equally doubtful whether Sadat himself ever intended to live up to the conditions of the treaty. Egypt, after all, was not a member state of the Warsaw Pact, it had no common border with the Soviet Union or any of its allies, and the Brezhnev doctrine of intervention simply could not be made to apply to it.

Podgorny's delegation left Cairo on May 8th, 1971; less than two months later Soviet-Egyptian friendship was put to a severe test as a result of the communist coup in the Sudan. In February the Sudanese dictator, General Gafaar al-Nimeiry, had announced his intention to 'crush' the local communists; they responded with acts of open defiance and he countered, in mid-March, by removing some sixty communists from key positions in the army, the police and the state apparatus. The communists then staged a coup on July 19th but within three days Nimeiry was back in power. The military plotters, as well as many leading communists, including the secretary general of the party, were executed. *Pravda* denounced the 'mass-scale bloody reign of terror' in the Sudan, while Nimeiry proceeded to expel the Bulgarian ambassador as well as a Soviet counsellor and to describe relations with the Soviet Union as 'extremely bad'. Subsequently it transpired that, as in Egypt, Soviet leaders had not been informed, let alone consulted, about the intended coup – perhaps because the conspirators feared they would veto it.

While Moscow was bitterly denouncing the repression in the Sudan, Presidents Sadat of Egypt and Qadafi of Libya were doing their best to help Nimeiry in his campaign to stamp out communist influence. In a speech delivered in Cairo on July 24th, 1971, Sadat said that the newly formed Arab Federation (involving Egypt, Sudan and Libya) had been born with teeth 'which in the Sudan were very sharp indeed'. Orders were given in Cairo for the immediate return of a Sudanese brigade from Suez to Khartoum to help Nimeiry in his counter-coup.

The next act in the unfolding tragi-comedy opened during Sadat's visit to Moscow in mid-October 1971. This was to be the first of three visits within seven months. Western observers noted at the time that Sadat had apparently moved closer to the Soviet line; he denounced anti-communist moves in the Arab world as 'prejudicing the peoples' urge for liberation'. The Soviet Union on the other hand gave qualified support to the new federation of Egypt, Libya and Syria, provided of course that it became 'a bulwark of unity of all truly progressive forces'. According to the Moscow communiqué, Sadat's talks with Brezhnev, Podgorny and Kosygin were conducted in a spirit of 'frankness and cordiality' – but in fact there was more double-talk than ever before. The Soviet leaders assumed, quite rightly, that they might as well give their blessing to the new federation since it was still-born anyway. Sadat, for his part, could safely issue a routine condemnation of anti-Sovietism since the procommunist forces at home and in the Sudan no longer constituted a danger. Soviet-Egyptian relations had turned into a farcical exchange of declarations.

Sadat returned to Moscow in the first week of February 1972. Once more there were the ritual incantations – the meeting was an 'outstanding success', 'an important turning point', friendship between the two countries was 'immortal' – yet according to all the evidence it was the worst conference so far. Sadat was now under great pressure at home; student riots in January had underlined the shakiness of his regime. The India-Pakistan war had caused apprehension in Cairo, partly because the Soviet Union had openly taken sides against a Muslim country, partly because of the temporary transfer of Soviet war material from Egypt to the sub-continent. If Sadat had hoped for a military-political escalation during the winter, the war in India clearly upset his timetable. Above all, his much vaunted 'year of decision' with Israel had come and gone and become the subject of many bitter jokes in Egypt and the other Arab countries.

What Sadat wanted now was offensive weapons: medium- or long-range ground-to-ground missiles, and MiG-23s ('Foxbats'), the most advanced Soviet plane. The Soviets ignored these requests for as long as they could, then finally told the Egyptians as diplomatically as possible that their army was not yet good enough to win a war against Israel, despite the fact that the Soviet Union had invested billions of dollars in Egypt's re-armament. In these circumstances a few Foxbats or missiles would not make that much difference. In addition, quite apart from the military assessment of the situation, there were weighty political considerations behind Moscow's coolness to the new Egyptian request: by February 1972 definite progress had been achieved in the talks with Washington, and at that stage no one in Moscow intended to see this progress undermined by a war in the Middle East.

All this should have been clear to the Egyptians long before; perhaps it was – but it became a topic of open discussion only after Sadat's return from Moscow, when it was made the subject of a seminar held in Cairo in the late spring and also of a feature article in *Al Ahram* written by Heykal.* Heykal cited no fewer than ten reasons underlying, as he believed, the mistaken Soviet policy of 'no peace and no war', and produced ten counter-arguments designed to show how the policy would be self-defeating from the Soviet's own point of view, and inferior to a policy of outright warfare. Characteristically, he ignored the most basic question involved,

* Heykal, adviser and confidant to Nasser, has been suspected by the Russians (wrongly it would appear) of being a mainstay of the pro-Western party in Cairo. He has the reputation of being the most accomplished journalist in the Arab world. Heykal has been a fairly accurate barometer of the political climate in Cairo, not an original or consistent political thinker; as a historical source his 'revelations' have to be read with the greatest of care.

namely, what would happen to Soviet interests in the Arab world after the expected victory over Israel had been achieved. Nor did he make clear exactly what, in the event, the Egyptians really wanted from Moscow: more planes and missiles – or the active participation of Soviet divisions and units of the Soviet Mediterranean fleet?

The last stage before the July crisis was reached when Sadat invited himself to Moscow for yet a third time (April 1972). The situation as he saw it was more precarious than ever. President Nixon was due to meet soon with the Soviet leaders; as far as Cairo was concerned nothing good could possibly come from their talks. Mrs Meir had been invited to Bucharest – another ill omen. And, lastly, Iraq, Egypt's main rival and antagonist in the Arab world, was about to sign a treaty with Moscow. Sadat's own speeches at home had meanwhile become progressively more violent. On the birthday of the Prophet, he solemnly announced another deadline for victory: 'When we celebrate the birthday of Mohammed next, not only Sinai but Jerusalem too will be liberated, and the Israelis reduced to the abasement and submissiveness decreed for them.' In Moscow Sadat met twice with Brezhnev and received Soviet approval to go to war – if he really wanted to. This new departure for the Soviets was actually less momentous than it appeared. Egypt was not yet ready for war, certainly not without the help of other Arab countries. After his return Sadat admitted there had been some differences with the Russians, but what did it matter? Agreement had been reached on certain 'important measures' to strengthen military cooperation.

During May and June news spread of a further deterioration in Soviet-Egyptian relations, but there is nothing to suggest that Sadat wanted a dramatic showdown with the Russians at this time. On the contrary, he went out of his way to denounce anti-Soviet elements inside Egypt. Marshal Grechko revisited Cairo in May, bringing with him a few MiG-23s. According to a statement by Colonel Qadafi, not published in Cairo, 'Grechko left nothing behind but public optimism and falsely raised hopes'.

On the events of June and July there is a semi-official version as well as several others. Sadat himself says he finally lost all hope of effective Soviet support in late June as the Russians continued to

15

ignore his demand for offensive weapons. On July 9th, President Asad of Syria arrived in Cairo quite unexpectedly in an attempt to mediate between Egypt and the Soviet Union. Sadat allegedly told him to mind his own business (Asad had just signed a military pact with the Russians). His own version was that he was further irritated by Soviet statements, made in talks with Syrian communist leaders in Moscow, that the Arabs would be well advised not to go to war with Israel since there could be few doubts about the outcome. On July 13th, Prime Minister Aziz Sidqi and Foreign Minister Murad Ghaleb flew to Moscow. They were scheduled to stay for three days but returned after only one. Again the Soviet issued an official communiqué saying that the Arabs could use 'all means at their disposal' to recover the lost territories. The day after Sidqi's return the exodus of Soviet military personnel began. On July 18th Sadat delivered a speech making the expulsion order a matter of public record.

That Sadat had for some time been feeling more than a little frustrated is beyond doubt. By promises and time-tables he had manoeuvred himself into an impossible position. To survive politically he needed a convincing explanation for the fact that 1971 had not been the 'year of decision' he had promised – and that 1972 was not likely to be either. The most obvious explanation lay at hand: the Russians had let him down. But this is only part of the story. There is reason to believe he was egged on in his decision by Colonel Qadafi, who had never made a secret of his feelings about the Russians. Qadafi had just survived an attempt by some of his fellow-officers to remove him from the political scene, and was now at his most aggressive. Above all, Sadat seems to have been confronted by an ultimatum from leading army officers, who for some time had wanted to limit Soviet interference in Egyptian military affairs. (The Russians for their part had asked for the removal of War Minister Sadeq.)* A great many stories were circulating in Cairo concerning the arrogant behaviour of the Soviet advisers towards the Egyptian military; there was even a report – perhaps apocryphal – that Sadat

* The Russians reportedly also requested the removal of Said Marei, the secretary general of the Socialist Union, the Egyptian State party, who had been instrumental in purging the pro-Soviet elements in the party.

himself no longer had access to Soviet bases on Egyptian soil.* The stories may well have been exaggerated, but what mattered was that the Russians were thoroughly disliked, and that the dislike was mutual. The army command, in brief, had reasons of its own for wanting to get rid of the Russians.

The Russians reacted with utter calm to the sudden expulsion. Their behaviour in fact seemed to bear out what Sadat had told Cyrus Sulzberger of the *New York Times* the winter before: that the Soviets were not at all interested in staying in Egypt, that they had repeatedly expressed the wish to leave, and that they remained only because Sadat insisted. But this, to put it mildly, was not the whole truth; the Soviets undoubtedly were not eager to man the Suez defence line against Israel, but the naval bases and the airfields were another matter altogether. Still, they had no alternative but to react calmly. A military take-over of Egypt was out of the question, and even a propaganda campaign of recrimination must have seemed rather pointless. The Soviet press quite sensibly described the troop withdrawals as the natural end of a mission which had been successfully completed: the rebuilding of the Egyptian Army. In his speech of July 18th, Sadat asserted that the expulsion would in no way affect Soviet-Egyptian friendship and he thanked the Russians for all their help. Heykal performed his usual tight-rope act, exhorting Sadat to safeguard friendship with the Soviets, 'for which there is no substitute', while at the same time disclosing that five planes flown by Soviet pilots had been shot down the previous winter by the Israelis in less than a minute. Heykal, and others, asked that serious talks be initiated with Moscow to put the relationship between the two countries on a new basis. But this was about the last thing the Russians wanted – at least in public.

During the following weeks there were hints pointing in different directions: notes were exchanged, ambassadors were withdrawn and then restored, and a new Cabinet was appointed in Cairo. In a speech in mid-August Sadat complained that he had been exposed

---

* Officially there were no Soviet bases, only 'facilities', including the major airfields at Mansura, Jiyanklis, Inchas, Cairo West, Beni Suef, Aswan, and some others, and the naval bases at Mersa Matruh, Alexandria and Port Said.

to Soviet pressure to capitulate to Israel, and that the Soviets had imposed a virtual arms embargo, intended to drive Egypt to despair. A letter he had received from Brezhnev was totally unacceptable in both form and content. But – *Inshallah*! – Egypt would receive the arms it needed for the blow against Israel. By late September, following additional exchanges and the efforts of half a dozen mediators from various countries, Sadat said that he felt a little happier about relations between the two countries. As a result, it was decided to dispatch the Egyptian prime minister for further talks in Moscow. The Russians, not surprisingly, made their continued support dependent on the satisfaction of some rather tough demands, and Sadat, after all the blustering of the hot summer months, acquiesced without a struggle: Sadeq, his war minister, was out, and so were the commander of the Egyptian Navy and other high-ranking officers. Soon thereafter, several hundred Soviet military advisers returned to Egypt to man the air defences along the Suez Canal and around Cairo.

After all these events President Sadat's position seemed weaker than ever before; the military men who had backed him were gone and it was not certain whether he could trust their successors. His fall from power seemed only a question of time to most outside observers. The Russians would surely have preferred someone more trustworthy, though they did not have an obvious candidate and, anyway, were not in a position to bring him to power. It was widely assumed that this was the end of the Soviet-Egyptian special relationship; from now on the Soviet Union would diversify its investments in the Middle East. Perhaps the Soviet exodus had only hastened a process that might otherwise have taken a little longer but was inexorable.

These assumptions were correct as far as they went; more will have to be said presently about the Soviet rapprochement with Iraq and Syria and the growing Soviet interest in the Persian Gulf with its enormous oil resources. But the crisis in Soviet-Egyptian relations did not mean that the break was radical and final, that as a result Egypt had been greatly weakened or that the danger of a Middle-Eastern war had receded or become altogether impossible. The opposite was true: the exodus of the bulk of Soviet military personnel only made the war more possible. Furthermore it was overlooked at the time that even though some of the most sophisticated military equipment was not left in Egyptian hands – for instance MiG-23, which was faster than any Western aircraft – the strength of the Egyptian armed forces which had been built up almost from scratch during the previous four years was unimpaired. Egypt still had its 1,700 Soviet standard tanks (T-54/5) not to mention the T-62; it had an enormous arsenal of guns and howitzers – 122mm, 130mm, 152mm and 203mm; it had 24 F R O G-3 as well as some F R O G-7 missiles, 'Snapper' anti-tank missiles, as well as a most effective anti-aircraft system with 130 S A M sites; it had a navy with 12 submarines and 5 destroyers (compared with 3 submarines and 1 destroyer on the Israeli side), it had an air force with 620 combat aircraft.[8] There was still great numerical superiority over Israel; could it be assumed that four years of intensive training by Soviet instructors had been all in vain? That discipline and training had not greatly improved and that the Egyptians were congenitally incapable of fighting? Soviet military supplies continued to stream into Egypt; not all advisers and instructors had been withdrawn and more were to return in 1972/3. Yet so unexpected and startling was the Soviet exodus from Egypt that little attention was paid to the fact that the Russians had left behind them a formidable war machine. Even if there was no longer the same warmth in relations between Moscow and Cairo, the two countries still needed each other. Egypt, despite all the set-backs, was still the biggest country in the Arab world; for Russia to cold-shoulder it would have had a detrimental effect on Soviet Middle-Eastern policy. Even if Sadat was not particularly liked in Moscow, there was always the chance that sooner or later he would be replaced by someone more reliable or pliable. Egypt on the other hand needed the Soviet Union for more supplies, for spare parts, for guidance and, of course, for political support. It could not afford to irritate too much its powerful protector. There were strains in the alliance, but there were still important common interests, and these, as future events were to show, helped to overcome the crisis.

Russia, Syria and Iraq

While Egypt was temporarily downgraded in the scale of Soviet priorities in the Middle East, Syria and Iraq began to figure much more prominently. Iraq had been ruled for more than six years by the Ba'ath Party. This was originally a group of army officers closely knit by family ties and common origin; subsequently some civilians also attained positions of command in the ruling group. The Baghdad dictatorship was cruel and ruthless even by Iraqi standards and it had few friends in the Arab world. But it was precisely this isolation which worked in Russia's favour, for the Iraqi leaders felt they needed the protection of a great power. As in Syria, several communists were members of the government, but they neither controlled the army nor the secret police, and these, of course, were the real levers of power.

The Soviet Union signed a treaty of friendship with Iraq in April 1972 and concluded several other specific military and political agreements later that year. The advantages of gaining a firm foothold in Iraq were immense. A well informed author wrote at the time that the Kremlin had gained a secure foothold in the Gulf from which to make her naval presence felt – if necessary on a continuous basis.[9] Iraq's geographical position has much to recommend it; it flanks Turkey and Iran, and borders on Syria, Jordan and the Arabian peninsula. It is a springboard for the oil-rich Persian Gulf area, including the tiny sheikhdoms and emirates which possess a substantial part of the world's oil reserves. It enabled the Soviet Union to extend aid to the 'Popular Front for the Liberation of Oman and Occupied Arab Gulf' and to combat Chinese influence among these rebels as well as in South Yemen. Above all Iraq meant oil; the North Rumaila oil-fields exploited by a Soviet consortium will produce twenty million tons a year by 1975 – a modest figure by present-day standards but one which promises to grow in time. The Soviet Union invested some $300 million in economic assistance and probably a much larger sum in military aid, including the delivery of some 1,000 T-54/5 tanks and about the same number of heavy guns, as well as an anti-aircraft system, combat aircraft, missile-carrying patrol boats and torpedo boats.

More important yet was the growing Soviet involvement in Syria. Syria is also ruled by the Ba'ath Party, although there is not much love lost between the Syrian and Iraqi branches of this party. Syria had maintained fairly good relations with Russia for a long time, but the ties had never been as close as those between Cairo and Moscow. In 1966 the Soviet Union had lent the Syrian Government $150 million for building the Euphrates Dam, and Marshal Grechko, the Soviet defence minister, visited Damascus almost as often as Cairo. About 1,000 Soviet military advisers were stationed in Syria between 1967-71; on the eve of the fourth Arab-Israeli war their number was probably closer to 3,000. Soviet warships began to call frequently at the ports of Latakia and Tartus and on occasion stayed there for weeks. These ports did not however become fully fledged Soviet bases, if only because they were small and did not possess the essential facilities needed to be of real help to the Soviet fleet. At the same time the Soviets began to construct a submarine base near Ras Shamra.

Though Syria was averse – for reasons that are not entirely clear – to signing a formal pact with the Soviet Union similar to those signed by Egypt and Iraq, collaboration between the two countries became much closer in 1972. Perhaps, following Egypt's temporary eclipse, the Syrians saw a real chance to strengthen their position in Arab politics and to assume the role of main champion of the Palestinian cause; perhaps they were frightened by a series of Israeli air strikes on their territory. In August and September 1972 the Soviet Union quite ostentatiously made major arms deliveries to Syria, including SAM-2 and SAM-3 missiles, to be followed later by the most up-to-date mobile SAM units. Altogether, by the outbreak of war, the Soviet Union had supplied to Syria several hundred T-34 and about 1,000 T-54/55 modern tanks, as well as an unknown number of heavy and light tanks and self-propelled guns, some 300 MiG-17 and MiG-21, IL-28 bombers and SU-7 fighter bombers. Shortly before the outbreak of war some of the most sophisticated Soviet weapons were delivered. Considering the fact that Syria has less than 7 million inhabitants in comparison to Egypt's 37 millions, Syria had become the most heavily armed country in the Arab world. For the Soviet Union it was a cheap price to pay for strengthening yet another foothold in the Middle East.

Peace Feelers 1967-72

The efforts to restore peace to the Middle East once the fighting in '67 had ended were protracted, highly complicated and ultimately futile, for the distance between Arab and Israeli demands was such that no formula however ingenious could bridge them. Since the Arab countries refused to deal directly with the Israelis, various go-betweens had to be called in, which did not help the cause of peace. The many rounds of negotiations of which only the briefest account can be given began with the Emergency Session of the General Assembly of the U.N. convened on June 19th, 1967, upon the initiative of the Soviet Union. Kosygin, who headed the Soviet delegation, demanded immediate evacuation of the occupied territories. Furthermore, Israel was to be explicitly condemned for its attack and it was also to indemnify the Arabs for the damage caused. But this proposal did not get majority support, nor did a Latin American draft which said that the termination of the state of war on the part of the Arabs was a precondition for the Israeli withdrawal. Deadlock ensued, but as a result of a fresh initiative taken by Dobrynin, the Soviet ambassador in Washington, a new formula was submitted which appealed to Dean Rusk, American secretary of state, and Arthur Goldberg, the chief U.S. representative at the U.N. This formula provided for unilateral Israeli withdrawal without delay from the territories in exchange for a declaration by all member states of the U.N. in the area that each enjoyed the right to maintain an independent national state of its own and to live in peace and security.[10] The Israelis viewed this as virtual American surrender to the Soviet-Arab position, for the formula did not even mention Israel by name. Israel would have been in serious trouble had the Arab states decided to subscribe to this meaningless and non-committal declaration. However, much to the relief of the Israelis and to the dismay of the Russians, the Arabs found this concession much too far-reaching and they rejected the resolution. Thus, after two months of futile talk, the Emergency Session broke up in disarray.

The Arab opposition even against verbal concessions had been led by Algeria and Syria. It was easy enough for the Algerians to be intransigent for they had not been affected by the defeat; Egypt and Jordan on the other hand had been hit hard and they had a far more urgent interest to 'liquidate the consequences of the aggression'. The Jordanians were apparently ready for negotiations with Israel right from the beginning, but they were the weakest of the

Arab states and could not take the political initiative. However, during October 1967 Nasser too seems to have had second thoughts about the wisdom of a purely negative stand. Mahmud Riad, Egypt's foreign minister, explained in meetings with Arthur Goldberg that the Egyptians were after all willing to make a number of concessions. They would let Israeli ships pass through the Gulf of Aqaba. They would also permit Israeli goods, though not Israeli ships, to pass through Suez. 'They were willing, though they never publicly said so, to give up the Gaza Strip. They would, if sufficiently pressed, in all probability agree to the demilitarization of the Sinai peninsula. They would accept a generally worded declaration of non-belligerence.'[11] In the meantime, however, the Israeli position had hardened, they asked for full maritime rights in the Suez Canal and they had the support of the Americans in demanding an end to all belligerency. King Husain was willing to accept these Israeli demands, but Nasser was not. Instead he decided, apparently on Soviet advice, to ask for the urgent convention of the Security Council. The Americans were dismayed by this move; in their view a good deal of progress had been made in the talks with the Egyptians and other council members; obviously, the Security Council was not the right forum to continue the dialogue.

The next two weeks witnessed hectic diplomatic activity which resulted on November 22nd in Resolution 242. This was based on a compromise draft prepared by Lord Caradon, the British representative; it combined a call for a withdrawal of Israeli forces from occupied areas with a declaration of non-belligerency, the definition of permanent and safe boundaries for all countries in the region, the demilitarization of certain zones, freedom of shipping and a just solution of the refugee problem. The Arabs tried hard to insert certain changes: they objected to the term 'recognized boundaries' and they wanted an explicit statement that the Israelis would have to withdraw their forces from *all* the territories occupied in the recent conflict. For this demand they had Soviet support on the very highest level; in a message to President Johnson Prime Minister Kosygin strongly urged that a change be made. But the Americans refused to yield and in the end Lord Caradon's resolution was passed unanimously. Resolution 242 is of importance because for many years to come it was the basic document figuring prominently

23

in all peace talks. It was accepted by Israel, Egypt and Jordan, though not by Syria, Iraq, Algeria and other Arab countries. However, as it was soon to appear the language of the resolution was – to put it mildly – not unambiguous, each side could read into it its own interpretation. Israel stressed the fact that Resolution 242 did not call for immediate, unconditional and total withdrawal (as the Arabs maintained), it demanded the cessation of hostile acts such as blockade and boycott. The Arabs on the other hand said, not without reason, that the resolution was to be considered as a whole; they would continue the blockade of Suez if Israel ignored that part of the resolution which dealt with the just settlement of the refugee problem.

The Security Council decided to appoint a special representative to work for a settlement in accordance with Resolution 242. Dr Gunnar Jarring, Swedish Ambassador to the U.S.S.R., was offered and accepted this thankless task. He travelled countless times to Cairo, Jerusalem, Amman and other capitals without making any noteworthy progress. The Arabs, to reiterate their position, insisted on Israeli withdrawal from *all* the occupied territories, refused to negotiate directly or to sign a comprehensive and formal peace treaty with Israel. The Israelis on the other hand demanded direct talks following an initial stage of indirect negotiations, and they refused to clarify what kind of border changes they had in mind when they talked about 'secure, recognized and agreed boundaries'. There were separate talks between Dr Jarring and Egyptian, Jordanian and Israeli representatives for five weeks in New York in summer 1968 but they only showed that there was no common ground. The attempt to institute a second round of talks in 1969 failed altogether.[12]

With the failure of the Jarring mission the initiative passed again into the hands of the U.S., the Soviet Union, Britain and France. Upon Soviet and French initiative quadri-partite meetings began in New York in February 1969 and continued in a desultory way throughout the year. But the only thing that emerged was the opposition of both sides to accepting an 'imposed settlement' (Nasser) and to becoming the 'object of power politics' (Israeli Cabinet statement). Shortly before the Soviet Union had submitted a six-point peace plan which the Egyptians, not surprisingly, accepted, whereas the Israelis refused to accept it even as a basis of discussions.

The next stage in the negotiations was reached with the publication of the Rogers Plan in December 1969. Following contacts with the Soviet Union, the American secretary of state suggested a peace treaty between Israel, Egypt and Jordan, calling for almost complete Israeli withdrawal, leaving open the question of the Gaza Strip and Sharm el Sheikh. Israel's rejection of it might have jeopardized its relations with the United States, but for the fact that the Egyptians too refused to accept it. Much to Washington's chagrin, even the Russians, having initially supported the Rogers Plan, had second thoughts on the subject.

During the next few months the conflict escalated, with the Israeli raids of deep penetration and the appearance in Egypt of thousands of Soviet instructors and other military personnel. Further messages were exchanged between Washington and Moscow, and the United States rejected an Israeli request for additional interceptors and strike aircraft in the hope that such gestures would halt, or at least slow down Soviet involvement in Egypt. But the Russians were too heavily committed to stop mid-way.[13] However, both Egypt and Israel gradually felt the effects of the war of attrition and after five more months had passed a certain shift could be detected in the attitude of both sides. Nasser's May Day 1970 speech was tough, even bellicose, but some observers interpreted it as an appeal to reason. Where do Israel's borders start, he asked, what do they really want? Why were they not willing even to mention the term withdrawal? Nasser had told Jarring that Egypt would agree to a package deal covering all provisions of the Security Council resolution which would be signed before withdrawal began. His main conditions were as follows:

1. No direct negotiations with Israel; contact would be maintained through a U.N. mediator.

2. There would be no formal peace treaty or diplomatic recognition of Israel but simply an end of the state of belligerency.

3. Israel would have to give up all occupied territories.

4. Egypt would accept demilitarized zones provided these were established on both sides of the border.

5. Free passage to Israel through the Straits of Tiran pending a decision by the World Court.

6. With regard to Jerusalem Nasser did not specify his demands; he was willing to leave this to King Husain.

7. A settlement of the refugee question.[14]

The Israeli demands can be summarized: no withdrawal without, or prior to a peace treaty, no total withdrawal, but only a retreat to secure and recognized borders, freedom of passage through Suez and the Straits of Tiran, a united Jerusalem under Israeli rule and a solution to the refugee problem mainly by resettling them in the Arab countries. Despite the fact that the positions of the two sides seemed irreconcilable, in fact they were less rigid than it appeared. In a speech on May 5th, 1970, Mrs Meir announced that for true peace Israel would make concessions that might 'surprise the world'; later that month she declared that Israel accepted the principle of withdrawal from territory occupied in 1967. It no longer insisted on negotiating with Nasser directly but was ready to have talks through a neutral intermediary, a concession which provoked much dissent inside Israel. Nasser promised that if the Israelis would withdraw, Egypt would recognize the State of Israel.

Thus conditions seemed auspicious for a new American peace initiative, the so-called Second Rogers Plan. It aimed at a ceasefire leading within a short period to a renewal of negotiations, Egyptian recognition of Israeli sovereignty and Israeli withdrawal from the occupied territories. Nasser at first rejected the plan, but following a long stay in Moscow and, apparently, new Soviet assurances, he changed his mind. The Israeli Government deliberated for a long time; there was a cable from President Nixon which said that Israel would have to withdraw only after a general settlement. The majority in the Cabinet accepted the plan but the right-wing Gahal ministers did not and resigned, thus causing the break-up of the government of 'national unity'. Mrs Meir and her associates felt that it would be politically most unwise to reject the American initiative, particularly since it was coupled with the promise of economic assistance and of military equipment. Thus the armistice came into being, but, as the deployment of SAM missile sites on the west bank of the canal continued the Israelis in protest left the talks which had again been initiated by Dr Jarring. They returned only three months later, towards the end of December, after the United States had given further promises to Israel both with regard to economic assistance and military aid, including the delivery of Hawk surface-to-air missiles and F-4 (Phantom) aircraft.

Great changes had occurred in the meantime on the Middle-Eastern scene following President Nasser's death and the civil war in Jordan. In the circumstances the Israeli Government saw no particular reason to hurry; it was not certain that Sadat would be able to remain in power, and in any case he was thought to be too weak to negotiate a peace settlement. Moreover, Jerusalem was not at all certain how much support there was in Washington for its demand that Israeli withdrawal should be partial rather than total. The only new initiative during the winter of 1970-71 was a suggestion put forward by General Dayan concerning an Israeli withdrawal of about twenty miles from the canal as an interim measure. This would have made it possible for the Egyptians to re-open the canal; there would have been no peace treaty but de facto peaceful co-existence. Once the canal was open, Dayan reasoned, the Egyptians and also the Russians would have a vested interest in keeping it open. President Sadat countered by announcing that he would accept the re-opening of the canal only if this would be the first step towards the realization of the other points of Resolution 242. Otherwise, he argued, the world would forget that the 'consequences of aggression' had not yet been liquidated, the Israelis would still be in Sinai and the powers would no longer be willing to bring strong pressure on Israel to withdraw to the lines of 1967.

The Dayan initiative had no success because Washington saw no particular advantages at the time in re-opening the canal. To make matters even more confused Dr Jarring soon after came out with a proposal of his own which was much more in line with Egyptian demands. He reiterated the call for an Israeli withdrawal to the former international boundary on condition satisfactory arrangements could be made with regard to the de-militarized zones, Sharm el Sheikh and the freedom of navigation. It is of course not certain whether the Dayan proposal for an interim settlement based on a step-by-step approach would have been accepted by the Egyptians; whatever prospects may have existed disappeared following Dr Jarring's well-meant but ill-timed intervention. The Jarring plan encouraged the Egyptians to press demands which even a sympathetic mediator found unrealistic – such as retreat from all occupied territory including the Gaza Strip. Cairo also announced that freedom of navigation would be granted only in accordance with the principles of international law; in other words, it would be up to the Egyptians to decide whether the Israelis would have this right.

The Israelis were angry with Dr Jarring who, they thought, had overstepped his brief and there were even tactless personal accusations against him. In its reply to his proposals Jerusalem stated that it would not retreat to the lines that had existed before the Six Day War. The Israelis did not accept American advice to ignore that part of the Jarring memorandum which offended them most. Thus a new deadlock was reached which the visits of Secretary of State Rogers and Joseph Sisco to Cairo and Jerusalem did nothing to break. The Israeli position hardened: the removal of their forces from the canal would *not* be a first stage leading to a further withdrawal. They would *not* permit Egyptian troops to cross the canal and there would have to be a permanent ceasefire. Egypt on the other hand was willing to consider the Dayan plan – if at all – only on condition that it would be able to dispatch its soldiers to the east side of the canal, and they were intransigent with regard to the passage of Israeli ships. Talks continued throughout 1971 despite the internal upheavals in Egypt and President Sadat's announcement that this would be the 'year of decision'. Much of these negotiations were taken up by efforts to find a compromise between the Israeli demand for direct negotiations and the Egyptian insistence on the use of go-betweens. Eventually, some agreement seems to have been reached in principle on having 'proximity talks' – for instance on different floors of a New York hotel. But no further progress was made because there was still that insurmountable obstacle: there was no common ground between the Egyptian demand 'that a partial settlement be linked to a general settlement and that Israel should declare her readiness, in principle, to withdraw from the whole of Sinai' – and the Israeli rejection of this demand.[15] Dr Jarring returned to Moscow and this was, broadly speaking, the end of the era of negotiations except for occasional statements, mainly on the part of the Americans, that efforts to reach a settlement should be renewed.

There were no contacts direct or indirect with the Syrians; the Israelis had declared early on that they would never give up the Golan Heights, and since the Syrians had not accepted Resolution 242 but continued to talk about the necessity of destroying the Zionist State, there was nothing to talk about. With Jordan, on the other hand, there were direct talks; King Husain met Israeli ministers and declared his readiness to make peace with Israel if the West Bank, or least part of it, were returned. He would have agreed to demilitarize the West Bank, but Jerusalem was a much more thorny issue. The Israeli Government stalled because inside the country there was strong opposition to giving up any part of Yehuda and Samaria, i.e. the West Bank. The internal crises in Jordan and the shaky position of the monarch gave plausibility to these doubts; even if Husain's good will and peaceful intentions could be trusted, what guarantees were there that eventually the West Bank would not be ruled by Fatah?

Mention should be made in passing of various unofficial mediators who offered their good services between the two wars. Most notable among them was Dr Nahum Goldmann, a veteran Zionist diplomat whose relations with the state of Israel were however somewhat tenuous. He advocated a more active dialogue with the Egyptians, and on at least one occasion volunteered to go to Cairo following a somewhat mysterious invitation. Dr Goldmann's past record as a political prognosticator was far from impressive and his faith in the effects of private diplomacy was, to put it cautiously, a little out of date. Had Dr Goldmann gone to Cairo, it is highly likely that his mission would have been a failure. But this should not have prevented the Israeli Government from giving him its blessing. There was nothing to be lost. Instead Dr Goldmann was bitterly attacked and there were articles in the press about the *galut* (diaspora) mentality of certain Zionist leaders who knew nothing about Arab psychology.

Missed Opportunities?

The melancholy story of the abortive peace negotiations leaves a great many questions open; above all, of course, whether Israel did miss any opportunities to make peace with its neighbours, or at any rate to defuse the conflict and to make a new round of fighting less likely. It would appear in retrospect that there might have been opportunities to normalize Arab-Israeli relations which were not pursued, and which should have been explored. One such opportunity existed immediately after the Six Day War, another in October 1967. It is possible, though not very likely, that an opportunity was missed in August 1970, at the end of the war of attrition; it is more likely that a less unyielding Israeli position during the first nine months after Nasser's death would have added to the prospects of a settlement. There were even chances for an accommodation in 1972. After the Soviet exodus from Egypt and the progress of détente Arab hopes for a successful war against Israel were at a nadir and Cairo might have been more receptive to new Israeli proposals. There is of course no certainty that greater Israeli willingness to make concessions would have achieved anything at all. All that matters in this context is that rigidity prevented progress on more than one occasion. There were admittedly no chances for peace with Syria. But if Egypt would have reached an agreement with Israel, Jordan would have followed suit, and Syria left to fend for itself might not have for ever persisted in its implacable hostility.

A unilateral Israeli withdrawal from most of the occupied territories would have been unique in the annals of history. But then Israel's position was unique and its foremost aim should have been to reduce the number of its adversaries. Israel in 1967 would have been able to negotiate from a position of strength: as a small country which had shown great military valour – and at the same time unprecedented magnanimity in victory. Egypt and Jordan were willing to make a number of important concessions after 1967 which would have been quite unthinkable before the Six Day War. There was the danger that if Israel had withdrawn its forces from the armistice lines it would have had to face a new attack from less advantageous positions. But there were all kinds of deterrent to reduce this risk. It is possible that the Arab states would have attacked Israel again, but it is at least equally likely that Egypt under a ruler less strongly orientated towards pan-Arabism than Nasser would not have taken part in such a dangerous venture. True, there was the humiliation of defeat, but there would not have been the same intensity of feeling, the additional stimulus of having to recover the lost territories. The rulers of Egypt faced a great many problems at home and abroad, the Arab world was rent by many bitter conflicts throughout the 'fifties and 'sixties. Had the Israeli danger loomed less large, had it not overshadowed everything else, there might not have been a new war in 1973. There would have been no peace, there would have been bellicose speeches and perhaps threats; the Arab leaders would still have promised to destroy the Jewish State one day. But there would not have been in Egypt the same feeling of over-riding urgency, and with the passing of time the conflict might have lost much of its acuteness. Fatah and its rivals would still have carried out sporadic attacks from across the border, and they might have hijacked a few planes; it would have been a great nuisance, but it would not have endangered the existence of the state. In the course of time the Palestinians would have realized that they could not rely on the Arab governments, and if they had been approached by Israel with some constructive proposals it is not impossible that they too would have accepted in the end the existence of the State of Israel.

Up to 1967 Israel was unable to make any territorial concessions to its Arab neighbours, for a smaller state would not have been viable. But after the Six Day War it was in the fortunate position of being able to give up something and it failed to do so. The borders of June 5th, 1967, were a nightmare from the military point of view, but they could have been improved upon and there would have been demilitarized areas. Psychologically, the Israeli attitude was not difficult to understand. The Arab leaders had threatened Israel with extinction for many years, and such threats could not easily be dismissed as idle talk. Few victories in history had been as sudden and as complete as the Israeli triumph in the Six Day War; surely it was most unreasonable of the Arabs to refuse even to meet the Israelis, let alone to discuss a firm and lasting peace. It was unreasonable, but the Arabs, as subsequent events were to show, could afford it. The question of Sinai was not one of ethics or morality; the desert is almost entirely uninhabited, it had been part of Egypt for a mere sixty years. Most wars throughout history have ended with the acquisition of territory by the victors. The Soviet Union, to give but one example, swallowed whole countries after the Second World War, and those who refused to accept the fact were denounced as fascist revanchists. But the victory of 1967 had not made a super-power of Israel and there should have been no illusions about its long-term political prospects. An Israeli general, one of the most capable and bravest, is reported to have said in an incautious moment in 1973, that Israel was stronger than all European armies, and that it could conquer the whole region from Khartoum to Baghdad and Algeria within one week. It was typical of a mood in which everything seemed possible. But in fact, Israel was not even a medium power; it had no fifty million inhabitants, no major oilfields, no developed nuclear arsenal. Its enemies, on the other hand, were many, they had unlimited manpower, their oil (and money) was a political weapon of increasing importance, and above all they had the backing of a super-power. True, Israel was backed to a certain extent by another super-power, but there was no symmetry in the relationship of the U.S.S.R. and its Arab clients and of the United States and Israel. The United States wanted to have good relations with some of the Arab countries too, whereas Russia had no incentive to woo Israel. These were the basic facts of political life which should have induced the Israeli Government in 1967 to make an all-out effort to defuse the conflict, to heal wounds, to calm and even to appease. De-escalation might not have worked, but it was not even really tried.

The outcome of the Six Day War had some unfortunate effects as far as Israel is concerned. 'A great victory is a great danger. For human nature it is more difficult to bear than a defeat.' * Before the Six Day War Israel had been a small country, but it had absorbed almost two million immigrants, its industry and agriculture had developed beyond all expectations, it was a flourishing concern. A few right-wing ideologists had argued all along that Israel had an historical right to everything that God had promised to the twelve tribes, meaning the whole land of Israel and a great part of Jordan ('Unto thy seed I give this land, from the river of Egypt unto the great river, the river Euphrates,' Genesis 15-18). But no responsible Israeli politician, not even the leaders of the extreme right, thought that Israel should pursue a policy of expansion. The war of June 1967 was defensive in character, against

* I chose Nietzsche's *obiter dictum* from *Unzeitgemässe Betrachtungen* as a text for the last chapter in *The Road to War*, written in 1967.

an enemy who had solemnly sworn to destroy Israel. Its aim was to save the country from annihilation, not to annex new territories. But so great was the victory that it had an unbalancing effect; it had been a miracle, it was said, it led to a mystical – quasi-religious – revival. All Jerusalem had been liberated, never again was it to be divided by machine-gun posts and barbed wire entanglements. The Jordan river was to be the natural frontier of Israel, never again were the links between the Jewish people and its historic country to be cut. Bethlehem was the home of King David's family, Hebron had historical associations with Abraham, and it had been King David's residence before the conquest of Jerusalem. In Sichem (Nablus) Joseph was buried and Gaza was the southern-most outpost of King Solomon's state. There could be found solid historical claims even for the Golan, for Jephta had once been judge there. Clearly it had been the divine will to fulfil the promise to his people. It was perhaps not surprising that the national-religious party and the orthodox religious establishment which had been quite dovish before the June war became one of the main-stays of the annexationist camp. In these circles the militarism of Joshua became much more popular than the pacifism of Isaiah – Joshua had conquered cities and hung up the enemy kings by their ears. At the end of October 1967 Sefardic Chief Rabbi Yizhak Nissim pronounced a religious ruling that no religious or secular authority, including the government of Israel, had the right to yield a single inch of the Land of Israel which was the heritage of every Jew.[16] But also non-believers and otherwise sane people were affected by delusions of various kinds, invoking holy texts and prophecies, divine injunctions and mystical bonds with the land. It was genuine, it was touching, and it was politically very dangerous. For even though Hebron had once been the residence of the Israelite kings, it was now an Arab town and the same went for the rest of the West Bank and Gaza (altogether about a million Arabs). This however did not unduly bother the Land of Israel movement or the right-wing Gahal (later Likud); the Jordan was to be Israel's political frontier, the Arabs were to be absorbed, some of them would no doubt leave, but in view of the future large-scale Jewish immigration there would be no demographic problem. The annexationists were caught on the horns of a very real dilemma: mass immigration was, at best, a hope, whereas the Arab presence was a reality. It was easy enough to talk about giving the Arabs in the occupied territories full Israeli citizenship. But in practice it would have meant the end of the Jewish State, Israel would have become a bi-national country. The annexationists, needless to say, had no intention of giving up *Hatiqvah*, the national anthem, nor did they want four or five Arab ministers in the government. They hoped to wake up one day and to find that the Arab problem had disappeared. Their sole preoccupation was with the new borders which they regarded as a guarantee for both security and peace as well as 'unprecedented horizons for an overall growth in the material and spiritual strength of the nation'.[17]

The public campaign for annexations which started soon after the end of the war produced a counter-drive. Thus in December 1967, an appeal signed by two hundred and fifty intellectuals was published in the Hebrew press headed 'Security and Peace – Yes; annexation – No'. The signatories stressed that unilateral annexation of the territories would be a perversion of the objectives of the last war and of Israel's policy, and would endanger the Jewish features of the state as well as its humane and democratic character. The prime objective of Israel's policy should be the search for peace, and any action impeding the chance for peace lacked all responsibility for the future of the Jewish people and the State of Israel.[18]

The polemical debates between the advocates of a greater Israel and the anti-annexationists were to continue right up to the outbreak of the next war. The hawks continued to argue that 'our right to our ancestral heritage is eternal', that all Palestine was to be settled by Jews, and that this was the only way to make the Arabs accept Israel's existence. On the other hand there were leading members of the Labour Alignment (a coalition of Left-wing parties) who favoured withdrawal, be it for pragmatic reasons – Finance Minister Sapir's fear that adding more than a million Arabs to Israel would strangle the Jewish State – or political motives.

Among the doves were Ben Aharon, the secretary general of the Histadrut, the Israeli trade-union movement, and above all Arye (Lova) Eliav, former secretary general of Mapai (the Israeli Labour Party), who in a widely discussed book submitted a peace plan of his own.[19] Eliav argued that peace with the Arabs was the supreme aim:

> Both the Arabs and ourselves have been caught up in a dangerous trap of fear, threats and psychological complexes. The Arabs who have not yet accepted our very existence, live in the shadow of Israel's 'unlimited expansionism', on the one hand, and the 'Crusader complex' of their numerical superiority (100 million against 3 million), on the other. We, who have suffered 2,000 years of exile, think 'the whole world is against us'. We live in the shadow of the Nazi holocaust, and fear the destruction of the Third Jewish Commonwealth.

Eliav decried the fact that the government was so vague about the future of the occupied territories and that no clear and unequivocal statements had been made about the Arab Israelis. He suggested the establishment of a Palestinian Arab state; if there was 'no one to talk to at present' this could well be the consequence of the fact that the Israelis had so far refused to discuss principles. He demanded a declaration to the effect that in principle Sinai was Egyptian, not Israeli, but that it would have to be neutralized and demilitarized for a long time to come. He thought that Jerusalem – the most complex and sensitive question of all – should remain undivided, the capital of Israel. At the same time the Arabs should be given sovereign rights over the mosques and other religious institutions; a territorial link could be established by means of a corridor linking these places with Arab Palestine.

This was not the only voice warning against 'intoxication with victory'. Abba Eban had said as early as 1967 that history had proved time and time again that military victory was unstable unless suitable political conditions were created. David Ben Gurion expressed the view that this was not the last battle, that while a strong army was vital, it was not sufficient to assure the country's future. He emphasized the need for a political solution – the West Bank should be returned under agreed terms, and Sinai should not remain in Israeli hands. But Eban's influence in the Cabinet was limited, and Ben Gurion, though still the country's elder statesman, no longer influenced the conduct of politics.

There were marked differences in the ranks of the government. Yigal Allon, deputy prime minister, recognized the Palestinian Arabs' right to self-determination and opposed all plans for creeping annexation.[20] According to a plan first outlined by him a few weeks after the end of the Six Day War Israel was to annex a narrow strip of territory along the Jordan and to establish settlements there to ensure security in this area. But the West Bank as a whole, linked to Jordan by a corridor, was to be under Arab rule. Dayan on the other hand gradually came to believe in the perpetuation of the status quo, which meant annexation, albeit with some reservations. The Palestinian Arabs were to remain Jordanian citizens. Living together would lead sooner or later to economic integration. One of Dayan's associates, Shimon Peres, minister of communications, suggested at one stage a Jewish federal state, consisting of a Jewish and an Arab canton. As time went on Dayan, and like him Mrs Meir and Israel Galili, became more and more pessimistic about the prospects of a peace settlement. If the Arabs were unwilling to talk, Israel was to stand fast and not give way to pressure. Peace by retreating was not a viable alternative, since nobody promised Israel peace if she retreated. There was growing reluctance even to discuss terms of a settlement: when the Arabs were willing to talk directly to the Israelis, proposals for a peace pact would be specified.[21]

As the Arabs at Khartoum had opted for immobilism, it seemed only natural that the Israelis would react likewise: any other course of action (they thought) would be interpreted as evidence of weakness and according to conventional wisdom Arabs respected only strength.

For the government the security interests were decisive. The Arab governments no longer openly advocated genocide, but then such threats would have sounded a little hollow after the defeat of 1967. Many Arab spokesmen still insisted that there was no room for a Jewish State in the Middle East whatever its borders. Even Heykal, one of the more moderate and sophisticated Arabs writers declared that there was no room in the Middle East for Arab nationalism and for Israel as well.[22] These speeches and articles were read in Israel and taken seriously, perhaps too seriously. Tension would not have run as high as it did, had it only been a battle of words. But the incidents on the borders and the terrorist activities abroad put the Israeli doves on the defensive. A violent public debate would have ensued if the government had made a moderate peace plan public. It would have been accused of criminal weakness, of treason and of blasphemy. Yet in the end the public would have followed the lead given by a strong prime minister, and his (or her) government. Such a lead, unfortunately, was not given. In a difficult situation fraught with dangers, Eshkol's government, and later Golda Meir's voted for immobility. It had no long-term concept for a settlement. True, the government made (or accepted) various peace proposals, but there was widespread relief when the Arabs in their intransigence rejected them, for the status quo seemed greatly preferable to any agreed settlement. The general philosophy (if any) behind this approach was that the Arab-Israeli confrontation, like every conflict in history, had to run its full course, that at some date, probably in the more distant future, there would be greater psychological readiness on the part of the Arabs to accept the existence of Israel. Then, but not earlier, it would be possible to find mutually acceptable solutions to all outstanding questions. This concept had much to recommend it in the light of historical experience. But it had one major flaw; it ignored the fact that the Arab-Israeli conflict was not purely regional in character, that big power interests were involved, that the Arabs had not only a great deal of arms but also weapons of another kind to bring indirect pressure on their enemy, and that as a result Israel found itself in growing isolation on the international scene. A major power could have watched this process with some equanimity, a small country could not.

Chapter Two On the Eve

The decision to attack Israel was taken in Cairo in the spring of 1973. It was no sudden decision nor the first such resolve. After the immediate shock of the defeat in 1967 Nasser had assumed that what had been lost by war could be restored only by war. The war of attrition in 1969-70, limited in scope, was regarded as a transitional stage; one day, soon, the Egyptian armed forces would be able to recover the lost territories. Some in Cairo proposed the crossing of the canal by a division or two: the enterprise would no doubt end in defeat, but it could be repeated after an interval; it would cause considerable Israeli losses, and would compel them to keep their army on the alert all the time. This would gravely weaken the Israeli economy even though it would not cause the downfall of the Jewish State. The idea was rejected; perhaps the Soviet advisers took a dim view of an exercise of this nature, perhaps it was opposed by the Egyptian generals who can hardly have enjoyed the prospect of sacrificing their men and materials for questionable political gains. Then on June 22nd, 1971, in a speech at the Alexandria Naval College, Sadat announced that this was the 'year of decision'. He was to regret this statement, for as 1972 came round there was no decision, only many jokes about the loudmouth whose promises were as foolish as those of the late Gamal Abdel Nasser. Sadat's explanation – that he had wanted to make war in November 1971, but that the Soviets had not agreed because their war material had to be diverted to India – was not given credence, though there may have been a grain of truth in it. It is doubtful whether Sadat could have gone to war in 1971, for his leadership at home was by no means uncontested. He may not have given up the idea of a political settlement; some observers of the Cairo scene believe that he considered rapprochement with the Americans after the Soviet advisers had been ousted in 1972.

Sadat expelled the Soviets because, like most Egyptians, he resented their growing hold on Egypt and, above all, because he feared for his own position. He did make half-hearted attempts to carry on a dialogue with Washington which lasted, broadly speaking, from August 1972 to March 1973. At the same time he continued to attack America in his speeches and threatened a renewal of hostilities against Israel. He believed that there was little if any sense in talking to the Israelis, directly or through mediators. Only America could possibly bring pressure to bear on the Israelis, and it was in all probability after the failure of the mission of Hafez Ismail to Washington in March 1973 that the idea of a new war began to preoccupy the Egyptian president. According to the Egyptian version Hafez Ismail, Sadat's adviser on security affairs, was told by President Nixon that he was willing to influence Israel only if Egypt would make a public declaration to the effect that it would accept concessions which went beyond the Rogers Plan. Meanwhile the American supply of Phantoms to Israel, a source of much worry to the Egyptians, would continue. The Rogers Plan, it will be recalled, was very favourable to the Arabs inasmuch as it envisaged a total Israeli retreat to the former international frontier between the two countries; only the future of the Gaza Strip and Sharm el Sheikh was to be left to negotiation. Nasser had rejected the Rogers Plan in December 1969, whereas Sadat three years later seems to have been willing to accept it provided further modifications could be made in Egypt's favour. But Washington felt itself no longer bound by this plan, and a new stalemate ensued. This was the stage when Sadat reached the conclusion that there was no way to break the stalemate other than war – not in the distant future, but within the next few months. In an interview with Arnaud de Borchgrave, a senior editor of *Newsweek*, Sadat declared in April 1973 that 'everything in this country is now being mobilized in earnest for the resumption of the battle, which is now inevitable.' Even before, on March 26th, he had announced in the Egyptian Parliament that he was taking over the premiership in order to prepare Egypt for total confrontation with Israel. The same determination recurred in countless speeches and interviews; in a talk on Libyan television he said, 'It has been always our conviction that what has been taken by violence can only be restored by violence.'[1] True, one could still find hints that a political solution was not entirely ruled out, but such statements were usually made in conversation with foreigners, not for domestic consumption. War was a necessity for Sadat's regime to overcome the credibility gap created by the failure of its promises.

The army did not have to be mobilized – it was ready for war. This is not to say that it was strong enough to tackle the Israelis single-handed. According to an appraisal by Shazli, the Egyptian chief of staff – made public much later by the Jordanian prime minister – Israel still had a 2:1 superiority. This could be partly offset by the moment of surprise, but full co-ordination with other Arab countries was needed. An Egyptian attack without the help of Syria and Jordan, and, if possible, other Arab states would have been suicidal. But there was also the question of détente; what help could Cairo expect from the Soviet Union in the case of an Egyptian attack? It would appear that Sadat could not quite make up his mind whether the international constellation favoured Egypt or not. Like other Arab leaders he thought of America's energy problem, and the great leverage which the Arab world could exercise in this respect.[2] But unlike King Faisal of Saudi Arabia he was not willing to wait until Western dependence on Arab oil would increase and could be used more effectively as a political weapon. Sadat's advisers seem to have taken a more pessimistic view of the world situation. As Heykal wrote in one of his famous Friday columns in *Al Ahram* in July 1973: 'We have altogether between three and five years to join forces and to develop a unified Arab policy.'[3] For the super-powers were exercising more and more control even on regional conflicts. Heykal warned against over-rating the effectiveness of the oil weapon; he believed the world financial crisis would be solved and that energy sources other than oil would be used by main consumers. According to some reports, the Russians too told Sadat not to put his trust in the 'oil weapon'. A general war had become impossible, détente was there to last – perhaps for three decades, as Brezhnev had informed Sadat in a personal message. There was, in other words, a real danger that the status quo would be frozen – including Israel's present borders with its Arab neighbours.

Egypt's relations with Moscow were a factor of crucial importance. Mention has been made of the attempts to patch up the alliance with Moscow after the crisis of summer 1972. A communiqué was published at the end of the Egyptian foreign minister's visit to Moscow in late May 1973; it pledged Soviet support for the Egyptian efforts to 'liquidate the consequences of aggression' and the possibility of military action was not ruled out. Following a talk with Brezhnev in Moscow in mid-June 1973, Hafez Ismail announced that there was agreement with regard to the next steps to be taken.[4] Did it mean war? Sadat made no secret of the fact that he still had certain reservations about Soviet policy: 'I told the Soviet leaders back in 1971,' he said on one occasion, 'that the present situation cannot be maintained. For if Israel does not feel that we can hit back it will cause an escalation of the situation.'[5] The Soviet Union, as Sadat and his advisers saw it, had a global strategy and was insufficiently aware of the regional problem that interested the Egyptians. Hence the conclusion that 'in our calculations we shall not consider the meetings of the super-powers and their discussions'. Even after Hafez Ismail's visit, when Soviet leaders had promised that military assistance to Egypt would continue, Sadat complained: 'We are not altogether satisfied with the arms deliveries but this is perhaps God's Will ...' Sadat always stressed that he was not in principle against détente, only against its consequences in the Middle East. Egyptian journalists were more outspoken. *Akhbar al Yom*, in articles by Ibrahim Saad and Ihsan Abdul Kuddous in August 1973, maintained that the Soviet Union had changed its foreign policy so that it no longer corresponded with the interest of the Arab countries. Such accusations were of course grossly unfair to the Soviet Union, which was willing to do anything for the Arabs, short of direct military intervention. In their reply to Egyptian critics Soviet spokesmen pointed to the Aswan High Dam, the Helwan steel plant, the Alexandria docks – 'not to mention the modern planes defending Egypt's skies'.

From what has been said so far a clear pattern emerges: while there were still tensions in Soviet-Egyptian relations, these in no way prevented close military collaboration. The Soviet Union remained Cairo's most important arms supplier and could also be relied upon to support Egypt in the United Nations and to put pressure on the United States. Seen from Moscow, Sadat's government was far from ideal: less 'progressive' than Nasser's, unreliable as far as Soviet interests in the region were concerned. Its increasingly close ties with the anti-Soviet and anti-communist regimes of Libya and Saudi Arabia must have caused further misgivings. But any failure to support the Egyptian Government would have greatly harmed the Soviet position in the Arab world, and perhaps even beyond it. There was always the hope that one day a more trustworthy regime would emerge in Cairo.

Libyan Interlude

In preparation for the military campaign Sadat had to establish closer relations with other Arab states, above all Syria and Jordan, Israel's neighbours, as well as Libya and Saudi Arabia who were to provide financial assistance. Mua'mar Qadafi of Libya was a most difficult partner. He had emerged as the leading figure after the coup of September 1969 in which the monarchy had been overthrown. A fanatical Muslim fundamentalist and equally staunch pan-Arab patriot, he was an impetuous, sometimes mentally unbalanced young officer. He had become a laughing stock for some: the intellectuals refused to take him seriously and Bourguiba called him a 'man from the stone age'. But for less sophisticated people in the Arab world he was the new saviour, Nasser's successor. The fact that he had a great deal of money to distribute was of considerable help in building up his reputation; he gave assistance to Muslim groups and assorted radical movements all over the world. Financial support went to insurgents in the Philippines, the I.R.A., the smaller African states, not to mention Malta and the Palestinian Arab groups. Radio Tripoli officially announced that it was financing attempts to assassinate King Husain and other undesirable Arab leaders. Qadafi was one of the main financial pillars of Sadat's regime and he declared himself in favour of immediate and total unity with Egypt, with Sudan and with Tunisia if necessary. Given Libya's wealth and its political and military weakness, it is one of the unsolved riddles of recent Middle-Eastern history why Nasser, and after him Sadat, did not accept this offer with alacrity and gain control of the oilfields; Qadafi could have been made minister for religious affairs or ambassador to the Philippines in which he had shown so much interest.

Qadafi saw his native Libya as the Prussia – or the Piedmont – of the Middle East, from which the Arab world could be effectively united. Seldom in history had there been such a discrepancy be-tween the power base of a politician and his ambitions: Libya, a vast desert country, has a population of less than two millions, almost half of them migrant Bedouins, who had not the slightest interest in Qadafi's far-flung ambitions, if indeed they had ever heard of them. Qadafi needed a much broader base for his projects; but at the same time he referred contemptuously to society in Egypt and other Arab countries as being rotten, inasmuch as it no longer obeyed the prescriptions of the holy Koran. He was equally outspoken with regard to the Arab governments: 'They are bank-rupt and paralysed,' he declared at a press conference in Benghazi in March 1973. It was not the only such statement and by no means the most offensive. A modern apostle of puritanism, he banned the sale and consumption of alcohol in his country, and had all inscriptions in languages other than Arabic removed. Foreigners were permitted to enter Libya only if their passports were in Arabic, thieves and other wrongdoers were punished by cutting off parts of their bodies. On the issue of Israel, only the most radical solution appealed to him, as to other non-combatant Arab leaders. The liberation of the occupied territories was a half-measure which he dismissed with contempt; his aim was the disappearance of the state of Israel. He also organized a 'cultural revolution', scheduled to liquidate all harmful foreign ideas incompatible with the Koran and Arab nationalism. Books were burned and the masses were called upon to take over the State radio and television. But since the masses could not run the radio, let alone the TV stations, everything returned to normal after a short period of chaos. A very few days before the outbreak of war Libya solemnly an-nounced a new punishment for adultery, defined as 'sexual inter-course between men and women not legitimately linked by marriage'. The transgressors would be given a hundred lashes with a 'single whip made of leather free of knots'; but in severe cases the 'penalty of death as a deterrent' was also mentioned.[6] This man, then, was Sadat's closest ally at the time, full of energy but always moody, given to manic activity and to fits of depression, for which he reportedly sought refuge from time to time in a nursing home. One day he would proclaim the most grandiose plans, the next he would declare that there was no point in convening a meeting of

43

the Arab Socialist Union, the Libyan state party, because it was good for nothing.[7]

In August 1971 Egypt and Syria had signed the constitution of the Federation of Arab Republics, announcing that the battle with Israel was at hand; in March 1972 Qadafi, Sadat and Asad of Syria had been sworn in at the first formal session of the assembly of the federation linking these states. According to schedule this union was to take full effect by September 1973. But, while asking for immediate and complete union, Qadafi behaved as if union did not exist; in January 1973, for instance, he announced the withdrawal of his troops from the Suez front because of the lack of action there.

The negotiations reached an acute stage in June 1973 when the Libyan leader came to Cairo and declared that he stood for a full merger; he was not interested in a mere federation. Again he complained: why was there no agreement between Cairo and Damascus about the coming battle against Israel? He thought that the Egyptian-Soviet friendship treaty should be cancelled since it fulfilled no useful function. Was it not true that Egypt had received more help before the treaty had been signed than after? Was it not equally true that the Soviets had exerted political pressure on Egypt – for instance at the time of the Communist coup in Sudan? Qadafi had misgivings about a war against Israel based mainly on Soviet help, for such a war would produce in the Arab States greater dependence on the Soviet Union, which would emerge as the leading power in the area. Attacking the negative Soviet attitude towards union between Libya and Egypt as expressed at this time in a *Pravda* article, one of Qadafi's spokesmen said that basically the Soviet Union was an imperialist power, no less anti-Arab than the United States.[8] Sadat on the other hand assured Qadafi that he was quite capable of handling the Soviet Union, i.e. of obtaining the maximum of Soviet help while giving the Russians nothing in return and preserving Egypt's independence.

Qadafi's stay in Cairo was ill starred. Egyptian women were not persuaded by the Libyan colonel who told them that their place was at home, that they should not preoccupy themselves with public affairs because they were congenitally inferior to men. He fared no better with the local intellectuals or the Egyptian politicians. And so after his return to Tripoli a mass pilgrimage was organized. Called upon by the radio and press, thousands of Libyan citizens in cars and trucks moved into Egypt, displaying slogans based on the speeches of Qadafi and the late Gamal Abdel Nasser. The purpose of this strange venture was to exert pressure on Sadat; perhaps the Egyptian masses would join the crusade? But for Sadat the whole idea of a cultural revolution was childish; worse, it could well mean chaos, about the last thing he wanted on the eve of his military campaign. Egyptian authorities stopped the convoy inside Egyptian territory not far from the border and only a small delegation was permitted to proceed to Cairo to hand over a petition written in blood. Though Sadat seems to have been greatly annoyed his public answer was in measured terms: such 'mass actions' were no alternative to serious consultations. He explained to Qadafi that the preparations for the confrontation with Israel had top priority and any action that would detract attention from this overriding aim must be considered harmful to the common cause. It is interesting that outside Egypt no one seems to have paid attention at the time to this statement; of course, Sadat had so often spoken about the coming war that these hints were no longer taken very seriously.

True to form, Qadafi countered by resigning from his post 'to remove the obstacles on the road to Libyan-Egyptian unity'. He had resigned several times before and the Egyptians were not unduly worried. Other members of the Tripoli revolutionary council announced that they too would resign if Qadafi did not change his mind. But according to another report the same day (July 21st, 1973) Qadafi had not resigned at all. Two days later he made a long speech in the Benghazi sports ground. At the beginning he said that the question of his resignation should be discussed in a calm atmosphere, not charged with emotion; demonstrations and strikes would not help. But the audience interrupted him, and for seven minutes there was pandemonium; whereupon Qadafi – though the atmosphere was no calmer – announced that he would not resign, at least not until full unity with Egypt had been achieved.[9] He was still most unhappy about the situation in Egypt: State control there was not successful, the country was run by the bureaucracy and this inspired anxiety in him with regard to the future of Egypt and the prospects of the union. Egypt needed a cultural revolution and 'direct democracy', not elections – otherwise it would not be able to face the enemy.

The negotiations about Egyptian and Libyan unity continued throughout August and September. But Sadat had lost patience; with an ally like Qadafi who needed an enemy? He no longer had time for endless and inconclusive talks with the Libyan, instead he sent one of his secretaries to Tripoli to keep Qadafi informed. On the eve of the Egyptian attack the Libyan leader once again appeared suddenly in Cairo, but fell ill and could not appear in public. Sadat had realized that the Libyan connection made it virtually impossible for him to put relations with the other Arab states on a normal footing. And so he decided as tactfully as possible to lessen his dependence on Qadafi and to turn elsewhere in his quest for additional financial support. To that end he visited Saudi Arabia and some of the little Persian Gulf states in late August.

Sadat and Faisal

The visit to Riyadh, the Saudi capital, was of considerable importance as far as the war against Israel was concerned. King Faisal's financial resources were considerably greater than Qadafi's, he was not a capricious man, nor would he try to dictate his policy to the Egyptians. Faisal welcomed the rapprochement with the Egyptians which was bound to strengthen his position in the Arab world. Until very recently Saudi Arabia had been rather isolated, a conservative regime increasingly out of tune with the radical forces in the Middle East. The Saudi ruling stratum, the king, a few hundred royal princes and their retainers had watched with apprehension the gradual encirclement of their country by a variety of enemies – from Aden in the south to Dhofar in the east and Baghdad in the north. Whatever the differences between Maoists and radical nationalists, both wished to bring down the Saudi dynasty. Its only potential ally was Iran, but, in view of the traditional distrust between Arabs and Persians, not to mention certain conflicting interests in the Persian Gulf, relations between Riyadh and Tehran were not in fact very friendly; the Saudis would turn to Tehran only in a grave emergency.

Of late, after years in the shadows, Saudi Arabia had suddenly become a very important country. It was thought to have the largest oil reserves by far in the world, as much as the United States, Iran and Libya taken together. It was gratifying for King Faisal to find himself treated as a statesman of great power and consequence but it must have also occurred to him that his country and his regime would in future be even more exposed to danger from without and within and he was desperately looking for new allies. He had never been able to get along with Nasser; Sadat was a man more to his liking. On Israel there was unanimity: something had to be done to evict the Israeli intruders from the occupied territories. The Saudi armed forces had not been involved in the previous wars and for this reason they did not share the acute sense of humiliation of the Egyptians and Syrians. On the other hand the Israeli conquest of Jerusalem had driven Faisal, a devout Muslim, into a veritable *odium theologicum*. The keeper of the holy shrines in Mecca and Medina felt a special responsibility for the holy places in Arab Jerusalem. He could not give much military help; the small Saudi Army consisted of four infantry brigades (36,000 men), of which 4,000 men were deployed in Jordan, and a small airforce which unfortunately was a hot-bed of political opposition and had been grounded for several years. But Faisal could give money, he could help to bring about a normalization of relations between Egypt and Jordan, and, above all, he could put pressure on the Americans.

Throughout the summer of 1973 spokesmen of American oil companies and various Arabists had stressed in meetings with the American administration the crucial importance of Saudi Arabia. Unless the Saudis were willing to increase their oil production, the United States and *a fortiori* the rest of the Western World and Japan would face an acute oil shortage in the near future. The Saudis (they argued) would be willing to oblige only if the United States changed its policy with regard to Israel. In years past the Saudis (as the Persians) had always stressed that unlike the Iraqis they had no desire to mix oil and politics. But as the West became more and more concerned about the energy shortage of the 'eighties and 'nineties there was a shift in the Saudi attitude. King

Faisal made it clear to his friends in Washington that he was under growing pressure by his fellow Arabs to impose an oil boycott. While he had no intention of cutting production such as, for instance, the Libyans had done, he could not possibly increase production to the extent the Americans wanted.

A great deal of bluffing was involved, for if America needed Saudi oil, the Saudi regime needed the political and military help of the United States even more badly. Without such help its chances of survival cannot be rated highly. But the intricacies of Middle-Eastern politics are not widely known, whereas the clamour for more oil has become universal; for this reason, if for no other, Faisal was bound to carry weight in Washington. Sadat seems to have accepted Faisal's suggestion that Arab policy should be to threaten non-expansion of oil production rather than sudden cuts. Sudden cuts might cause a shock in the capitals of the Western world; if pressed too hard the Americans and the Europeans might take drastic action, perhaps even seize and internationalize the Arabian oilfields. Applying gradual pressure on the other hand would probably result in greater willingness on the part of the West to fulfil the demands of the Arabs.

One does not know to what extent Faisal was drawn into Sadat's confidence about his plans. It is possible (but unlikely) that he discussed with the king the October campaign in detail; it seems more probable that he talked with him about the possibility of a war in the not-too-distant future and various eventualities that could arise in this context. Some of Sadat's advisers, such as Heykal, had suggested that Egypt should try to get Saudi support without getting too closely tied up with Faisal, for a Cairo-Riyadh axis was bound to create difficulties elsewhere in the Arab world.

The Eastern Front

In discussions about the war against Israel the idea of the 'reactivation of the Eastern front' had always played a central role. It will be recalled that the reconciliation, after years of bitter attacks, between King Husain and President Nasser less than a week before the Six Day War was one of the milestones in the pre-history of that war. Suddenly, late in the morning of May 30th, 1967, Husain had arrived in the Egyptian capital together with his prime minister and several high army officers. A few hours later the text of a new defence agreement was announced and at five in the afternoon Husain was already back in Amman – together with Ahmed Shukairy, the head of the Palestine Liberation Organization and Husain's pet aversion. The crowds were cheering and now it was all kisses, 'brother Nasser' and 'our sincere Husain'. Perhaps it was inevitable that Husain would rejoin the camp, but he was to pay dearly for his decision. During the Six Day War his Arab legion fought courageously, but it was no match for the Israelis, and when the fighting was over he had lost the entire western half of his kingdom.

Worse yet, his country was saddled with hundreds of thousands of refugees. The more militant among them soon began to behave as if the state of Jordan did not exist. They would engage in hit-and-run attacks against the Israelis, or more often shoot at them from Jordanian territory. When the Israelis retaliated they had disappeared and the regular Jordanian army had to bear the brunt of the counterblow. There were some 15,000 Iraqi soldiers in Jordan and a Syrian armoured brigade; the king seemed to be no longer master in his own house. There were constant clashes between regular forces and the Palestinians in the autumn of 1968, in February 1970 and then throughout the summer of 1970 ending in a draw. In September 1970 the small but effective and loyal Jordanian army turned against the insurgents who showed little military prowess in activities more exacting than hi-jacking. The result was bloody; Nasser in a cable to Husain talked about a 'ghastly massacre', General Numeiri of Sudan of 'genocide' committed by the Jordanian army, Qadafi asked for immediate military sanctions, and Iraq and Syria gave the Fatah military help to fight Husain. All this did not make the king disposed to be friendly towards his Arab brethren. The Iraqis, the Sudanese and the Libyans had sent him encouraging messages when he was fighting for survival but that had been about all. How to explain the curious fact that every Arab country, including much stronger ones, such as Egypt, refused to give the para-military forces bases on their territory while insisting at the same time that Jordan must do nothing to limit their freedom of action? The bloody fighting in September 1970 – from which 'Black September' was to derive its name – ended in a compromise in which the Palestinians just saved face. There were further clashes in April 1971 and in July of that year the last pockets of Palestinians were driven out. During that phase of fighting alone more than a thousand Palestinian irregulars were killed or wounded; more than 2,000 captured and a few dozen crossed the Jordan into Israel, preferring the Zionist monster to King Husain.

King Husain effectively restored his rule in Jordan but found himself ostracized as far as the rest of the Arab world was concerned. He still had the tacit support of the Saudis who wanted to bring about a reconciliation between him and the Palestinian irregulars; they might have succeeded but for the murder of Wasfi el Tal, the Jordanian prime minister, in Cairo by a group of Palestinians who announced that they wanted to drink his blood. The debate as to whether this was intended metaphorically preoccupied the Arabists for a long time; Sadat decided not to prosecute the murderers, for which Husain could not, of course, forgive him. Meanwhile many Arab countries had broken off relations with Jordan; Syria had even closed its borders. In March 1972 Husain announced a plan for a new federation uniting Jordan with the West Bank once the Israelis would withdraw from it. There would be a governor general and a Cabinet for each region, with Amman and Jerusalem as capitals. Husain regarded his project as the only feasible plan to break the deadlock; it was clear that it implied peace with Israel. Egypt reacted by severing diplomatic relations with Jordan.

King Husain, it will be recalled, had met Israeli leaders several times since 1967 and he had, albeit reluctantly, reached the conclusion that in view of the total lack of Arab solidarity there was no alternative but an accommodation with Israel. This coincided with the policy of open bridges sponsored by Dayan. Arab-Israeli produce was freely exported to Jordan; tens of thousands of Jordanian visitors crossed into Israel every year. There was de facto a state of peace between the two countries and Husain would have been ready to sign a peace settlement, 'for another war would be disastrous', as he told the representatives of an American television network in January 1973. Nevertheless, when the Egyptians indicated their willingness to be reconciled with Jordan, Husain was only too willing to meet them halfway.

The gradual Egyptian-Jordanian rapprochement began with two visits of the uncle of Jordan's prime minister to Cairo in June and July, and another visit by the same envoy to Damascus. (According to some reports Said Rifai, the Jordanian prime minister, also paid secret visits to the Egyptian and Syrian capitals.) In early August Sadat's personal representative Hassan Sabri al Khouli went to Amman; upon his return he declared that he had tried to create the conditions 'for the sake of the cause for which we work on all levels – namely the battle'.[10] When Mustafa Tlas, the Syrian defence minister, appeared in Amman on August 29th, it should have been clear that something was in the air, for Jordan's relations with Syria had been exceedingly bad. These contacts culminated in a meeting on September 12th in Cairo between the leaders of the 'frontline states', Sadat, Husain and Asad; diplomatic relations between Jordan and Egypt, and Jordan and Syria were renewed. The possibility of restoring the financial assistance of the oil states was also mentioned; Sadat apparently offered his good services to intervene on Jordan's behalf with Kuwait and Abu Dhabi.

There was no hope of persuading Qadafi, who was firmly opposed to the alliance with Jordan. As the official Libyan newspaper *Al Balag* wrote, 'The rapprochement would give the Hashemite government merely a pretext to hasten the liquidation of the Palestinian resistance.'[11] That Qadafi disliked the Jordanians goes without saying, but the real target of his attack was King Faisal. As Qadafi saw it, Saudi Arabia was a state similar to Libya before the revolution – its rulers had always opposed the radical measures demanded by Libya against the oil-consuming countries. They had treated him as an upstart and in many parts of the Middle East and in Africa they had discreetly pre-empted Libyan activities by actually distributing money where Qadafi had merely given promises. But the Saudi rulers were devout Muslims and their anti-Israeli fervour was second to none; it would have been unwise to attack them directly, whereas Jordan was a much easier target. It is however more than doubtful whether Sadat was still willing to listen to the unsolicited advice offered by Qadafi.*

The Jordanians commented on the Cairo meeting with considerable caution. The stress was on 'national responsibility', on 'dialogue' and 'consultations'.[12] They were glad to note that relations with other Arab countries had again been normalized. According to some Arab sources Husain promised at the Cairo meeting that his armour would attack the Israeli town of Bet She'an, a few miles across the border. But he made this conditional on the Syrians seizing the Golan Heights.

While the war was discussed at the Cairo meeting it is doubtful whether Sadat in conversation with Husain committed himself to a certain date and whether Husain committed himself to a certain strategy. In view of what had happened in the past Sadat and Asad could not possibly trust Husain; even if they did not keep the secret from him, Husain may not fully have believed them. After all, it was not the first time that the beginning of the battle had been announced, only to be postponed at the last moment. In an interview with a leading Beirut newspaper Husain talked about 'setting up the basis for a firm building', of evading hasty action 'so that we do not suffer shocks and defeats as in the past'.[13] It is unlikely that he would have used this language had he known that war was impending. Husain gave instructions to release most of the Palestinians from prison including 'Abu Ayad' (Salah Khalef) one of the main Fatah leaders arrested in September 1970. His army was small, it had to defend a very long border, it lacked heavy tanks and effective air support; Husain probably did not commit himself in Cairo to taking part from zero hour in the attack against Israel. On the other hand, by making threatening noises he would compel the Israelis to keep some forces in readiness along the Jordan river and also south of Jerusalem. These forces would not be able to participate in the battles in Sinai or the Golan Heights; thus he would provide indirect assistance to his Arab brothers. He could have gone no further; for it remained to be seen whether Sadat and Asad really meant what they were saying. With all the talk about the restored solidarity and the regained fraternal

* Qadafi: 'Sadat and Asad have taken their decision [to go to war] without my agreement, without consulting, without even informing me.' (*Le Monde*, October 23rd, 1973)

feelings, the Voice of Palestine radio, stationed in Cairo, continued to attack Husain in violent terms: Husain was 'feverishly moving towards the enemy'. The Zionist-Royalist co-operation continued, a meeting had allegedly taken place in Aqaba between Israeli and Jordanian officials to discuss the building of a highroad connecting the Gaza Strip with the port of Aqaba. The king was serving the enemy, he was plotting behind the back of the Arab nation, Arab détente (i.e. the Cairo meeting) was simply a smoke screen behind which he was hiding.[14] A great deal of calumny and vituperation – and the attack was just five days away. The understanding reached in Cairo was, according to all the evidence available, tentative in character.

It seems in retrospect possible that the conflict between Egypt and Israel could have been reduced to manageable proportions but for Nasser's ambitious pan-Arab schemes and Israeli unwillingness to compromise after 1967. It is quite likely that there could have been a lasting settlement between Israel and Jordan. For pan-Arabism had reached Egypt comparatively late in the day; many Egyptians continued to regard themselves first and foremost as heirs to a specific national heritage and only secondly as Arabs. As far as the Syrians were concerned, the war was inevitable, there was no willingness on their part to compromise. They were the most fanatical advocates of Arabism; Palestine to them was 'Janub-Suria' – South Syria. Fighting on the Israeli-Syrian border had always been more bitter than elsewhere; the Israelis had not forgotten the almost constant bombardment of their settlements in Upper Galilee before 1967. At the time of the Six Day War Syria was ruled by a pro-Soviet junta, the extreme wing of the Ba'ath Party, which was ousted in November 1970 by Asad, former minister of defence and commander of the air force. His was the twenty-second regime in twenty-eight years; he stood for a more nationalist Arab policy, slightly more liberal at home.

Once the bases of the fedayeen in Jordan had been destroyed and their freedom of action was curbed in Lebanon, Syria was under pressure to let them operate from its own territory. This the Syrians did though they must have known that it would provoke Israeli retaliatory action. There was heavy fighting on the Syrian-Israeli border in November 1972 and a day-long battle on January

8th, 1973; Damascus radio called the other Arab countries to go into battle immediately and not let Syria stand alone and take the enemy blows. There were more battles in the following months, the most spectacular on August 13th, 1973, when thirteen Syrian planes were shot down over the Mediterranean not far from the Syrian coast by the Israelis, at the loss of one of their own. This was a severe blow to Syrian self-esteem and to Asad personally; the air force after all had been his original power base.

Asad was drawn into Sadat's confidence soon after the failure of Hafez Ismail's mission in Washington. Ahmed Ismail, Egyptian war minister, visited his colleagues in Damascus on April 2nd, and again on May 8th. In June Sadat flew to the Syrian capital for talks with Asad, and in July it was announced by the Syrian foreign minister that Egypt and Syria were agreed on a common policy. This referred probably to Asad's acceptance of Resolution 242 of the U.N. as his war aim; up to that date the Syrians had rejected the U.N. resolution and insisted on total war and the destruction of Israel. During the weeks of August there were several meetings between high-ranking Egyptian and Syrian military leaders, and by the time the tripartite pact was signed with Jordan on September 12th, the details of military co-operation between Egypt and Syria had been worked out.[15]

Iraq did not figure in Sadat's planning. At one time or another it had quarrelled with all other Arab countries. Furthermore there were serious doubts about Iraq's internal stability below the façade of 'national unity'; the head of the Iraqi secret police had attempted to overthrow the regime in a coup on June 30th, but only succeeded in assassinating the minister of defence. Iraq was involved in a conflict with Iran, and there was always the danger of civil war in the Kurdish regions. The Iraqi army was not rated highly; if Sadat told the Iraqis anything at all about his campaign, he did so, in all probability, at the very last moment.

Inside Israel

Foreign and Israeli observers were in full agreement that never in its history had the country felt so secure, never was a new war thought less likely. True, the Arab leaders continued to talk about

54

the coming battle against Israel, but this was thought to be mere rhetoric, part and parcel of the Arab political style. No one attributed any importance to bellicose statements, because without massive Soviet help the Arabs would not possibly dare to attack. No one expected that such help would be forthcoming at a time when Nixon and Brezhnev were announcing the arrival of a new age of true, peaceful co-existence. Israel, some argued, was now the only military power that counted between Paris and New Delhi. Forgotten were the difficult days of 1969-70 when the Israeli air force had suffered substantial losses over Suez, when it had appeared that the Soviet SAM missiles were a most formidable – temporarily insuperable – obstacle to Israeli air superiority. Ignored was the fact that though many Soviet military instructors and advisers had been withdrawn from Egypt, quite a few had remained or returned. If Soviet arms supplies had decreased over the last year or two, the main reason was no doubt that saturation of the Egyptian and the Syrian armies had been reached. Given the limited number of trained personnel it is doubtful whether the Egyptians and Syrians could have used more planes and tanks than they had.

Little attention was paid to these facts, understandably no doubt, because this was, after all, the age of détente. A wide-ranging understanding had been reached between Moscow and Washington; as a result the two super-powers would not only refuse to be drawn into a regional conflict, they would do their utmost (as it was said in solemn declarations) to prevent any situation arising that could endanger world peace. Surely, this applied to the Middle East as well as to other regions; the Russians after all could not participate in a Middle-Eastern war while preaching peaceful co-operation in Europe. These and other arguments seemed altogether convincing and they all proved that there would be no change in the Middle East in the foreseeable future. The centre of gravity was shifting for obvious reasons from Sinai to the Persian Gulf, an area infinitely more important for the super-powers and the rest of the world – except Egypt, Syria and Israel.

There were other reasons for Israeli optimism. The economic situation was better than ever before; between 1969 and 1972 the real increase in the G.N.P. was on the average almost 10 per cent,

55

a rise paralleled in very few other countries. Per capita annual income had reached $2,000, which put Israel in eighteenth place in the world: equal with Austria and ahead of Italy, an astonishing achievement for a nation poor in natural resources. In 1969-70 it had been predicted that the country faced bankruptcy because its holdings in foreign currency were dwindling at a rapid rate as the result, mainly, of the enormous defence budget. But in 1972 foreign currency holdings were almost three times higher than in 1969. New industries were established, new suburbs and settlements built, there was an alarming increase in private cars considering the small size of the country and the few first-rate highroads in existence. The boom showed no signs of diminishing, and there was virtually no unemployment. Immigrants from Russia began to arrive in ever-increasing numbers; more than 30,000 had come during the last year before the war. This too, had been unthinkable even a few years previously. Partly under the pressure of Western public opinion, partly for somewhat obscure internal reasons, the Soviet authorities had decided to get rid of most of the trouble-makers. True, there were difficulties with regard to the absorption of the newcomers in Israel; culturally, socially and even professionally the new immigrants underwent an often painful process of adjustment. But this had been the lot of every immigration wave in the history of Jewish Palestine; some of the newcomers would move on to greener pastures but the great majority would stay.

Internal security in Israel, too, was greater than ever before. Many thousands of workers from the occupied territories had found permanent work in Israeli towns and settlements, their economic situation had considerably improved since 1967. Israeli authorities believed in a minimum of intervention in internal Arab affairs; Arab newspapers in Jerusalem could bitterly attack Israeli politics with impunity, Israeli soldiers in the occupied territories were kept in the background. Even the Gaza Strip, which for a long time had been a hotbed of terrorist warfare, had become very quiet indeed. The Arabs had not come to love and admire their Israeli conquerors, but most of them had reached the conclusion that there was no alternative but to accept the situation and to make the best of it. Few would have quarrelled with Moshe Dayan when he detected a mental shift in favour of a peace settlement in the occupied territories.[16] Whichever way one looked at it there seemed every reason for Israeli confidence. They had 'played a *Klaf meshuga*' (drawn an ace) for six years running, an almost unbelievable strain of luck.

True, there were some dark clouds on the political horizon, but these seemed small and distant. Increasingly, Israel found itself in political isolation on the international scene. This was particularly felt in Africa where more and more countries had severed diplomatic relations with Israel. In the United Nations and *a fortiori* in regional Afro-Asian meetings there would be heavy majorities for increasingly violent anti-Israeli resolutions. Israelis felt bitterly disappointed and hurt particularly by the decision of African countries to whom they had extended a great deal of help in years past. The reasons for this change of heart were obvious. Chad, for instance, had been paid a hundred million dollars by the Arabs in compensation for its political reorientation, a sum almost twice the yearly income of the country. This was an offer the Israelis could not possibly match. In Asia they had few friends anyway. India, which counted among its citizens more Muslims than Egypt, Syria, Iraq and Jordan together, had been hostile from the very beginning; in recent years its foreign policy had become as predictable as that of a Soviet satellite.

Loss of sympathy for Israel in Europe had been less far reaching; there was a widespread belief in Europe that the Middle-East conflict was a nuisance and a potential danger to world peace. Some thought it was one of the main obstacles on the road to genuine détente between West and East and that the Israelis were more at fault than the Arabs. But even if Israel's cause had been without blemish it would still have been blamed, for there were many Arabs and few Jews, and the former had the oil on which Western Europe's industry depended. British foreign policy was surreptitiously pro-Arab, French policy openly so, Italy had the interests of its citizens in the Arab world to consider; even Chancellor Brandt, who had visited Israel earlier in 1973, had talked about a new chapter in German-Israeli relations. Israel could not count any longer on a special relationship with West Germany, whose Middle-Eastern policy would be even-handed.

Once upon a time it had been argued that Zionism owed its

political successes to the influence of the moneyed Jews. It was not quite true because most Jewish millionaires had always dissociated themselves from the Jewish national movement. Be that as it may, economic assistance to Israel by world Jewry was dwarfed into insignificance by the wealth of the oil sheikhs which all over the world was used as a political weapon.

Israelis followed their progressive isolation with incredulity. Surely it was the failure of their emissaries abroad who had been unable to present Israel's position and aims in the right light? There was a touchingly naive belief in Israel in the omnipotence of the information services, as if these could make the oil-fields of Saudi Arabia, Libya and Iraq disappear or transfer them to the Negev desert. The Jews had always been an argumentative people, there was a curious inability to accept that in politics there were stubborn, objective facts which no amount of reasoning, explaining or persuading could possibly change or remove. Israeli incredulity turned into cynicism, some of it justified, some not. The Security Council had an inbuilt anti-Israeli majority; if the Arabs were to submit a complaint that Israel had attacked Okinawa and poisoned the local wells, it was virtually certain that the great majority would accept this. Russia would maintain that Israel should be severely punished, China would argue that Russia simply wanted to appease Israel by suggesting half-hearted measures, the British and French representatives would at best ask for more time to study these serious allegations and only the Americans would dissent from an otherwise full consensus. What many Israelis failed to realize in their analysis of, for instance, French policy, was that France, after all, acted according to what it thought were its best economic interests. It had not greatly benefited from this policy so far, but neither had it suffered any harm, and there was always the chance that its pro-Arab stance would be rewarded one day. The Israelis found it difficult to accept that most countries act in accordance with their economic interests rather than lofty ideals or abstract justice; as far as Western Europe was concerned Israel was expendable whereas the Arab oil was not – at least not for some time to come. Of course, in the last resort it was of no great consequence what the British or French foreign ministers said or did, for Europe had ceased to count in world politics. An economic giant, it was in no position to assert its interest in the Middle East.

There was only one power that could counterbalance Soviet influence in the region and this was, of course, the United States. Israeli relations with Washington were close and there was undiminished support for Israel in Congress and in public opinion. There was no danger, Israelis felt, that the administration would sell Israel down the river as the French had done because the international constellation had changed. Israelis watched with anxiety the internal tribulations of the Nixon administration during the summer months of 1973; they feared that Watergate would have a direct impact on America's foreign politics. Who in Washington cared about the state of the world while the epic battle of the tapes was fought? The Israelis, like other Western nations, feared that the president's freedom of action during the years to come would be greatly restricted. But on the whole they felt so secure that when Ambassador Rabin's turn came to return home in 1973 he was replaced by someone of very different stature. This appointment was of some significance for Washington was the key position in the Israeli diplomatic service.

There were undercurrents which did not justify Israeli optimism. Between American support for Israel and Soviet help to the Arabs there was no symmetry. America had to consider its other interests in the Middle East, whereas the Soviet Union could give all-out assistance to its clients. Quite frequently Americans found to their embarrassment that no other country was willing to speak up for Israel in the U.N., irrespective of the merits of the case. American diplomats, too, had argued for a long time that close identification with Israel was detrimental to America's interests; they found support in Congress and also in the media. President Nixon with all his sympathies for Israel had declared a few weeks before the outbreak of the war that both sides were to blame for the lengthy stalemate. The oil companies had launched a public relations campaign to explain to the public that if America wanted a secure oil supply American foreign policy had to comply with the justified national aspirations of the Arab peoples. But the Israelis saw no cause for alarm; the real energy crisis was a number of years ahead and in the meantime a great many changes could take place in the Middle East.

Israeli isolation was perhaps felt most acutely in their struggle against terrorism in which they received no foreign help. Palestinian para-military groups had existed well before the Six Day War but it was only after 1967 that Fatah and the other terrorist organizations became factors of some political importance. Israel needed no outside help to cope with terrorist activities inside the country and they would have been quite willing to weather the storm in the Security Council whenever they hit back against the bases of the terrorists in Lebanon and Syria; unlike true guerrillas the Palestinians had failed to establish such bases inside Israel. There was insufficient support on the part of the Arab population and furthermore geographical conditions did not favour guerrilla warfare. Thus, but for the occasional bomb in a supermarket or bus station there was no armed resistance inside Israel. When this had proved impossible, the Palestinians had begun to concentrate on the hijacking of planes and on attacks against Israeli embassies and individuals abroad. It began with the hijacking in Rome in July 1968 of an El Al plane which was taken to Algiers. Then in December 1968 passengers of another El Al plane were attacked in transit at Athens airport; there was a similar attack in Zurich in February 1969 and in Munich in February 1970. When El Al introduced stringent security measures the terrorists transferred their activities to the airlines of other countries. By this time killing by proxy had become a widespread practice; Japanese terrorists were enlisted by the Palestinians to kill a group of Puerto Rican pilgrims at Lod airport, on the assumption that this would deal a severe blow to the Zionist occupiers. A T.W.A. Boeing was hijacked in Damascus in August 1969, an Olympic Airways plane in Beirut in July 1970, to list only a few of these incidents. Forty-seven persons were killed in February 1970 when a Swissair plane was exploded by a bomb activated by barometric pressure. In quite a few of these cases the hijackers were arrested by British, French, Italian, German or Greek authorities, but they were invariably released from prison after a short time because their comrades threatened retaliatory action against B.E.A., Air France and Lufthansa. No European country wanted to become the battleground between Arab terrorists and Israeli counter-terrorists; the governments thought it was the wisest as well as the most responsible and humane course of action to give in to such blackmail whenever facing it. Thus the killers of eleven members of the Israeli team at the Olympic games in Munich were released by the German authorities seven weeks later. A Lufthansa plane had been hijacked by Arabs who demanded that their Munich colleagues be set free. The Israelis' claim that there had been connivance between Germans and Arabs was probably untrue; the German authorities (and the French and the Italians) would have acted the same way if their own nationals had been involved. Like all bureaucrats they wanted above all peace and quiet, and the way of least resistance to cope with blackmail was of course to give in.

The inability on the part of the international community to reach agreement, even in principle, to combat air piracy caused some despondency among Israelis. Objectively, the activities of the terrorists were of no consequence; they did not even affect tourism to or from Israel. But psychologically they were important because they caused a hardening of Israeli attitudes towards the Arabs; Israeli doves could not expect sympathetic audiences in the wake of the Munich massacre. As security precautions became more effective, attacks against Israeli institutions were made more difficult; other means of 'guerrilla warfare' had to be employed, such as letter bombs, but these too, after a brief scare had little effect. There was much internal dissension in the ranks of the Palestinians and by 1973 their activities had become on the whole rare, and ineffectual. But it was, of course, not humanly possible to prevent attacks against Jews and Israelis altogether; just eight days before the outbreak of the war Israel suffered its heaviest psychological defeat in its war against the terror. Two Arabs armed with hand-grenades and submachine-guns attacked Russian Jewish immigrants on the train from Czechoslovakia to Vienna and held a group hostage. They had boarded the train in Czechoslovakia and since this was their second attempt in a month it stands to reason that the Czech authorities were not altogether unaware of their intentions. However, the attack happened on Austrian soil and Austrian authorities had to face the agonizing problem of how to treat the kidnappers.

The Austrian government of the day was headed by a veteran socialist of Jewish origin, Bruno Kreisky. A man of intelligence and integrity, but not a Churchill or De Gaulle, Mr Kreisky broke down under pressure and promised that Schönau, the transit camp for Soviet Jews, would be closed if the Arabs released their hostages, which they promptly did. This concession was all the more surprising since the attackers had not even asked for it, they merely wanted a plane to fly with their hostages to an Arab country. Mr Kreisky was not however willing to admit that his nerve had failed him and that a promise extracted under duress was invalid. He announced that he would not change his mind and 'give in to pressure' – meaning that he would not give in to moral pressure, only to the threat of violence. While there was a great outcry about Kreisky's behaviour in most Western capitals, his action was approved by a majority of Austrians, a fact which would not have surprised the late Sigmund Freud, who knew his compatriots only too well.

As the Israelis saw it, the Kreisky affair was a dangerous precedent. Other means of transporting Russian Jews to Israel could have been found. It was perfectly true that Austria was under no obligation to help the Russian Jews in any way; Kreisky would have been justified if he had objected to the establishment of the transit camp in the first place. But he could not give in to the carriers of two hand-grenades and submachine-guns without causing grave damage to the standards of political behaviour. Mr Kreisky faced the storm philosophically: 'Let them rage,' he said, 'the world will forget.' He could not have known how soon his prediction would come true. Eight days later everyone had forgotten about Mr Kreisky.

Seen in retrospect, the Kreisky affair was of little consequence. But it was symptomatic and it helps to understand Israeli psychology between the two wars. During the Second World War when one-third of the Jewish people had been massacred, the peoples of Europe had shown indifference. Israelis, needless to say, understood that no further holocaust was planned in Europe, but they were equally aware that it would be futile to expect any help from Europe if Jewish existence were to be threatened again. Hence the Israeli resolution to put their trust only in their own military strength. Such an assessment of European attitudes seemed to be altogether paranoiac, but as subsequent events were to show, it was not altogether unrealistic: M. Jobert and Sir Alec Douglas-Home would not have saved them.

The Israeli electoral campaign was nearing its end in early October. The elections to the eighth Knesset, the Israeli Parliament, were contested by twenty-two lists, more than ever before in the history of the country. There were some last-minute additions such as the 'Civil Rights Movement' sponsored by a leading Tel Aviv lawyer and television personality Mrs Shulamit Aloni, a Black Panther list of young militants mainly of North African origin and a rival group of Blue-White Panthers, an Iraqi and a Yemenite immigrants list, two communist factions, an Arab Bedouin and Villagers list, not to forget the indefatigable Rabbi Meir Kahane, a recent but very militant arrival from the U.S., and his Jewish Defence League. The two main rivals were the Labour Alignment which had been the central force in Zionist and Israeli politics for four decades and, on the right, the Likud which united the General Zionists, Mr Begin's Herut, as well as some smaller groups. The initiative for the establishment of Likud had come from General Sharon, former O.C. Southern Command, who had resigned from the army a few months earlier. Israeli military leaders were traditionally men of the left; in recent years, however, a certain shift to the right had been felt. General Ezer Weizman, former airforce commander, had thrown in his lot with Begin and so had General Lahat, a former Sinai tank commander who was running for mayor in Tel Aviv. True, the Labour list also had a fair share of generals such as Dayan, Rabin (the chief of staff in 1967) and Yariv (former chief of military intelligence). Nevertheless, the fact that a few military men now supported the right was of some significance; it was interpreted as yet another manifestation of the swing to the right in Israeli politics which had taken place since 1967. Others simply regarded it as the natural reaction of military men gravitating to the party which stood for a tougher line as far as the country's security interests were concerned.

There were indications that the elections would result in a certain weakening of the Labour Alignment; this at any rate was what the pollsters were saying during July and August. But as the date of the elections drew nearer what had seemed to be a landslide by Israeli standards became a mini-trend and in the end it was no longer visible to the naked eye. Israeli voters were traditionally conservative in their political behaviour, there had been minor fluctuations in elections but never a major shift and there was no good reason to assume that there would be one in late October of 1973. An Israeli political commentator reviewing the election propaganda noted that all parties assumed that the voter was basically conservative and preferred a central position to extremism; all parties were in favour of social justice and combating poverty, no one advocated a retreat from the present defence lines.[17] If no significant political change was to be expected, was it really worth spending between fifty and a hundred million dollars to get a few new faces into parliament? Nevertheless, the parties and their candidates went dutifully through the motions, there were public meetings, enormous advertisements in the newspapers and in the streets. But there was not a great deal of excitement; the average Israeli went to see *The Day of the Jackal* in the nearest cinema; at the Habima theatre *Cat on a Hot Tin Roof* was performed and, in a more cheerful mood, *The Merry Wives of Windsor*. The public issues which preoccupied the community were questions about who should be head of the Israeli aviation industry and whether or not a modern hotel called El Al should be built in the Omariya olive grove facing Mount Zion. Many private citizens as well as the Knesset Ecology Committee opposed the idea, but the Jerusalem District Planning Commission and the Hotel Workers' Association were in favour. There was an unprecedented heatwave with temperatures well above 100 degrees in many parts of the country during the Jewish New Year weekend of September 27th. Most people stayed home but several tens of thousands went to the south, to Eilat and to Sharm el Sheikh. The Israeli newspapers reported tersely that during the four days of holidays things were absolutely calm. Not one incident or a single case of suspected activity was reported during that time either in Israel, along the borders or in the administered areas.[18] It was the proverbial silence before the storm.

During the last few weeks before the outbreak of the war there had been two new foreign political initiatives, both sponsored by Dayan. During the summer the minister of defence had changed his stand on the future of the occupied territories and in a memorandum to his colleagues he had suggested what critics unkindly but fairly accurately called 'creeping annexation'. Up to that date the government had not favoured Jewish settlement in the occupied territories, and it was opposed to the sale of land to Jews in these territories as the right-wing political parties demanded. The consensus in the Cabinet was that Israel had no interest in creating *faits accomplis* but wanted to retain in a future peace settlement only what was essential for its defence. Dayan, on the other hand, having reached the conclusion that there would be no peace with the neighbouring Arab states in the foreseeable future, suggested that Israel should act unilaterally; perhaps it would help in convincing the Arabs that time was not working in their favour. He suggested the allocation of money for establishing new Jewish settlements in the occupied regions, both urban and agricultural, including the building of Yamit, a coastal town south of Gaza.[19] The project was debated at great length and with considerable passion in the Cabinet and what emerged was the so-called Galili document, Israel Galili being a minister without portfolio in the government and a past master at wording resolutions. Despite the opposition of Pinhas Sapir, the finance minister, and Abba Eban, Dayan largely had his way. The decision on Yamit was postponed for a few years, but, subject to government control, Israeli citizens were to be allowed to buy land in the occupied territories. There were to be new settlements on the Golan Heights, in the Rafah region and a five-hundred-acre enclosure was to be established on the West Bank to house Jerusalem's expanding industry. This was certainly a turn in Israeli policy; the Labour Alignment may have feared that with a moderate platform, it would not be able to compete successfully against Likud (which was in favour of outright annexation). Moreover, Dayan's veiled threat that he would not support the party unless his proposals were accepted was probably taken very seriously. Mrs Meir was not in principle opposed to Dayan's suggestions anyway, though she may have preferred a different timing.

If Dayan's action and the acquiescence of the Israeli Cabinet revealed a hardening of attitudes, news about a plan to divide Sinai with Egypt ascribed to Dayan pointed in a different direction. It will be recalled that Dayan had been unhappy with the Suez Canal as Israel's border from the very beginning. 'If the army reaches the canal, the war will never end,' he had said in G.H.Q. and in the Cabinet soon after the end of hostilities in 1967 when the question of where to halt in Sinai was discussed.[20] It was tantamount to 'keeping a foot on Egypt's neck'. From a military point of view, the canal was not the only, perhaps not even the best line of defence for Israel. Now, six years later, on the eve of fresh negotiations with the Americans, he returned to the idea in a speech at an officers' academy and on several other occasions in September. He had suggested to his Cabinet colleagues two months earlier a plan to define boundaries in Sinai but there had been no further discussions. The speech was reported in a London newspaper and subsequently in Cairo; the Egyptian press rejected the idea in both form and substance. It conflicted with Egypt's position that not one inch of Arab land should be surrendered. No political solution was in sight, there was only the hope that Dr Kissinger, the new American secretary of state who had worked such miracles in other parts of the world, would provide a fresh initiative.

American Attitudes

The Soviet Union, for obvious reasons, was not surprised by the outbreak of war; it had after all thousands of military advisers in key positions in Damascus and Cairo. Not a tank unit or a missile base could be moved without its knowledge, unless, of course, one assumes that the Soviet officers were afflicted by both blindness and deafness. The United States on the other hand was no more prepared for the combined Arab attack than Israel. The spy satellites must have supplied a steady stream of pictures accounting for what happened on every square foot of ground, but apparently those who interpreted the news did not see anything ominous in the troop concentrations. Dr Kissinger later revealed that both U.S. and Israeli intelligence had informed their superiors on three separate occasions during the week preceding the war that 'hostilities were unlikely to the point of their being no chance of it [war] happening'. They were aware of the troop concentrations but there was miscalculation with regard to the intention behind them. This failure will no doubt be pondered for a long time by intelligence services and policy makers, because it showed that there is no early warning system in case of a surprise attack.

When the war broke out Dr Kissinger had been in office for a few weeks only. Quoting President Nixon as his authority, he had said in one of his first interviews that the Middle East was 'perhaps the most dangerous area'. There were rumours that he was to take a peace initiative soon and the idea seems to have appealed to the Arabs; Arab diplomats in Washington said that it would be easier for Kissinger to bring pressure on the Israelis precisely because he was himself of Jewish origin and thus less exposed to attacks from his co-religionists. The London *Times* published an article which purported to present a plan ascribed to Kissinger for solving the Arab-Israeli dispute. It was neither better nor worse than any previous such plan; but it was by no means certain that it had really emanated from Dr Kissinger. In one of his first appearances as secretary of state, Kissinger met representatives from several Arab nations for a luncheon session. The atmosphere was described as relaxed and very friendly; Mahmoud Riad, former Egyptian foreign minister and now secretary general of the Arab League, reiterated the Arab claims for total Israeli withdrawal. In his reply Kissinger said that the U.S. understood that the Arab nations viewed aspects of the present situation in the Middle East as unacceptable. He would try to do his best but one should not look to the U.S. for miracles. Naturally, there was not the slightest hint on the part of the Egyptians about their impending action. On the contrary, an editor of *Al Ahram* upbraided the five countries who had boycotted the luncheon (Iraq, Libya, Algeria, Syria and South Yemen); why did they turn their backs on Kissinger if he had taken a step which could be regarded as the beginning of a new phase in U.S. policy? A few weeks earlier, commenting on Kissinger's appointment, Heykal had written that Kissinger would do what the Arabs wanted, but only if there was 'massive action', if the situation in the Middle East were to become so dangerous that American political intervention became imperative. Ihsan Abdul Kuddous, another leading Egyptian commentator belonging to Sadat's entourage, also wrote in September that the Arabs would have to go to war to bring pressure to bear on Kissinger.

It is idle to speculate what kind of peace initiative the new American secretary of state would have sponsored but for the outbreak of war; probably he had no clear idea at the time. Israel in all likelihood would have been urged to make concessions. Since it could ill afford to offend its main benefactor, Israel would probably have accepted the American plan; whether this would have satisfied the Arabs is a different question altogether. All that can be said with certainty is that the American administration was worried about the Middle East situation and that it was about to do something about it. Assuming that without substantial Soviet support the Egyptians and Syrians would not be able to move very far, it did not think war was imminent. And since there had been a dramatic improvement in relations with the U.S.S.R., it was unthinkable in Washington that the Russians would allow a situation to arise – let alone deliberately foment it – that would endanger all the progress that had been made during the past two years. If the Russians knew that a dangerous situation was about to arise in the Middle East, surely they would inform Washington, and a common effort would be made to prevent a war; or, if that should be impossible, to limit the fighting and to bring it to a speedy end.

Détente and the Soviet Union

These American assumptions were profoundly mistaken, not because of some miscalculation on the tactical level but because it had become the fashion in Washington to attribute aims to Soviet détente policy which were quite unreal. True, by October 1973 there were less illusions in this respect than a year earlier, when according to conventional wisdom the Soviets had forsworn the cold war and engaged on a policy of close co-operation with the United States. A number of developments had made the Americans a little more suspicious of Soviet motives: there were second thoughts in Washington about the benefits of SALT I (Strategic Arms Limitation Talks) and about the grain deal. The Soviet persecution of dissidents had caused annoyance among American liberals; already the rhetoric of 1972 – about 'generations of peace' and Soviet willingness 'to co-operate in establishing an international system in which the participants would operate with a consciousness of stability and permanence' – seemed a little out of date. But though many American policy-makers realized that their concept of détente and peaceful co-existence was not identical with the Soviet concept, they were not aware of the extent of the difference.

The Soviet leaders shared the American concern for removing the danger of a military confrontation between the super-powers and they were all in favour of agreements such as SALT I – especially if these might give them long-term advantages. They genuinely wanted an expansion of trade between the two countries, or, to be precise, massive long-term American loans at low interest and the infusion of American technology. This would have made it possible to develop much more quickly both the civilian and the military sector of the Soviet economy. To achieve these important aims, the Soviets were quite willing to tune down anti-Western propaganda, but, as Dr Kissinger wisely noted before he became secretary of state, a change in atmosphere did not necessarily amount to a change in substance. In this respect no one could fairly accuse the Russians of bad faith and double dealing, for they had maintained all along that the ideological-political struggle would not only continue during détente, it would in fact be intensified. American observers had assumed, for no good reason as it was soon to appear, that 'ideological war' meant no more than the ritual incantation by professional ideologists of certain basic tenets of Leninism, such as the ultimate victory of the Soviet system over the West, declarations which would not have the slightest effect on the pragmatic, businesslike and on the whole peaceful Soviet leadership.

We shall have to return to the subject of détente at a later stage. All that needs to be emphasized in the present context is that in Soviet eyes peaceful co-existence and cold war were not irreconcilable opposites but two sides of the same coin. They genuinely wanted détente in the sense just outlined, but this did not in the least affect their overall goal of a gradual change in the global balance in their favour. Nor did the Soviet leaders ever make a secret of their intention to support wars of national liberation even during détente; the famous dictum of a former Soviet foreign minister about the indivisibility of peace simply did not apply any longer. A war of national liberation can be interpreted in many ways; obviously an Arab war against Israel belongs in Soviet eyes to this category. But so presumably would a Croatian irredentist movement in Yugoslavia after Tito's demise; every separatist movement in Europe and in other parts of the globe could be regarded, in principle, as a war of national liberation, worthy of direct or indirect support. Potential wars of liberation could be discovered if necessary in the United States and China, for these countries too have their minority problems. Open Soviet support for a war of national liberation in North America or Western Europe or China would of course be counter-productive because it would effectively put an end to détente – it could even mean a world war. A war in the Middle East on the other hand must have appeared far less risky; if cautiously managed it could cause great damage to the West without seriously affecting détente. The Arabs after all did have a case against Israel, and they had considerable international support for their claims. Such a war was not bound to result in the breakdown of détente, provided the two super-powers collaborated in finding a just and equitable solution. Arguments of this kind would appeal to politicians in Washington and Bonn, in Paris and London; after a few weeks it would be forgotten that the Soviet Union had been deeply involved in the preparation of this war. Everyone would be concerned with reducing world tension and this could only be done with the Soviet Union playing the role of peacemaker. The Soviet dilemma with regard to the war was not whether it should support it, but how far its involvement could go without unduly antagonizing Western believers in détente.

Soviet support for the Arabs had not been whole-hearted in recent years. In view of the volatile character of the Arab regimes, the frequent government changes, the absence of firmly entrenched, reliable allies in the area, Soviet policy-makers have manoeuvred with circumspection, especially since Nasser's death. They have not been too happy with developments in Egypt since 1970; they preferred the former regime in Syria to the present one. The chances of survival of the Iraqi regime, their closest ally, were uncertain and they had reservations even about the Algerians who had been counted at one time among the avant-garde of the progressive camp. Their feelings about Qadafi and the Saudis were known. Nevertheless, for a variety of reasons there was no doubt from the very beginning that they would assist the Arabs in the war against Israel. They cordially disliked the Jews and Israel who for many years now had caused them so many difficulties on the international scene. Though Soviet policy is not as a rule dictated by

70

emotional considerations, Soviet anger did no doubt play a certain role and the opportunity to teach a lesson which they would not easily forget to the 'Zhids' must have strongly appealed to the Kremlin.* There were other, more weighty considerations. The Arabs were, potentially at least, the stronger battalions; given sufficient guidance, war material and political assistance, they would win the war, and the Soviet Union would gain much prestige as the power which had made the victory possible. The United States would be isolated in their support for Israel, they would have all the Arabs against them, there would be dissension in N A T O and in the end American prestige would have been badly shaken because it would have been shown that the Russians took better care of their protégés than the Americans. The Russians were not interested in a total Arab victory and the annihilation of the State of Israel – not for humanitarian reasons, but simply because they had few delusions about the lasting effects of Arab gratitude once Soviet help would no longer be needed. But there was not, as the Russians saw it, any real danger that the Israelis would be wiped out; at a critical juncture the two super-powers would get together and, if necessary, step in. If on the other hand the Arabs suffered defeat on the field of battle, the result would be far from disastrous as far as the Soviet Union was concerned. It could not possibly be a total, lasting defeat and everyone would know that the Russians had done their utmost to arm Egypt and Syria; everyone also knew that they had their ideological differences with Sadat and the Syrians. A new Arab defeat would in all probability trigger off a process of radicalization in the Arab world from which the Soviet Union could only gain. Whichever way one looked at it, the risks involved for the Soviet Union were small, the possible gains considerable.

It is, of course, impossible to establish with absolute certainty the date on which the Russians were told when war would begin. Soviet envoys and military advisers must have known about Sadat's preparations from the very beginning though they played no part, as far as can be ascertained, in the talks with the Syrians and the

* 'The Russians are not entirely rational on Israel ... When Kissinger was in Moscow in 1968 he found he could talk to the Russians rationally on all subjects, even including Vietnam – except for Israel.' Kissinger in conversation with C. L. Sulzberger.
C. L. Sulzberger, *An Age of Mediocrity* (Macmillan, New York, 1973).

Jordanians. They were involved in working out Egyptian and Syrian strategy; this was, after all, what they were there for. On September 22nd Sadat saw Vinogradov, the Soviet ambassador, and handed him a letter to Brezhnev; it seems reasonably safe to assume that this message contained the date that had been set for the attack. Brezhnev answered almost immediately; the contents of his reply are unknown. Sadat saw Vinogradov again on October 4th, presumably to report on the latest preparations for the attack. Thus the Soviet leaders had at the very least two weeks to decide about their tactics vis-à-vis the West.

The difficult part was how to treat the Americans; Europe presented no particular difficulty because most European leaders were only too willing to believe that this was a regional dispute which did not directly concern them. But there were explicit agreements with the United States according to which one side would not look for advantages over the other. There was a solemn commitment – the third principle of the Soviet-American accord – that both sides should take upon themselves the responsibility 'to do everything in their power so that conflicts or situations will not arise which would serve to increase international tension'. The Russians could argue that they had not known about the impending attack, but in view of the presence of 3,000-4,000 Soviet military advisers in the Arab armies no one would have believed them. They had after all a defence treaty with Egypt according to which Sadat should consult them. Either he had done so, in which case they had not lived up to their commitments to the Americans, or – which is most unlikely – he had refrained from doing so, in which case they were under no obligation to support his war. Observers leaning over backwards in trying to understand Soviet policy argued that Moscow faced the agonizing choice either of betraying the confidence of their Egyptian and Syrian clients or of living up to the Basic Principles which were to guide Soviet-American relations. In this situation, rashly perhaps, out of excessive loyalty to their Arab allies, or because they did not think that the regional conflict would spread, they made a wrong decision. But such an explanation was rapidly overtaken by events, for once the war had started, far from trying to localize it, the Soviet leaders did their utmost to fan the conflagration. They called on countless governments in Africa and Asia to give Egypt and

Syria maximum support. On October 8th President Boumediene received the Soviet ambassador, who handed him a message saying, according to Algiers radio, 'Arab fraternal solidarity must, more than ever before, play a decisive role. Syria and Egypt must not be alone in their struggle against a treacherous enemy. There is an urgent need for the widest aid and support of the progressive regimes in these countries who, like Algeria, stand for hope and freedom in the Arab world.'[21] The message went on to say that the Central Committee of the Communist Party of the Soviet Union was firmly convinced that the Algerian leaders would use every means and take every step required to support Egypt and Syria in the face of the common danger – as would the Soviet Union. Similar messages went to many other capitals; when Mr Zakharov, the Soviet ambassador to Uganda, went to see President Amin, he was told that he, Amin, had been justified when he had said some time ago that Hitler was right to burn six million Jews in Europe during the Second World War. 'The President told the ambassador that if Hitler had not burnt the six million Jews, the present problem in the Middle East would be in the Soviet Union and the whole of Europe, including Britain.'[22]

President Amin's statement was not given publicity in the Soviet Union and when asked about the message to Boumediene, Soviet officials replied that they did not have sufficient information to comment about it.[23] Unofficially Western diplomats and newsmen in Moscow were told that the Soviet Union was opposed to the escalation of the war and that the Western interpretation which saw it as a Soviet attempt to widen the war had been far from the mark. Even the Brezhnev message, an American correspondent reported from Moscow, was reread by some Western diplomats as essentially a defensive measure, a plausible Soviet effort to fend off Arab efforts to involve the Soviet Union directly in the war.[24] The Russians had not informed Washington that the Egyptians were about to attack because had they done so, the Israelis would have been told and would have forestalled the Arabs. This version too found some believers in Washington. First Western reactions must have convinced the Soviets that their basic assumption had been at least partly correct, namely, that it would be possible to combine aggressive actions with statesmanlike postures, calls for restraint, responsible action and the continuation of building a durable peace. Dr Kissinger would be assured that Soviet-U.S. friendship would not be affected and meanwhile Soviet broadcasts would announce that conditions were ripe to exploit the energy crisis in the capitalist world.

It may not be possible for a long time to establish with any degree of certainty whether and to what extent the Soviet Union had encouraged the Egyptian and Syrian attack. Certain indications show that it did so, such as the delivery of purely offensive weapons and of equipment to cross the Suez Canal; the first ships with war material to replenish Egyptian and Syrian arsenals reportedly sailed from Odessa even before the attack had been launched. But the evidence, for the time being, is incomplete; all that can be established with certainty is that the Soviet Union had advance knowledge of the attack, that it did nothing to stop it, but on the contrary tried to spread the conflict.

According to the official Egyptian and Syrian version the war started with Israeli attacks in the Gulf of Suez and in the Golan Heights which were immediately rebuffed by successful Arab counter blows. Once the war had got under way it was of course no longer of decisive importance to maintain this version, but it is of some interest that Cairo and Damascus did not entirely neglect propagandistic preparations for the attack. Towards the end of September the Arab media began to publish news items about 'heavy Israeli troop concentrations', including tanks and heavy artillery. According to the Syrian press, Israel was preparing for a new military adventure; the Iraqis reported Israeli violations of Lebanese air space; other Arab sources announced that 1,800 members of the Moroccan expeditionary force had now taken position on the Golan Heights. 'Israel will not frighten us,' said the Arab press. This kind of Israeli blackmail and demonstration of military strength was bound to fail because it ignored world public opinion which demanded the restoration of peace in the Middle East.[25] The Arab media had frequently reported Israeli troop concentrations and impending attacks; such news items would not attract much interest in Israel unless they were given very prominent publicity. The alarm sounded in early October in Cairo and Damascus was normal by established standards. The Israeli press merely noted in passing the fact that the Egyptians declared a state of alert on October 2nd in the northern and central sectors of the canal 'due to Israeli concentrations';[26] they had been advised by military spokesmen not to give it undue publicity. In a speech on the anniversary of President Nasser's death, Sadat left to the very end the question of the confrontation with Israel which had so prominently figured on past occasions. 'I have deliberately not broached the subject of the battle,' he said, 'because there has been enough talk.' He was promising nothing, nor was he willing to discuss any details. All they should know was that the liberation of the land was the first and main task facing Egypt, and, God willing, they would achieve this aim.[27]

Such restrained language was unaccustomed and might have aroused Israeli suspicions. But the Israelis thought that it was just another stage in Sadat's retreat from his promises to go to war. A few days before the attack Egyptian soldiers were seen to play around with rubber dinghies and other small craft; the Israelis were puzzled, perhaps the Egyptians wanted to go fishing? It is easy in retrospect to collect much evidence pointing to an impending attack. But at the time the situation seemed very quiet indeed. In view of the Syrian troop concentrations a state of emergency was declared in some of the new settlements in the north of Israel but this too had happened many times before and produced no particular disquiet in the country. The most explicit warning that the Arabs were concentrating troops along the armistice lines was made on Wednesday, October 3rd, in a speech by the Israeli chief of staff on the occasion of Parachutists' Day in the Maccabiah Village. The news item rated exactly eleven lines in the press; it stated that General David Elazar had said that the enemy should know that through the parachutists Israel could reach objectives far in the enemy's rear.[28] General Elazar may have been aware that some trouble was brewing but the last thing he expected was a major war. Everyone in authority in Israel seems to have shared this view on the eve of the Day of Atonement, Friday, October 5th, 1973.

Chapter Three   Operation Badr

At the weekly meeting of the Israeli Cabinet on Wednesday, October 3rd, 1973, Mrs Meir reported on her recent visit to the Council of Europe at Strasbourg and her attempts to persuade Mr Kreisky, the Austrian Chancellor, not to close the Schönau transit camp. For a few days military intelligence had reported troop concentrations on the Egyptian and Syrian borders, but the Cabinet had not even been informed; Mrs Meir's 'Kitchen cabinet' decided that these were the usual autumn manoeuvres. But news about further concentrations continued to arrive during October 4th, and on the morning of Friday, October 5th, half of the Cabinet met informally at the Prime Minister's Tel Aviv office. The ministers were asked to leave their addresses behind so that they could be reached if necessary at short notice. It was still believed that neither the Egyptians nor the Syrians would dare to attack; to be on the safe side a few reserve units were called up on Friday afternoon. The front line in Suez was manned by 600 officers and soldiers, on the Golan Heights there were some 70 tanks. The air force and the communication units were in a state of readiness but the infantry was quite unprepared.*

* The circumstances of the Arab attack became a topic of heated debate in Israel after the end of the war. Sadat had kept the secret well; even Egyptian brigade commanders learned of the war only the day it broke out. Five Egyptian infantry and two armoured divisions attacked on the afternoon of October 6th. According to General Bar Lev, a former Israeli chief of staff, the soldiers on the front line were doing their laundry and wearing slippers, some were playing football. General Elazar, the present chief of staff, sharply dissented: as far as the regular army was concerned the alert had begun ten days earlier and reached its peak on Friday morning. The entire army was put on full battle alert at 11 a.m. on Friday, October 5th. General Elazar admitted however that there were serious failures in observing the order for full alert at the lower echelons. Some reserve units were insufficiently equipped when they moved into battle: 'But there were two sides to be heard on this point.' He cited the case of an armoured brigade commander who decided to send his tanks to the front line as quickly as possible with only part of the ammunition each tank could take, rather than hold up his tanks until they were fully loaded. He announced an internal army inquiry to investigate the shortcomings on the eve of the Yom Kippur war. (*Jerusalem Post*, November 12th, 1973)

Which takes us to Saturday, October 6th. Mrs Meir met Dayan and David Elazar, the chief of staff, in the morning. General Elazar had advocated general mobilization the night before but had been over-ruled by Dayan. Twelve hours later there was no room for any more doubt: the Egyptians and the Syrians were about to attack, but it was not yet clear whether this would happen in the evening under the cover of darkness to reduce the risk of the Israeli air force attacking the advancing Egyptian and Syrian columns, or whether the offensive would be launched the next morning. More reserve units were called up. The choice of Yom Kippur – in contrast to the New Year celebrated ten days earlier – was not a good one from the Arab point of view: almost everyone could be reached at home or in synagogue. The American ambassador was informed that an attack was imminent, but that Israel would not fire the first shot. The idea of a preventive air strike was discussed and rejected during Mrs Meir's meeting with the military leaders in the morning. At noon the government met in Tel Aviv; all the Cabinet meetings during the war were to take place in Tel Aviv rather than in Jerusalem so as to enable the army high command to participate. While Dayan reported about the military situation, news came in that the attack had started. This was the beginning of the Yom Kippur War, which Sadat named 'Operation Spark'; some Arab publicists were to call it 'Operation Saladin', a reference to the great Muslim leader who led the war against the crusaders. The official Egyptian code name was 'Granite Two', according to the Israeli chief of staff, but the Egyptian war minister said it was 'Badr', a reference to the first battle fought by the Prophet Mohammed against his enemies.

War, we are told, makes rattling good history. The war which began on October 6th, 1973, will no doubt be studied for a long time for the strategic and tactical lessons it offers. There were individual exploits of great intrinsic interest: manifestations of courage and cowardice, of headless confusion and of brilliant improvisation. These will no doubt be described in great detail by other writers but are not relevant to the present account which is devoted to a critical analysis of the main stages of the war. Such an account can be written for the time being only as seen from Israel, with an occasional glance at Arab strategy. For in Israel a great deal of material has already been published on the course of the war, much of it critical in substance, whereas on the Arab side the announcements and reports have been almost entirely official in character. They stress the fact that the Arab armies fought well, which is certainly true, especially in the first stage of the war; but they are not of much help in a detailed appraisal of the war. To understand the predicament facing the Israeli Army Command, and to evaluate its strategic concepts, it is necessary to look back at the development of the Israeli armed forces, the kind of war they expected and were prepared for.

Israeli Military Doctrine*

The time factor has always been of paramount importance in the Arab-Israeli wars and has been reflected even in the names they were given. The Sinai War of 1956 became in common parlance the 'war of the hundred hours', followed in 1967 by the 'Six Day War'. The 1973 war ended inconclusively for one and only one reason: the Israeli forces had not sufficient time to win a decisive victory over the Egyptian and the Syrian armies, and this was rightly interpreted by the Arabs as an important achievement. Arab strategists had paid great attention in recent years to analysing the time factor in their wars against Israel and they reached the conclusion that Israel was not capable of conducting a prolonged war. Hence their attempt to force on Israel the war of attrition. They assumed that Israel could be defeated because it would not be able to shoulder the burden of an extended war effort in view of its limited material resources and lack of manpower. Subsequent events did not bear out these assumptions for in the war of attrition Egypt suffered no less than Israel and this, in effect, brought the war to an end in August 1970. Nevertheless, the belief of Arab strategists in the advantages of a prolonged war did not weaken; in their view Israel had not been compelled to employ most of its reserves in the war of attrition whereas in a full-scale war Israel would not be able to hold its own for any length of time. They

* The following section is based on a study prepared for this book by Major-General (retd.) Dr M. Peled.

found confirmation for this belief in various studies published during the 'sixties according to which the Arab countries could win a war against Israel even without engaging in actual fighting if only they managed to compel Israel to keep its forces mobilized. Their belief was further reinforced by the experience of the early 'sixties when a substantial part of the Israeli forces was mobilized in response to the threat of Egyptian troop concentrations in eastern Sinai. Serious dislocations were caused in daily life in Israel and the Israeli economy was affected. The Six Day War was regarded as further evidence: Israel had to gain a speedy victory simply because it could not engage in any other form of warfare.

There was an element of truth in these assumptions: a small country like Israel is bound to face serious difficulties as a result of a general mobilization of its forces over a long period. On the other hand it was no more than a half truth, for the 'war of liberation' of 1948-9 had shown Israel's ability to wage war for a relatively long time – and its resources were then much more limited. But for the intervention of the powers the war of 1948-9 would have ended with the occupation of Sinai, Eastern Jerusalem and the Hebron and Samaria districts. To this extent the war of 1973 resembles that war: but for the intervention of outside forces Israel would have won a decisive victory on the battlefield and the Egyptian forces would have suffered a major defeat. The two wars demonstrate the crucial importance of the time factor and its impact on the outcome of the war.

The Israeli high command had been aware for a long time that in any war it had to force a decision before the powers could intervene and prevent a military decision, imposing a ceasefire. This was, in fact, one of the basic tenets in Israeli strategic thinking. Unless Israel gained a decisive victory within the limited time span at its disposal, the Arabs would continue to believe that there was a military solution to the Israeli problem. In other words, the Arabs had to be shown that they had no chance of destroying Israel. Victory in the field of battle thus became an aim in itself even though, as in 1957, Israel might have to withdraw from the territories seized in the course of the war.

Israeli strategic thinking had to take into account moreover the possibility of a war on two fronts. Other countries have had to face similar situations and like them Israel needed a plan to cope with this eventuality. The obvious way to do so was to take the initiative and first to hit the more dangerous enemy; subsequently the forces would be concentrated on the other front. Recognition of the fact that Israel had to take the initiative in every war became official doctrine when David Ben Gurion, Israel's first defence minister, stated in his instructions to the high command that the Israeli Army had to carry the war into enemy country from the very first moment, whenever hostilities broke out. An enemy attack resulting in penetration into Israel, its containment on Israeli soil, and a subsequent counter-attack were contrary to the spirit of this doctrine. It was of course realized that there could be an exception, namely if, in a war on two fronts, one of the enemies succeeded in advancing before Israel had been able to force a decision on the other front.

This doctrine had a direct impact on the structure of the Israeli Army, its tactics and its equipment. Since the main strength of the Israeli Army is in its reserves, these had to be mobilized within forty-eight hours. A logistic system had to be developed to carry the reserves to the theatre of operations safely and within the shortest possible time. Such protected movement involved in turn an air-defence system in a permanent state of high alert. The possibility that Israeli reserves would have to be mobilized in conditions less than ideal as far as air cover was concerned was taken into account, but every effort was made to prevent this. Hence the necessity of maintaining a strong air force within the framework of the regular army. All this was not however sufficient to ensure Israeli combat-readiness before the enemy could make his preparations and launch an attack. To gain more time Israel developed a very effective warning system enabling it to have the necessary information about enemy intentions and movements at the earliest possible moment. Lastly, Israel needed an excellent system of internal lines of communications which would make it possible to transfer men and equipment from one front to another without any delay. All this was practised many times both in manoeuvres and on occasions when there was reason to assume that a war was impending. But the decisive tests came in 1956 and in 1967. In 1956 there was no second front for Israel but in 1967 Israeli forces were transferred from the south to the Syrian front very quickly and efficiently. The Jordanian front did not constitute a problem because it did not involve the concentration of major forces for any length of time. The lesson of the Six Day War was very important because it demonstrated that the Israeli strategic concept was basically sound and also because the tactical approach and the combat technique corresponded with the strategic needs, namely a short and decisive war. It also showed that a massive victory in the field enabled Israeli diplomacy to postpone relinquishing the gains that had been made and to demand a real *quid pro quo* for any concessions. Lastly it demonstrated that Israel's fears that it needed an ally in the case of war were unfounded; on the contrary, Israel could pursue a far more independent line precisely because it acted without outside help.

On the negative side, it appeared that the Israeli Government had not been at all familiar in 1967 with the strategic concept that had been developed on Ben Gurion's inspiration and under his supervision. Ben Gurion had regarded matters of defence more or less as his private bailiwick and his activities in this field were not brought to the knowledge of the government. As a result no other government minister knew about the strategic concept of the army high command, not even those who had played a leading role in the war of 1948-9. While Ben Gurion was minister of defence this did not matter greatly, but when he was succeeded by Levi Eshkol Cabinet ministers began to participate in discussions on national defence and a certain degree of confusion ensued. There was no experience in dealing with these matters, there was hesitation in accepting responsibility, and vital decisions were likely to be postponed. Eshkol himself did not feel particularly at ease in these discussions; furthermore there was no one to help and advise him when he had to consider the recommendations of supreme headquarters. He felt that he had to act on the basis of advice given by a body whose modes of thought and action were strange to him.

This state of affairs reached a climax on the eve of the Six Day War. It suddenly appeared that the government had failed to understand the great danger inherent in the situation; the Israeli Army had been almost fully mobilized for some considerable time but no decision was taken as to the objectives of its operations. Nor was there full understanding of the fact that it was vital that Israel should take the initiative instead of waiting for an enemy attack. Eventually the ministers accepted the strategic concept of the high command. Dayan had been chief of staff during the Sinai Campaign and when he accepted responsibility for the decision it was easier for his colleagues to follow suit. His appointment as minister of defence in June 1967 no doubt helped; he discontinued Eshkol's policy of making other ministers participate in deliberations on defence. The government was again cut off from direct contact with issues pertaining to national security and the mode of thought of the high command and this was to have fateful consequences.

Consequences of the Six Day War

Soviet intervention was another novel feature of the Six Day War. It was of course known in Israel that the Soviet Union had supplied arms and instructors to Egypt since 1955. A considerable effort had been made in Israel to study Soviet war doctrine, its strengths and its weaknesses. But at the time of the Six Day War the Soviet Union also began to plan and direct Egyptian and Syrian military operations and this caused grave concern among Israeli leaders. The fact that military action against Egypt and Syria was tantamount to a direct confrontation with the Soviet Union was to them like a bolt from the blue. It made it more difficult for them to accept the recommendations made by the military on how to deal with the situation created by the Egyptian blockade and the troop concentrations in Sinai.

Despite its hesitations, the government in the end decided to take the initiative, and the results of the war proved that the decision had been correct. The blow dealt to the Arab forces and the shock given to the Russians created a new situation, advantageous from the Israeli point of view. It is a pity that the Israeli Government did not use this advantage to make progress towards a political settlement with the Arabs; this could have perhaps brought about the neutralization of the Middle East between the two superpowers. There was such a possibility and it continued to exist for some time afterwards, but the leadership did not use the opportunity.

The most dramatic result of the Six Day War was psychological in character. The country had suffered for twenty years from claustrophobia and the very fact that Israel became a larger country helped to remove the feeling of being 'fenced in'. There was a feeling overshadowing everything else that somehow the situation of the country and its future prospects had undergone a qualitative change. There was a desire not to return to the old claustrophobia, and ideological rationalizations to justify this instinctive urge were easily found. Some invoked the 'historical rights' of the Jewish people, others stressed that the territories were of vital importance for the absorption of immigrants. In the past such claims had been rejected by the Zionist movement as expansionist and altogether unacceptable. Above all, it was now argued that the territories were essential for the defence of Israel; they suddenly acquired a central importance in Israeli strategic thought. This consideration, more than any other, was accepted – quite wrongly – by most of the public as altogether convincing; the country was still besieged by enemies, and the territories would help to remove the outside danger to a certain extent. This was a misconception; far from making Israel any stronger, the occupied territories weakened its position. It was apparently the first and only case since the Second World War when an ideological concept has distorted strategic thought and adversely affected the whole defence fabric of the country. The feeling that the acquisition of territories had made the country a safer place to live in and easier to defend made it impossible to achieve a political solution of the Arab-Israeli conflict. Nor could the political leadership show that there had been any gain to national security which could justify the fact that a political solution had become impossible. The maintenance of the territories constituted an additional burden. The borders had to be manned by a bigger standing army, and billions of Israeli pounds had to be invested in creating a new infra-structure. Arab terrorist activities did not decrease in comparison with the pre-1967 era. The defence budget constantly increased, from 15 per cent of the G.N.P. in 1967 to 25-30 per cent in later years.

Defence on the Suez Canal constituted a particularly heavy burden. Before the Six Day War Dayan had been opposed to establishing the Israeli forward line at the canal. He had wanted

Israeli troops to stop some seven miles east of the canal in their pursuit of the Egyptian forces. This was an unrealistic proposition; eventually the Israeli forces did reach the canal. Once this had happened Dayan changed his view, and the Israeli defence forces did not retreat from the water-line despite the fact that for tactical reasons these forces should not have been left within the range of the Egyptian artillery. An Israeli withdrawal from the water-line would not have meant giving up any tactical advantage, for the terrain is such that the water-line can be controlled from a ridge at a distance of 10-13 miles, and the penetration of small units could have been prevented by means of roving patrols. There were dissenting voices in the high command but these were ignored by Dayan. Before the war the defence minister had been opposed for political reasons to keeping the water-line, whereas after the 1967 war he regarded it as a political advantage and made the army command extend its forces accordingly, thus putting it at a tactical disadvantage vis-à-vis the enemy. Even in 1967-8 the Egyptians still had enough artillery to make life for the Israeli forces very uncomfortable; subsequently when the Russians had resupplied more than 80 per cent of the equipment that had been lost, the Egyptians could subject the Israelis to very heavy shooting warfare – the war of attrition. Since the Israeli forces had orders to keep within the effective range of the Egyptian guns enormous fortifications had to be built not once, but thrice, for the last time in August 1970. As these became stronger and bigger, they turned into shelters and ceased to be fighting positions. Thus the Bar Lev line had all the drawbacks typical of a static line of fortifications.

It was not the aim of the Egyptians during the war of attrition to cross the canal or to oust the Israeli forces from Sinai but simply to make their stay very costly indeed. The Israeli decision to stick to the water-line could not be logically justified; it was a question of prestige. The Israeli forces were stuck in the fortifications, they had to be supplied and the casualties had to be removed. Since the Egyptian artillery was stronger, Israel had to bring in the air force in order to silence the Egyptian guns. This amounted to an escalation of fighting; in response the Egyptians had to establish an anti-aircraft defence system to protect their gun positions. This in turn led to the Israeli deep-penetration air raids, whereupon

Nasser called in the Russians, who established an anti-aircraft defence system which eventually covered the whole Egyptian air space. In this way the war spread, and all this (as a senior Israeli officer said) to supply tomatoes to the soldiers on the Bar Lev line.

During the last weeks of the war of attrition the Soviets reached the conclusion that the canal area ought to be hermetically closed to Israeli air attacks because it was to become the main zone of deployment for Egyptian forces. The Israeli air force and the Soviet missile bases were locked in a bitter fight over the fate of the canal zone. The details of the struggle are known; Dayan announced that it was Israel's aim to prevent the deployment of Soviet bases within a zone some thirty miles west of the canal. Israel accepted the ceasefire precisely because it prohibited installation of missiles in this zone; but it was immediately broken by the Russians who moved their S A M bases into forward positions. What chiefly matters in this context is the fact that the struggle for the canal was the first battle since the Six Day War in which Israel was defeated, even though Israeli spokesmen denied this. True, the Egyptian forces failed to oust the Israelis from the water-line but the Suez Canal became a 'defended zone' despite all the efforts and sacrifices of the Israeli air force to prevent this. It was an intellectual and political defeat, for by obstinately clinging to the water-line Israel caused an escalation of the conflict, strengthened the Egyptian anti-aircraft system and involved the Soviet Union in the Arab war effort far more deeply than before.

In Israel, on the other hand, the war of attrition was interpreted as a victory for the Israeli strategic concept, which was to put the emphasis on a fortified defence system manned by a limited number of regular forces; their presence would make it possible to mobilize the reserve forces whenever necessary. This dangerous concept contained almost all the harmful and negative elements of defence theories developed since the beginning of the century: the reliance on a static line of defence to withstand a major, well prepared attack and the dependence on small regular forces. Such ideas had been universally rejected by military planners since the end of the Second World War, but in Israel they enjoyed a curious belated revival – mainly due to the political desire to stress the absolute value of the territories as far as the country's defences were concerned. The political arguments put forward in military terms were briefly as follows: in the past it had been necessary to mobilize some of the reserves whenever there was reason to fear that the enemy planned offensive action. In the new conditions, on the basis of a static line of defence and a bigger regular army, there was no need to be so sensitive. Furthermore, the fact that Israel had water obstacles on most of its new borders (the Suez Canal and the Jordan) increased the feeling of security: on Israel's eastern border the establishment of civilian settlements was thought to contribute to the country's defensive strength. Such settlements were also established in the Golan.

These arguments collapsed within six hours on October 6th, 1973. It appeared that the high command had not only permitted the politicians to use pseudo-military arguments for political purposes, it had managed to deceive itself. This was most pronounced on the Suez front, the most important one for Israel. Only at the end of the war, when the chief of staff tried to explain the failure of the warning system, was it admitted that with the acquisition of the Sinai Peninsula by Israel the warning system had disappeared. Before May 1967 the Egyptian Army for practical reasons had been kept in permanent quarters west of the canal and only small forces were on the border with Israel. Thus every Egyptian troop movement to the east was a warning sign. The Israeli chief of staff was no doubt correct when he admitted that this advantage no longer existed as the result of the new deployment of the Israeli forces. He should have added – which he failed to do – that if this was the case, the basic assumptions of the post-1967 period about greater security for Israel as the result of the acquisition of Sinai – rather than its demilitarization – had been wrong.

This takes us back to the general issue of civilian-military relations. Under Dayan no attempt was made by civilian bodies to understand, let alone to control, military thought and policy; no cabinet sub-committee was established to deal with these affairs. Dayan's personal prestige was such that the ministers gladly left everything to him. It was a return to the Ben Gurion period, with, however, one important difference: Ben Gurion was a man of principles and great intellectual stature. The same did not apply to his successor – a man of strong instinctual urges, which he found difficult to control, an indecisive character and mediocre intellectual capacity. The fact that this man alone decided military policy, without any civilian control, was a bad sign for the future. Under his leadership there was a marked qualitative decline in the high command – intellectual clarity gave way to confusion, there was a general politicization of the atmosphere in the army and instead of the good personal relations which had prevailed in the past there was competition.

This gradual deterioration was kept from the eye of the public both by a number of showy military operations and Dayan's personal prestige; his very personality was thought to be the best guarantee for the security of the country. Popular opinion was placated by reducing the length of the period of military service; there was also the feeling that the great defence budget was giving value for money inasmuch as it made the country more secure.

According to Ben Gurion the regular army should consist of a very small body of professionals, unable to carry out any military operations without substantial assistance from the reserves. This was a very sensible policy for, among other things, it perpetuated the concept of a citizen's army. Under Dayan, on the other hand, with the growth of the regular army a military caste came into being; this became a matter of considerable concern both in view of the intervention of senior officers in politics and their prominent role in the administration of the occupied territories. At a time of intellectual, moral and professional decline, and in the absence of any civilian control, there came the Yom Kippur War.

The Campaign of 1973

Whoever prepared the Egyptian-Syrian attack in 1973 must have been aware of the changes in Israeli strategic thinking since 1967, for the attack made use of all its weaknesses. It is difficult to know whether the selection of Yom Kippur was intentional. Few people in Cairo and Damascus knew that the date chosen was the Day of Atonement, just as few people in Israel knew that it was the tenth of Ramadan (the day when Mohammad set out to occupy Mecca, which he accomplished ten days later; as a result, all of Arabia became Islamic). Too much importance should not be attributed, however, to the date chosen, for the decisive factor was very simply that a big force, which had been well trained for the purpose, went to attack much smaller units who had no knowledge that war would break out and who were tied down to a static line of fortifications. In view of the fact that Sinai no longer served as a warning zone for Israel, military intelligence should have been particularly sensitive with regard to the intentions of the enemy. But such sensitivity could not exist in an atmosphere of self-confidence and smugness; the warnings which were given by American intelligence were dismissed for the same reason. Beneath this neglect was the assumption that even if there was a mistaken evaluation there would still be time to correct it in view of that great defence line in which one had got accustomed to believe.

The fact that Israel would mobilize its reserves only after the outbreak of hostilities must have been known to those who prepared the attack; commando units were dispatched deep into Sinai to seize strategic positions to prevent the advance of the reserves to the front line. Simultaneously with the crossing by Egyptian forces of the canal, the Egyptian air force carried out some major attacks against Israeli bases in Sinai, evidently to hit the command and control system while the crossing was in progress.

A different kind of operation was prepared by the Syrian command in the Golan. In the absence of a water obstacle the Syrian Army decided to sweep with vastly superior tank forces into Golan and from there into the valleys. This attack too took into account the small number of defenders manning the Israeli fortifications, their surprise and low state of alert. They hoped to prevent the arrival of reinforcements by a swift and deep penetration, whereas the Israeli strategists were firmly convinced that the reserves would always have sufficient time to get organized while the regular army was holding the forward defence line. It would be interesting to know what made the Egyptian and Syrian command believe that Israel would not launch a preventive air strike at the very last moment, for the Israeli air force does not depend on reserves to carry out operations at very short notice. Such a preventive strike, even on the morning of Yom Kippur, would have affected the Syrian operations and could have caused a great deal of dislocation and confusion among the Egyptians. The Egyptian defence system based mainly on SAM missile sites would have made such an attack difficult (as it was to appear subsequently) but a strong surprise attack from the air would have nevertheless caused serious damage to the forces about to cross the canal. Needless to say, had the Egyptian and Syrian forces encountered Israeli forces in a state of alert, the whole course of the war would have been different.

The confidence with which the Egyptian and Syrian leaders prepared their complicated operations shows that they assumed that there would be no Israeli preventive strike and not even a state of alert at the front line. If this was indeed their appraisal, they were frighteningly correct. Israeli spokesmen later on tried to explain this failure, but their arguments were neither logical nor sincere; this was merely *post factum* rationalization. The prime minister provided several conflicting versions to explain the decisions not to launch a preventive strike – one on the evening after the attack, another after the war in the U.S. television programme 'Face the Nation'. In the first she implied that she had not wanted to hurt American sensibilities. This argument was not repeated, for Kissinger had made it clear meanwhile on two separate occasions (on October 12th, and October 25th) that the Israeli Government did not expect an attack; thus the issue of a preventive strike did not arise and the Americans had not been consulted in the first place.

The earliest date on which the subject could have been possibly discussed was the morning of October 6th. The Israeli Government knew by that time that an attack was imminent, but it had no idea exactly when. The news that hostilities had broken out came when the Cabinet was in session dealing for the first time with the steps that had to be taken in case of war. The evening before, Mrs Meir and several ministers had decided not to mobilize the reserves. The chief of staff said in an interview later on that he had been convinced that mobilization was necessary but he had been over-ruled.

Dayan maintained on several occasions that the central issue since 1967 had been whether to keep reserve forces in the forward lines or whether to accept a certain risk and leave this task to relatively small regular army units. The public had accepted the big investment involved in establishing the network of fortifications in order to release the reserves from the burden of serving for lengthy periods in the forward lines. However, the issue at stake was not one of principle but far more specific: should the Israeli forces not have been mobilized several days before the attack in view of the evidence that the Arab armies were preparing for some major operations? Dayan did not answer this question.

It seems that the Arabs' immediate targets were restricted in scope from a military point of view. The Syrian forces intended apparently to occupy a substantial part of the Golan, whereas the Egyptians hoped to advance beyond the Mitla Pass to the line Ras Sudar-Jebel al Didi-Jebel Gadeira and from there in a straight line to the north up to a point east of Romani. This line would have given the Egyptians full control of the Suez Canal.

These achievements alone would have been a sufficient reward from the Arab and Soviet point of view. The reconquest of this territory would have been of considerable military importance and Arab military prestige would have recovered from the defeat of 1967. At the same time the prestige of the Soviet Union as the friend and saviour of the Arabs would have soared, it would have had the free use of the Suez Canal, whereas other countries would not have been certain whether they would receive similar rights. The results of the war would have greatly strengthened the Arab countries in the political negotiations following the armistice. However, as it emerged, even these limited targets could not be achieved. From October 6th to October 9th, the Arab forces were tactically in a superior position and their gains were impressive. The Syrians seized most of the Golan and they threatened the approaches to the valleys to the west. The Egyptians crossed the canal in an impressive operation showing mastery of the techniques applied in such operations. However, the Israeli forces mobilized quickly (more quickly even than the standing orders envisaged), and on October 10th they reached the front lines. The initiative to a certain extent passed into their hands: a counter-offensive against the Syrians was already under way on the 9th, and within six days they were thrown back beyond the 1967 armistice lines up to a point near Sassa on the Kuneitra-Damascus axis. Heavy losses were inflicted on the Syrians as well as on the Iraqis and the Jordanians who had come to their aid. According to Israeli military intelligence estimates on October 10th, the Syrians had already lost 800 out of 1,500 tanks; most of them were of the T-54 and T-55 type, but there were also some newer models (T-62) and many of them were seized intact by the Israeli forces. 'For every Syrian tank that had been hit we found two that were deserted,'[1] said General Raful, commander of tank forces on the northern front.

While the fighting continued in the north, the Egyptians continued from October 6th-14th to build up their positions at a curiously slow pace along a narrow strip east of the canal. Its average width was five miles, and in the south the third army succeeded in advancing to Ayun Mussa and installing itself at a point south of it. The Egyptian build-up proceeded in an interesting fashion: for several days they refrained from transferring their armoured divisions to the east bank; they apparently wanted first to put up bridges and to widen the strip which had been occupied by infantry divisions of the third army in the south and the second army in the north. These two armies, which had been operating well in the stage of crossing the canal, were reluctant to advance any further, for by doing so their units would have moved beyond the zone defended by the missile sites and would have opened themselves to attack by the Israeli air force. This was a decisive consideration for the Egyptian command, which, despite the superior position it had gained on the ground, did not even try to challenge Israeli air superiority outside the zone defended by the missiles. Within that zone the Israeli air force suffered serious losses in its attempts to thwart Egyptian operations in the immediate vicinity of the canal. The Egyptian infantry began to dig itself in and to install its air defence which was not too difficult in view of the mobile character of SAM-2 and SAM-3, not to mention the SAM-6 which is operated from vehicles.

But the armoured divisions preferred to wait until the strip on the east bank had been broadened to at least ten miles, so as to enable them to prepare themselves for the second stage of attack, which should have carried them some twenty-five miles into Israeli territory. The Egyptian concept involved operating very slowly and cautiously, and this at the very time when the Syrians were under the constant pressure of the Israeli counter-offensive which gradually pushed them back towards Damascus. On the 11th the position of the Syrians had become so difficult that the Egyptians felt they had to speed up their operations to reduce the pressure on their allies in the north. The armoured divisions therefore began to cross the canal without waiting for the broadening of the strip on the east bank or the installation of the air-defence system. On the 13th they were on the east bank and the day after they launched a major attack. There had been sharply dissenting views in the Israeli high command as to how to cope with the Egyptian forces; the Egyptian attack brought this internal debate to an end.

From the moment the Israeli reserves had reached the Egyptian front some commanders had advocated an immediate counter-offensive in Sinai parallel to the one in the Golan. They assumed that general headquarters were not likely to send reinforcements from the Golan front. For this reason it would be foolish to permit the Egyptians to fortify their positions and to install missiles on the east bank, for this would only make an Israeli counter-offensive more difficult later on. According to this concept, the fact that most of the Egyptian armour was on the west bank would be an advantage in the initial stage for these units would not be able to intervene effectively early on during the battle. As for the second stage of the proposed Israeli counter-offensive, the Egyptian armour about to cross into Sinai was in a disadvantageous position; an Israeli surprise attack would upset all plans and preparations and force the Egyptian command to improvise – traditionally their weakest spot. Those who advocated an immediate Israeli counter-attack also argued that this was the only effective way to liquidate the Egyptian missile sites which had made it so difficult for the Israeli air force to operate in the battle zone. With their destruction the full weight of Israeli air superiority would be felt and would more than counter-balance any disadvantage (i.e. the presence of Egyptian armour on the west bank) as far as further stages of the battle were concerned.*

This was a daring concept, but the Israeli command preferred a more cautious approach. It did not want to remove substantial forces from north to south, and feared that if the Israeli units suffered heavy losses crossing the canal, the offensive would come to a halt before reaching its destination; this would mean an end to the hopes of forcing a decision on the southern front. The Israeli high command preferred therefore to wait until the Egyptian

* The chief advocate of an early attack was General Arik Sharon; the fullest statement of his views is in an interview with *Ma'ariv* (January 25th, 1974).

armoured forces crossed the canal to the east and launched an attack in which they would no doubt suffer heavy losses. Only then would the Israeli units stage their counter-attack across the canal and seize the west bank in the best possible conditions, i.e. in the absence of major Egyptian armoured forces. There was no reason to fear that Egyptian armour would be withdrawn to the west bank, for the Egyptian air-defence system would be weakened to such an extent that the Israeli air force would be able to prevent the re-crossing of the Egyptian forces to the west. Underlying this concept was the assumption that in a tank battle the Israeli forces would prevail, because all the difficulties encountered earlier by Israeli tanks in the fighting were caused not by Egyptian armour (which was found to be slow in movement and inaccurate in firing) but by the massive application of anti-tank weapons by the Egyptian infantry units. The Israelis knew that there were no strong Egyptian infantry units on the west bank and they would have to face only relatively small tank units which could be easily defeated.

The superiority of Israeli tanks was clearly demonstrated in the fighting of October 14th. The Egyptian division which had been thrown into the battle quickly – by Egyptian standards – suffered heavy losses and did not succeed in making any headway at all. At the end of the day they left two hundred tanks behind, realizing that they could no longer hope to regain the initiative which they had lost on October 9th. The Israeli forces suffered surprisingly few losses that day and the Israeli command decided there and then to counter-attack in the early morning of October 16th. Strong parachute units landed on the west bank and operated against missile sites on October 16th; simultaneously tanks crossed on rafts and extended vital support. On the 18th a bridge had already been constructed on the northern end of the Bitter Lake and from now on Israeli forces continued to build up their strength on the west bank, steadily but somewhat slowly. When the armistice came into force on the evening of the 22nd, the Israeli forces held territory 25 miles in length and 20 miles wide. However, since the fighting continued for some more time with both sides trying to improve their positions, the Israeli forces eventually succeeded in advancing southwards to the Red Sea at Ras Adabia, south of Suez, and to the north up to the suburbs of Ismalia.

Hostilities ceased on October 25th. On the Syrian front there had been no major fighting since the 15th; shortly before the cease-fire the Israeli forces reconquered the Hermon position. As the war ended two features of its progress emerged for the Israelis. The first was that the Israeli fighting forces were again superior; they had won every battle which took place after the Israeli mobilization had been carried out. Israeli tactics, battle techniques and the ability of the individual soldier had not changed for the worse since 1967. It was simply not true that there had been a tremendous qualitative change as far as the Arab soldier was concerned or that the new arms used by the Egyptians and the Syrians had had a revolutionary effect. The veterans of the war of 1948 had to remind their young colleagues that when an infantry company had attacked a defended Egyptian or Syrian position in that war it had suffered about 30 per cent casualties. This shows that the Arab soldier is effective when favoured by circumstances. Up to the Yom Kippur war the Israeli Army planned its wars in such a way that the Arab soldiers did not have the chance to show their full abilities. For this reason some had drawn the wrong conclusion – that the Arab soldiers lack fighting ability. This was a mistake which should not have been made by professionals.

The new weapons were not as new as the apologists made them appear. General Haim Bar Lev said in an interview after the war that all the weapons systems used by the Arab armies were well known to the Israelis.[2] The responsibility for the set-backs early on in the war should be put where it belongs, not on military intelligence. This brings us to the second feature that emerged for the Israelis: the high command was not intellectually prepared for the war and had no clear conception of how to conduct it once hostilities had started. The war was not conducted from the Israeli side according to any central strategic idea. This was clearly shown by (among other things) the deployment of Israeli forces at the end of the war.

The reasons for the complete surprise of the Israeli staff have already been discussed. But they had sufficient time to work out a strategy even after the war had begun. Operations during the first three days proceeded in effect according to standing orders: mobilization of the reserves went on as planned, the air force went into action to assure its supremacy in the air and to defend the skies of Israel. This was brilliantly accomplished by the Israeli airmen, operating both against the advancing enemy and against targets in enemy territory. The navy showed from the very beginning great ability and it carried out its assignments with an efficiency which surprised even those who knew it well. Despite its numerical inferiority vis-à-vis the Arab navies it had complete freedom of action along the shores of enemy territory.

During these three days the general staff should have analysed the strategic problems and the ways to tackle them. But this was not done. The minister of defence was ineffectual and almost panicked, his ideas and recommendations were of help to no one. The war in actual fact went on without him; it was conducted by the general staff and its chief without the assistance of any advance plan and without any guidance from the government. The great problem facing the general staff was the fact that the war had to be fought at the same time on two fronts. This meant that the Israeli Army could not achieve two of its traditional aims: it could not concentrate its forces on one front, and it could not bring the war to an end before the great powers intervened. In these circumstances the general staff should have decided on a scale of priorities, to force a decision at least on one front, and after that, if there was still time in hand, to try to do the same on the other front. Sufficient forces could have been concentrated to accomplish this task, had the staff planned it. The Syrian front had to be given priority because the Syrian penetration constituted a greater danger to Israeli settlements, and also because it was easier to defeat the Syrians. The general staff realized this but it did not understand how vital it was to force a decision on this front. Instead of penetrating deeply into Syrian territory, which would have caused Syria's collapse, Israeli operations were basically defensive in character, directed against the Kuneitra-Damascus axis, the most fortified part of Syria. This operation proceeded rather slowly and eventually came to a standstill.

It could be argued that political considerations caused the slowing down of the advance towards Damascus and prevented any deep penetration into Syria. But there is every reason to assume that the government would have accepted the advice of the general staff, had the army command taken a firm stand. The defeat of the Syrian Army, the cutting-off of Damascus and an advance towards Jebel Druz would have given Israel several far-reaching advantages. Firstly, it would have removed Syria from the fighting. Secondly, an advance towards Jebel Druz would have opened up positive political possibilities; traditionally, many Druze have been favourably disposed towards Israel. The Syrians were very much afraid of this; it was surely not accidental that the first senior officer executed by the Asad government during the war was a Druze brigadier-general. Meanwhile a holding action could have been fought on the Egyptian front which would not have been so difficult to accomplish. If troops had to be withdrawn from the south the risk involved was not very great in view of the fact that Sinai gave Israel strategic depth; even a further Egyptian advance would not have materially affected the situation, for the main value of Sinai to Israel is not in the twelve miles east of the canal. On the other hand a real defeat of Syria would have made it possible to concentrate subsequently most Israeli forces in the south. This would have been politically advantageous; their position would have certainly been much less exposed should fighting be resumed. If Syria had been defeated first, it is quite possible that the ceasefire would have come into force later than it did and this, too, would have been to Israel's advantage. For the Soviet Union, which was mainly instrumental in bringing about the ceasefire, was concerned above all with Egypt. Energetic action against Syria might have left Israel with enough time to turn against Egypt and to repel the Egyptian forces at least up to the canal.

Since this line of action was not adopted by the general staff (and there is reason to believe that it was not even seriously considered) G.H.Q. should have attempted to reach a more decisive outcome on the Egyptian front. In other words, once it had become clear that the war on the Syrian front was at a stalemate, the defence there should have been organized in such a way as to release strong forces which could have been transferred to the south. Once a breakthrough had been effected in Sinai and a bridgehead established, much stronger armoured forces should have been dispatched in the general direction of Cairo and the Nile delta; they would have rolled up the Egyptian front, from north to south. When the Israeli tank units crossed the canal in force on the 18th and 19th, they moved westwards hardly encountering any resistance. Armoured units which ventured some thirty-five miles west of the canal did not spot any enemy forces. However, the general staff was still in a defensive mood following the impact of the Arab surprise attack. It hesitated to accept risks; it prevented any further advance to the west and preferred less ambitious operations such as the building up of a more stable bridgehead west of the canal. But this proceeded too slowly because tanks were operating against defended positions as they had done on the Syrian front where great caution had again been a pronounced feature of the conduct of warfare. This could be understood perhaps in view of the fact that Israeli forces operating west of the canal were as yet not very substantial, but it is also possible that the strategy was influenced by political considerations, the fear of approaching too near to Cairo. It appeared as if the Israeli military leaders had forgotten all about the time factor, only to remember its existence suddenly after the ceasefire of October 22nd. True, on October 22nd, and even more so on the 25th, the Israeli forces were in a better position to liquidate the besieged third army.

In 1949, the Israeli forces were prevented from reaping the fruits of victory at the very last moment. The whole military doctrine of the Israeli Army had been founded on this necessity for speed, which was only to be forgotten after 1967. For this reason it is not good enough to talk about 'being deprived of the fruits of victory'. Everyone knew in advance that this would happen if the time factor was ignored. But even if the Israeli forces had been able to defeat the third army within two or three days, it would not have amounted to a full victory. The second army was still in a strong defensive position and to destroy it the Israeli Army would have needed at least one more week, perhaps ten days. For this reason it did not really matter, in the last resort, when the war ended; for in its last stages, after October 22nd, fighting went on for prestigious rather than real achievements. In professional military terms Israeli achievements were considerable, its army had shown a rare fighting spirit and the ability to turn the tables when facing a difficult tactical situation. But the overall result was less than satisfactory; it is the political function of an army to provide the government with a good starting point for future action. According to General Elazar, the chief of staff, the army did enable the government to proceed from a position of strength, but this simply does not correspond with reality. The government was in a difficult position owing, *inter alia*, to the failure of a general staff which had ignored certain lessons of the past.

It is too early to analyse in detail operations in the two theatres of war, but it would appear that the obsession with the 'territorial issue' which distorted strategic thought prior to the outbreak of war also bedevilled the conduct of the war. Despite the strategic depth offered by the Sinai desert, the high command was not willing to take the risk of a retreat in this region in order to make significant gains in Syria. On the other hand the command continued a frontal attack against the Syrians after these had already been thrown back beyond the 1967 armistice lines, as if it were important to make any further territorial conquests. The Israeli counter-attack at Suez was launched before the Syrians had been totally defeated, as if it was strategically important that the Egyptians were holding a narrow strip of land.

Various sacred cows had to be sacrificed during the war: for example, the settlements on the Golan Heights which had been established, as it were, in order to contribute to Israel's defence. This house of cards collapsed and the settlements had to be evacuated immediately. The civilian population had also to be evacuated from Sharm el Sheikh after it appeared that Egyptian commando units were operating in the area. It had been assumed that Sharm el Sheikh was of vital strategic importance because it safeguarded the approaches to the Red Sea; even a cursory glance at the map should have shown that the Red Sea could be sealed off at Bab el Mandeb, as indeed it was at the outbreak of the war. Since Jordan effectively stayed out of the war, Israel was spared yet another bitter lesson, that the settlements which had been established in the Jordan Valley in recent years would have had to be evacuated too.

The 'territorial illusion' was particularly pronounced in the case of Dayan, who eventually favoured wholesale annexation. His political views obtruded on strategic thought and virtually prevented a balanced defence policy commensurate with Israel's specific position. The general staff underwent a process of intellectual decline after 1967, uncritically accepting the views of the defence minister. This did not remain unnoticed, but most outside observers believed that the professional level of the general staff was not affected. They came to regard the general staff not so much as an institution with ideas of its own (which it had been for twenty years, from General Yadin to General Rabin), but as a technocratic body capable of ensuring the technical and tactical supremacy of the armed forces. However, in the course of the war it appeared that such a differentiation was in practice impossible; for in the technical and tactical fields, too, the general staff was not on the same high level as in the past.

Mention has been made of the defensive approach which affected strategic thinking. Mistakes were made in other respects even though the consequences were not as serious – for instance in the constitution of ground forces. This is an issue of great importance because the Israeli Army is mainly based on ground forces, and the general staff consists almost entirely of ground-force officers. The navy and the air force staffs are, in theory at any rate, an integral part of the general staff, but in actual fact they have a high command of their own. This involves certain dangers but in the event both the navy and the air force were much less affected by the decline of the general staff. One may not entirely acquit the air force staff of not being better prepared to cope with the enemy air-defence system, but on balance the air force, in spite of great difficulties, showed operational readiness and carried out its assignments in a brilliant way. Many observers underrated the achievements of the air force in 1973 simply because it did not destroy enemy aircraft on the ground as in 1967. But the Arab commanders had learned the obvious lesson from their débâcle in the Six Day War: their planes were dispersed all over the country and hidden in fortified hangars which prevented, needless to say, the destruction on the ground of the Arab air force. Nevertheless, the tactical superiority of the Israeli air force was not challenged, the Arab air command kept its planes on the ground whenever there was a danger that Israeli aircraft would appear in the vicinity; when dog fights did take place they ended with heavy losses to the Arabs.

The performance of the Israeli Navy came as a surprise not only to Egyptians and Syrians but also to the Russians, who discovered that their various types of missile boats could not compete with the Israeli vessels. This will no doubt act as a spur to the Russians to improve their naval equipment and affect the future organization of the Egyptian and Syrian naval forces. This could be the challenge facing the Israeli Navy in a future war.

The fighting capacity of the Israeli ground forces was hardly affected by the way of thought of the general staff which forced them to move into battle in unfavourable conditions. The general staff had decided in 1969, without apparent justification, to base the ground forces mainly on the tank brigades to the detriment of the infantry units and the parachutists. This decision had nothing to do with the lessons of the Six Day War; it so happened that former tank commanders were prominently represented in the general staff after 1967. The same tendency was reflected in a combat technique which caused some problems; the Israeli tank forces were unpleasantly surprised when they encountered Egyptian infantry excellently organized and equipped for anti-tank warfare. This in itself should not have been surprising, the only novelty in the situation was that the Israeli forces were not prepared for it. If the importance of the armoured units was over-emphasized, night combat was neglected. In the past this had been one of the strong points of the Israeli Army and it had been developed and improved to a high degree. But in October 1973 the Egyptian and Syrian tanks were better prepared for night fighting, and the Egyptian infantry, unlike on past occasions, was not afraid of night fighting either. Israeli infantry on the other hand was only seldom involved in night fighting, despite the fact that they had been well trained for the purpose.

The positive influence of Soviet training was most palpably felt in these tactical aspects. It emerged that in conditions which the Egyptian and Syrian soldier had been led to expect, the Soviet military doctrine was of more help than any other approach. Similar experiences had been gained in Vietnam, Korea and elsewhere. This should not have been a startling discovery for the Israeli armed forces, for the experience of wars in distant countries should have been studied. However, the general staff did not imagine that the Arab armies would ever reach a stage in which they could fully show to what extent they had benefited from Soviet training. This, in turn, was not unconnected with the change – or the absence of it – in Israeli strategic thought.

As for the deeper significance of Soviet intervention, there was an inclination in the Israeli Army – as in the country in general – not to face reality. The full seriousness of Soviet intervention had become known only on the eve of the Six Day War. This frightened the government, which previously was not aware of the full extent of this process. Levi Eshkol thought he could induce the Russians to help in settling the conflict in the 'Spirit of Tashkent', which, seen in retrospect, was a very naive assumption indeed. But the outcome of the Six Day War was so unequivocal that the politicians were tempted to forget the lesson of the possibility of Russian intervention and it was generally assumed that the Soviet Union and the United States would again co-operate and compel Israel to retreat as in 1956. As this did not happen there was a tendency to ignore the long-term implications of Soviet intervention. This attitude did not change despite the fact that the Soviet Union re-equipped the Arab armies after 1967 on an unprecedented scale and that it directly and massively intervened in the war of attrition. Privately the politicians were perhaps willing to admit their concern but they would not do so publicly because it would necessitate a change in attitude to the settlement of the Arab-Israeli conflict. For the same reasons they regarded the Soviet exodus from Egypt in 1972 as evidence of the decline of Soviet influence in the Middle East. Which did not prevent Mrs Meir, after the outbreak of hostilities, from denouncing the Soviet Union as the force mainly responsible for the war, and for Israeli setbacks during its early stages. This is reminiscent of Nasser's declaration in 1967, when he refused to admit that he had been defeated by Israel and instead accused the United States. If Nasser was surprised in 1967 that the two super-powers would not collaborate against Israel as in 1956, Israel on the contrary was shocked in 1973 by the fact that there was such co-operation towards an armistice.

There were surprises for Israel all along the line, even on the battlefield, and they caused a great many losses even though, on balance, Israel did not lose its superiority. But weapons were used and units thrown into the battle which were unsuitable in the circumstances. Officers and men faced conditions on the field of battle for which they were not prepared. This was the fault, in the final analysis, of those who had made strategy subservient to political doctrine. The loose talk by senior officers on the value of 'secure borders', the boasting about the omnipotence of the tank forces which through their superior fire power would sweep away and utterly crush enemy infantry, the belittling of the ability of the enemy to learn, slowly but steadily, a new combat technique and to carry out complicated operations which it had rehearsed countless times – all this was bound to create illusions in Israel and in its army.

It must be admitted that the men in the field were quicker to adjust themselves to the new conditions than the staff; and with an extraordinary capacity for improvisation they overcame the difficulties. The pilots learned how to evade the missiles, the tank crews mastered the technique of getting out of the rain of anti-tank missiles. If the general staff had shown a similar capacity to rethink it might have complied with the first commandment of Israeli strategic thought, namely to end a war within the limited period at its disposal; all the excuses about the 'very few days' which were needed were no compensation for a full victory. The feeling of urgency was somehow absent among the senior army staff in this war. Suddenly they discovered that the best course of action was not to engage in pursuit after the rapidly vanishing time. Suddenly army spokesmen explained that there was no necessity to conclude the war quickly, but that there was time enough to finish the job without hurry. They had the support of the government which likewise failed to understand the supreme strategic necessity. Such mistakes would not have been committed by a more capable leadership.

The Two Sides of the Hill

The first announcements by Israeli leaders after the outbreak of the war showed a serious misjudgment of the military situation. Preceding Ironside on Israeli television, Dayan declared on Saturday evening that Israel would smite the Egyptians 'hip and thigh'; the present transition phase would lead to victory 'within a few days'.

The Egyptians had engaged in a 'very, very dangerous adventure'. The officer commanding southern command, General Gonen, announced on Sunday that the Egyptians had failed to achieve their objectives along the entire front; General Mendler, the commander of the armoured forces in Sinai, declared in his order of the day on October 7th that before this day was out the enemy would be 'utterly routed'.[3] Everyone thought the war would be over soon. On Monday, October 8th, Israeli correspondents reported that the Golan soldiers hoped to be home by Sabbath and that the decisive push to the canal was expected the same day.[4] Also on October 8th, the chief of staff, General Elazar, said at a press conference that the turning point was just ahead: 'Our aim is to teach them a lesson and to win a decisive and significant victory, in short, to break all their bones.'[5] The Israeli counter-offensive in the Golan made good progress but when Dayan visited Sinai the next day the overall picture was not at all encouraging, and he returned in a dark mood; his report to the government was pessimistic. He was to appear in a televised press conference that evening but it was decided to let General Aharon Yariv, former director of military intelligence, appear in his place. Yariv provided the first honest and realistic account: he revealed that Israel had evacuated most of the Bar Lev line. There was no danger to the existence of Israel, but it would be a long and hard war, and one should not have 'soaring visions of elegant and rapid conquests'.[6] The first Israeli reaction as reflected in countless speeches was that the Arab attack was a 'mad adventure'; at the end of the first week of war it no longer seemed that mad. On Thursday, October 11th, Mrs Meir admitted that she had had to face very difficult and bitter hours of late. On the second day of the war the Israeli Cabinet had decided that there would be no truce until all invading enemy forces had been driven back across the borders. On October 13th, Mrs Meir again vowed victory but at the same time made it known that her government would consider a ceasefire any time the Arabs were ready.

Thus during this first week of fighting there were many official speeches and declarations in Israel, most of them far too optimistic in character; later on, when things were going well the compulsion to make public statements was no longer felt. The fantastically high Arab claims were not believed in Israel; the Syrians, to give but one example, claimed to have downed sixty-eight Israeli aircraft on one single day (October 11th).[7] But there were rumours about heavy losses and the authorities did little at first to counteract them.

Israel quickly prepared itself for a war: blackout came into force; buses stopped at 6 p.m., blood donors were queuing up, strikes were shelved for obvious reasons and housewives stormed the grocery stores. Schools were closed on October 7th and 8th but reopened the day after, radio and TV were broadcasting around the clock, the elections were postponed. There was much volunteering for all kinds of jobs; two ex-generals were driving garbage vans in Tel Aviv and scientists of world renown were sorting the mail in Jerusalem. The postal service functioned as it had never before; letters from soldiers on the Golan were distributed in Haifa twelve hours later. On October 9th, Finance Minister Pinhas Sapir announced a national loan of a billion Israeli pounds to help finance the war; he said that during the first week alone the war had cost eight times this sum. While the war continued El Al went on flying from Lod to Europe and America; all other airlines stopped their flights to Israel. While Jordanian soldiers were fighting with the Syrians, the bridges over the Jordan remained open and hundreds of Arabs crossed every day in either direction. Cotton was harvested in Galilee, after the initial rush there was again plenty of food in the supermarkets, rationing was not envisaged. The settlers who had been evacuated from the Golan returned to their homes and began to repair the damage that had been caused. There were more volunteers than work and the Jewish Agency offices outside Israel were told to hold back on sending volunteers. The Arabs in Israel were very quiet indeed; heeding Fatah radio appeals they did not turn up for work at the beginning of the war but returned a few days later.

After a week of confusion life in Israel returned to normal, there was a patriotic upsurge and the same spirit of volunteering as in previous national emergencies; the police chiefs of both Tel Aviv and Cairo announced a most startling decline in theft. The fishing fleet was back at work and the astrologers reported that when the Arabs made their attack Venus had been close to Neptune, which, of course, had forced the Arabs to make mistakes. By October 12th, the Syrians had been defeated, three days later the turning point on the Egyptian front was in sight. On October 16th in her Knesset speech Mrs Meir mentioned for the first time the presence of Israeli units on Egyptian soil. The Egyptians maintained that this was a propaganda stunt; seven amphibious tanks had tried to cross the canal, four had been immediately destroyed, the others were encircled and would be liquidated within the hour. They continued to encircle the three tanks for a whole week but without apparent success. For when the ceasefire came there was a whole Israeli army west of the canal and the Egyptian third army was cut off. Yet with all these successes, after a week of set-backs there was no jubilation in Israel. The public was aware, some acutely, some dimly, that something had gone wrong – and not just that Israel had been unprepared the day the Arabs attacked.

On the Arab side, the first news the public got was communiqués that the Israeli enemy had launched a treacherous air and naval attack (at Sokhneh and Za'afarana) against Syria and Egypt. But the Arabs had immediately counter-attacked and inflicted a heavy defeat on the enemy, over-running the Suez Canal and the Golan Heights. In the evening President Asad made a speech in which he said:

> Today we are waging the battle of honour and dignity in defence of our dear land, our glorious history and the heritage of our fathers and forefathers. Israel had been despotic and arrogant. They persisted in crime and indulged in aggression. Their hearts are filled with black hatred for our people and mankind. They are thirsty for bloodshed.
>
> Grandsons of Abu Bakr, Umar, Uthman, and Ali may God be pleased with them; grandsons of Khalid, Abu Ubaydar Amr, Sa'ad, and Saladin; the conscience of our nation is calling us and the souls of our martyrs are urging us to take examples from the battles of Yarmuk, Qadisiah, Hittin and Ayn Jalut. The masses of our nation from the Ocean to the Gulf are focusing their eyes and hearts on our great stead-fastness ...[8]

And on he went, not one *Khalif*, not a single battle was left out;

a *Jihad*, a holy war, was declared. Yet compared with 1967, Arab rhetoric was restrained, especially in Egypt during the first week of fighting. Despite successes, the Egyptian people were warned that they faced a 'hard and protracted battle'.[9] The more responsible papers predicted in their editorials a 'long war'.[10] The main slogan was: 'Kill the myth that Israel is an invincible state.' (General Ahmed Ismail in his first message to the Egyptian armed forces crossing the canal.) There were no premature announcements of 'final victory'. It was only during the second week of fighting when things were going much less well that Arab propaganda reverted to its old bad habits: typical was the story about the Israeli pilots who had been found chained to their seats so that they could not parachute to safety.

Since Arab expectations with regard to military successes had not been too high, the subsequent disappointment was not too great. The Egyptians after all were still in Sinai and the Israelis had been unable or unwilling to make any further advance towards Damascus. When President Sadat made his first appearance during the war on October 16th, before the People's Assembly, he exuded confidence: Egypt was prepared to accept a ceasefire on the basis of an immediate Israeli withdrawal from all occupied territories under international supervision to the pre-5th June 1967 lines.[11] Egypt was willing to attend an international peace conference at the U.N. as soon as the withdrawal had been completed. The American sea and air bridge to Israel did not frighten Sadat. Ten days later he was to admit that he had to accept the ceasefire because he could not fight the American war machine – the same declaration that had been made by President Nasser in 1967.

In Syria the war was virtually over after eight days of fighting. But Syrian official announcements were still full of optimism and President Asad, speaking to the nation on October 16th, painted a picture of a state of affairs which had little in common with reality: 'Our forces continue their advance, they have expelled the enemy from Kuneitra, Jibbin, Khushniya, Awl Al, Jukhadar, Tal al Faras and a great many other places.' He added, 'Our forces continue to pursue the enemy and strike at him and will continue to strike at enemy forces until we regain our positions in our occupied land and continue then until we liberate the whole land.'[12]

Since the Syrian Army was no longer able to attack, this did not mean much in military terms, but it signified that Asad regarded the Egyptian-Syrian agreement about limited war aims (Resolution 242) null and void: the target, as far as Damascus was concerned, was the liberation of the whole (Palestinian) homeland.

Foreign observers in Cairo and Damascus agreed that the mood was serious; there was little traffic in the streets, and few private cars around. Cairo airport was closed, those wanting to get in or out had to travel by taxi to and from Benghazi. The minister of culture anticipated that the war would last for a long time; he commissioned playwrights to write on martial themes so as to replace the comedies performed on the Cairo stage.[13] Schools were closed in Egypt, the radio carried chantings from the Koran and martial music. The street cafés were open – even at night the temperature did not fall below 30° centigrade – but some of the cabarets had been closed. The mood after forty-eight hours of fighting was one of confidence; according to one observer, 'all Egyptians notwithstanding their social origin have shown a phlegm, even a sang froid which one should not mistake for indifference'.[14] The next day a reporter from Damascus wrote about a 'disconcerting serenity' prevailing in the Syrian capital; and a few days later: 'Damascus no longer expects the troops of General Dayan.'[15] Soviet observers conceded that there were difficulties: 'Damascus goes through difficult days just now.'[16] Damascus had been heavily bombed and considerable damage had been inflicted on Homs, Latakia and Tartus during the first week of the war. The decision to bomb civilian targets in Syria – in contrast to Egypt – had been taken after the Syrians used F R O G missiles to hit settlements deep in Israeli territory. Tuesday, October 9th, was the worst day for Damascus – there were six air raids between morning and evening. But the post and the public services continued to function, electricity and telephone lines were repaired; Damascus too, came to terms with the war.[17] The Damascus government had never admitted that Israeli forces had penetrated well into Syria, and while the thunder of the heavy guns was heard in the suburbs of Damascus, the population of the city was not aware of any particular danger. Syrians were encouraged by the success of the Soviet ground-to-air missiles against the Israeli Skyhawks and Phantoms.

The fact that the average Syrian and Egyptian was not too well informed about the real state of affairs helped to keep up morale at home. Perhaps he would not even have minded hearing the truth; so great was the military prestige of the Israelis after the war of 1967 that the fact that Arab armies were holding out and inflicting casualties on the Zionist enemy would have been considered a triumph. But the fact that they had been misinformed was bound to backfire in the end; only yesterday they had been the victors and then all of a sudden a ceasefire was agreed upon which left the Israelis, at least for the moment, in possession of more Arab land than they had on October 6th. Why did Arab leaders accept this truce after having sworn they would not stop fighting until the last inch of Arab territory was liberated? If the whole world was with the Arabs, who could force Sadat and Asad to accept an armistice of this sort? There was a feeling of anti-climax, and euphoria gave way to disenchantment.[18] For once Arabs and Israelis agreed – both felt deprived of victory.

The Lessons of the War

The lessons of the fourth Arab-Israeli war will be discussed for a long time to come. At the beginning it was widely assumed outside the Middle East that the war would be over within a few days, in a week at most; when this did not happen there were second thoughts on the quality of the Israeli Army and its leadership: perhaps its efficiency had been greatly over-rated? Perhaps its successes in 1956 and 1967 had been entirely due to the advantage of surprise? Had it rested on its laurels and deteriorated? The Prussian Army under Frederick II had been the greatest fighting force in Europe, yet twenty years after the death of the monarch Prussia collapsed at Jena and Auerstädt. Had there been a similar process in Israel?

Such an appraisal was, of course, unfair. The world had become accustomed to thinking that no Arab-Israeli war would last longer than a few days. But for the moment of surprise it would have taken the Israeli forces much longer to win the wars of 1956 and of 1967. If expectations at the beginning of the war were much too high, the negative reappraisal at the end of the first week of fighting was no less erroneous. For on the sixth day of the war Israeli columns had already crossed into Syria; on the ninth day the major Egyptian tank offensive had been repulsed and had suffered heavy losses; on the twelfth day there was an Israeli bridge across the canal and when the ceasefire came into force the Egyptian Army was on the brink of disaster. Once the Israeli reserves were fully mobilized there was no doubt about the military outcome of the war. This is not to say that all was well with Israeli strategy, and that Israeli set-backs during the first few days could be explained (as some later maintained) simply by reference to the fact that the country was taken by surprise.[19] There was brilliant improvisation on the part of some senior commanders, but basically the Israeli forces were successful owing to the excellence of their field officers and fighting men. There had been the feeling after 1967 that Israel was invincible, that the Arabs would not dare to attack, and that they would suffer a crushing defeat within a few days – if not hours – if they were foolish enough to try their luck on the field of battle. This theme returned in countless speeches by military leaders after 1967 and it reappeared even during the first days of the war in 1973, when it no longer carried much conviction. It was perhaps significant that the Israeli Navy, which had not excelled in 1967, acquitted itself so well six years later; the navy commanders had carefully studied the lessons of the 1967 war and had made the most of them. The experts in the general staff knew all about the existence of SAM-6 and the 'Sagger' anti-tank missile (a more recent version of 'Snapper', the wire guided missile; it is 2 feet 6 inches long and has a 11.5 lb. warhead). But they did not anticipate that Saggers would be massively used by the Arab forces and thus have a major impact on tank warfare. Above all, the commanders and the soldiers in the field were not aware of these innovations; there was a breakdown in communication and this caused serious and unnecessary losses.

It would not have been an easy war in any case, for the forces involved were considerable by any standard: the Egyptians and the Syrians brought into battle some 4,500 tanks (T-34, 54, 55, 62) and 3,300 guns (of more than 120 mm) – more than in the whole of NATO Europe. Israel had some 1,700 tanks and 900 guns; 1,000 Syrian and 850 Egyptian tanks were destroyed or damaged, and of their air force of about 1,000 planes, the two countries lost some

420. Israeli losses were estimated at more than 500 tanks and more than 100 planes. Nevertheless both sides had about as much war material at the end of the war as at the beginning; within ten days some 7-8,000 tons were sent by way of the Soviet air bridge – the greatest ever in military history – and much more by ship.[20] The American supplies to Israel were smaller but also of vital importance. The Sinai tank battle was the second largest in history after the battle of Kursk on the Eastern Front during the Second World War.

It is easy in retrospect to point to Israeli weaknesses and mistakes; it is more difficult to point to alternative strategies that should have been pursued once hostilities had started. An Israeli advance deep into Syria and/or Egypt might have brought the Soviet Union into the war. This depended almost entirely on the way America would react; it is unlikely that the Russians would have entered the war if there was a risk that this would lead to American intervention. America's position was not quite clear; Israel was heavily dependent on American supplies, and this dependence, which the strategists had vastly under-rated, had obvious political implications. Thus, in the final analysis, Israel's options were narrowly restricted. The military objectives of the Egyptians and the Syrians in launching the war were limited, not out of humanitarian reasons but because they realized that total military victory was not in their reach. It was merely to be the 'spark' (to use Sadat's term), not the real conflagration in which Arab oil was to play a central role. As far as the Arabs were concerned, the war was merely the overture to negotiations, which they regarded as the continuation of warfare with other means. Whatever the outcome of the battle, its impact on the conduct of negotiations was strictly limited, provided only that the Arab armies did not immediately collapse or that Israel did not suffer a decisive defeat. These eventualities were most unlikely, and for this reason the war, for all its sacrifices, was only an interlude between two periods of political warfare. This takes us back to the politics of the confrontation; but before taking leave of the military aspects of the war some general observations on the wider military lessons of the war seem to be called for.

Intelligence*

After initially spreading the story that 'we knew of the coming attack, but could not pre-empt it owing to political considerations' (e.g. Mrs Golda Meir in her first television talk), most sources now agree that, while Israeli and American intelligence had both registered Arab preparations for war, the information at hand was misinterpreted. Arab military measures, such as the construction of roads, the setting-up of crossing points along the Suez Canal, the massing of bridging equipment, the establishment of anti-aircraft missile umbrellas, and finally the mobilization of reserves, were registered, but wishful thinking led to their being mistaken for defensive measures, part of a game of bluff, or ordinary manoeuvres. It is not yet clear whether the failure to understand measures for what they were, i.e. preparatory steps towards the launching of a large-scale offensive, was the responsibility of military intelligence proper or of higher, political, echelons.

Taking a broad view, it would seem that this combination of a knowledge of the facts with their misinterpretation was by no means accidental. While technological advances in the last thirty years have made it practically impossible for war preparations of any size to escape aerial photography, radar and electronic surveillance, gauging the intentions behind these preparations has become increasingly difficult. The reasons for this are as follows:

1. The sheer amount of information to be processed. One might perhaps venture to say that while the quantity of incoming information has been growing by leaps and bounds, few really important advances in processing this information have been made in recent years. There are indications that the problem of how to cope with the enormous quantity of incoming information and make use of it is a major difficulty facing many intelligence services.

2. The perfection of means of communication and consequent centralization of the decision-making power has greatly reduced the number of people in the know and made it possible

* The following sections in this chapter were written by Dr Martin van Creveld.

to postpone the moment when the executive levels are made aware of what is going on. Thus the number of potential leaks is greatly reduced.

3. The widespread use in communication of 'one time' codes based on random numbers.

On the whole, these developments lead to the conclusion that, in spite of the perfection of means of surveillance and detection, surprise attacks are now more feasible than ever.

Offence versus Defence

In regard to this crucial problem, the last war seems to have reconfirmed the old lesson, perhaps somewhat obscured by the Six Day *Blitzkrieg*, that the best possible method of waging war is to combine the strategic* offence with a tactical defence. A comparison of the last war with the previous ones brings out the advantages to be gained by launching a strategic surprise attack, i.e. striking before the enemy can bring his forces to bear, in overwhelming fashion. Not only do the speed and range of modern weapons make it possible to gain advantages by means of the initial blow, but once these advantages are won it is exceedingly difficult to cancel them out again. Thus, during the first two days of the war, the Egyptian and Syrian armies possessed all the advantages of strategic offence without having to do very much fighting tactically. From the third to the ninth day the Israelis, while strategically on the defensive, had to take the initiative tactically, and it was in this period that they seem to have suffered their heaviest losses. A brilliant move – crossing to the west bank of the Suez Canal – enabled the Israelis to overcome this handicap on the tenth day of the war. After that, things became somewhat easier for them.

Given the fact, demonstrated by the last war, that it is very difficult to deny the aggressor a territorial advantage once gained, the temptation to launch a surprise attack in order to make some gains against which the other side will then have to wear itself out is enormous. This, it seems, was just what the Egyptians (and perhaps the Syrians) had in mind; and for a few days it looked

* Here used to include everything between the grand-strategic and tactical, i.e. in a sense equivalent to the German *operativ*.

as if their objective of grinding down the Israeli Army by forcing it to engage in a tactical offensive might well be achieved.

Static versus Dynamic Defence

In so far as the initial Arab breakthroughs on both fronts were made against almost ridiculously small forces, it is doubtful whether the war can really lead to any conclusions as to the value of fixed lines of defence. Had the Bar Lev line been held at greater strength, and had there been proper reserves immediately behind it, the initial stages of the war might well have assumed a different character. If the war has demonstrated anything in this respect, it is not the worthlessness of fixed fortifications but the amazing speed with which immensely strong defensive lines can be improvised. Within thirty-six hours of the crossing the Egyptian Army had dug in sufficiently to repulse all Israeli counter-attacks. The lesson to emerge from this would seem to be that reserves should be concentrated immediately behind the line, not far in the rear as was done in the present case. For Israel, this presumably implies that a larger part of her forces will have to be kept in constant readiness, i.e. as a standing army.

The Role of Armour

The history of the tank is essentially the story of an attempt to adapt a machine, originally invented for the purpose of breaking through fortified trenches, to an armoured cavalry role. On two occasions did it appear that this attempt was vindicated: during the German successes of 1939-41 (although it has been argued that, given any kind of defence, those successes would not have been possible) and during the Six Day War. Western military doctrine, however, had begun to doubt the value of the tank in this role from about 1943 onward, and the last war seems to have confirmed these doubts.

The essence of cavalry warfare is movement, and free movement for armoured cavalry – the tank – depends on the absence of weapons effectively able to stop it. In the past, anti-tank weapons either could not be made sufficiently numerous and mobile (as in the case of the anti-tank gun) or they suffered from a very short range (as in the case of the bazooka, the P I A T, the *Panzerfaust*, and the various types of anti-tank rifles). The development of a relatively cheap, easily manufactured anti-tank missile has enabled the individual soldier to engage the tank at considerable range. Moreover these missiles, in contrast to earlier anti-tank weapons, are guided, and thus help to neutralize the tank's advantage of speed of movement. As a result, all attempts to use the tank in a cavalry role – breakthrough first, exploitation second – have run into a rain of missiles and failed. Instead, tanks are being kept more to the rear and used with greater care, their main function (on the Israeli side, at least) being to engage enemy armour and troop concentrations at intermediate range by sharp-shooting.

The last war has also confirmed armour's vulnerability to air power or, rather, the fact that not even 'the best tankmen in the world' can operate without air cover. This was a lesson which the Israelis should have learnt from the Six Day War, if from nowhere else;* at that time complete mastery of the skies enabled their own armour to storm forward in the Sinai, while the fact that Jordan's crack armoured forces had no air cover to speak of led to their quick annihilation by the Israeli Air Force using its second-line aircraft. In the last war the Israelis did not possess complete mastery of the sky; initially, however, they made the mistake of using their armour as if they did. The results were disastrous.

Trying to get a glimpse of the future, one might conclude that we are unlikely to see armour resume its 1967 role of charge, breakthrough and exploitation. Whether the tank can for long justify its existence in the more limited role it is playing now appears problematical. It may, however, prove possible to cancel out the advantage of the guided anti-tank missile by replacing the tank by some faster and more manoeuvrable vehicle.

The Future of the Air Force

In this field, three observations should be made:

1. Any hope Israel may have had of rendering Arab anti-aircraft missile defences ineffective simply by relying on the excellence of her pilots had to be given up. The new weapons,

* The same lesson was apparent from the last years of World War II and the war in Vietnam.

particularly the relatively small s a m 6 and s a m 7, have been proved highly successful against the fighter bomber. While air-to-ground missiles such as the American Shrike may be effective against the larger targets presented by stationary s a m 2 and s a m 3 bases, it is doubtful whether they will be very effective against far larger numbers of small, mobile s a ms 6 and 7 dispersed all over the place. Neither is it certain that electronic counter-measures will solve the problem, since some at least of the recently introduced missiles can be guided optically or carry infra-red homing devices that are immune to jamming.

On their side, the Israelis did apparently succeed in scoring hits on Arab fighter-bombers simply by large volume of fire. Numerous Syrian and Egyptian planes were reportedly brought down by Israelis firing small arms, mainly machine-guns, against them.

In so far as TV and laser-guided bombs may enable planes to escape some of the effects of the new weapons by allowing them to attack ground targets from a greater altitude it would be premature to conclude from these facts that the fighter-bomber is finished. Still, its freedom of action has certainly been diminished. In the future, ground forces will do just as much to protect planes as planes will do to protect them. In this connection it is useful to recall that it was only after the Israelis crossed the canal and destroyed a large number of anti-aircraft missiles on the ground that their air force regained anything like its accustomed freedom of action.

2. The war may have strengthened doubts as to the combat value of super-fast aircraft. In recent years, it was reported that such planes, including the Soviet made MiG-23 and MiG-25, were stationed in Egypt and were making an occasional reconnaissance flight over the Sinai. Whether these planes, capable of Mach 3 as they are, are really suitable for anything else is doubtful. Operating at 80-90,000 feet, they are practically useless against ground forces; while descending to a lower altitude will presumably involve a loss of speed, it does bring other qualities, such as manoeuvrability, into play. In view of the role played in reconnaissance by satellites, it is questionable whether the speed of present-day aircraft may be

increased to serve any useful purpose. It is significant that the F-4 Phantom, commonly regarded as the best all-round fighter and fighter bomber in the world, is now fully eighteen years old, and that perhaps the only aspect of its performance which has not been greatly improved since it first flew is its speed.

3. Finally, the war has demonstrated the crucial importance of air-lifting capacity, if the super-powers are to intervene quickly and effectively anywhere outside their own borders. The American C-54 'Galaxy' may have been a controversial plane, but it has fully proved its worth by enabling the United States to safeguard its global political and military interests.

The Place of Infantry

The last war has shown that weapons hitherto regarded as dominating the battlefield, such as the tank and the aircraft, are vulnerable to relatively unsophisticated weapons operated by infantry in small groups or even by individual soldiers. If, during the last six years, the Israelis have ranked their infantry a poor fourth (behind air force, armour and navy) in the order of priority, this order may well have to be changed as a result of the war just behind us. Furthermore, the introduction of more powerful weapons in the hands of the infantry may well cause the adaptation of new tactics and bring the motorized foot-soldier, instead of the tank, to the forefront of the attacking force.

Destruction versus Manoeuvre

Wars, as Winston Churchill once observed, are won by either slaughter or manoeuvre. The question as to which form any particular war assumes depends on generalship and a variety of logistic, technological and even social factors. The Six Day War was a war of movement *par excellence*; many Egyptian units in particular were not engaged at all but found themselves passed by and isolated dozens of miles behind the front. During the last war, by contrast, advances on both sides were slow and laborious, seldom if ever exceeding ten kilometres a day. With the exception of the Israeli crossing to the west bank of the Suez Canal (itself a very slow affair by Six Day standards) no deep penetrations, imaginative flanking operations or great encirclement battles have been seen, as is reflected also in the relatively small number of prisoners. On the whole, tactics have predominated over strategy; attrition over movement; and wholesale destruction over manoeuvre. It has been a *Materialschlacht* on a scale unprecedented in the Middle East. In so far as this development is not the result of the accidental absence of generalship but stems from clearly identifiable factors there is reason to believe that in this respect the fourth Arab-Israeli war provides a much better indicator of the future than the Six Day War.

Army and Society

The Six Day War, according to one authority, 'was won by a disciplined, technologically skilled people against a well equipped but badly led army without the educational or social infrastructure to fight a machine war.' Whether the 'educational or social infra-structure' of either the Egyptian or Syrian armies has changed very much during the last six years may be doubted, but the performance of both forces, though perhaps not brilliant, has certainly improved a great deal. Part of the improvement is probably due to higher morale (the fact that the Arabs were fighting for their 'homeland', the desire to avenge their military honour, and the timing of the attack to start during Ramadan) and as such may be temporary, but such factors clearly cannot account for their undoubted, if unexpected, ability to maintain and use sophisticated equipment, nor for the technical and organizational ability displayed by the Egyptian Command in carrying out a huge canal-crossing opera-tion. The Arab performance was certainly assisted from the outside by *matériel*, training and doctrine (although it is arguable that Soviet doctrine, far from speeding the Egyptian advance, actually delayed it). It may also have something to do with the fact that the most effective of the recently introduced weapons, such as the anti-tank and anti-aircraft missiles, are not necessarily the most complicated ones to operate. Looking beyond these facts, however, the war may have shown that, given time and certain other condi-tions (e.g. unlimited manpower) it is possible for a state to build up armed forces considerably in advance of its social, economic, educational and technological infrastructure. It is true that while the Soviet Union, which is another example of this phenomenon,

117

has pulled itself up by its own bootstraps, the Arabs have had their straps pulled for them; but the very fact that this can be done may, in the long run, prove the most ominous lesson of the war.

Chapter Four   A Test for Détente

'Do grown-up people have to be on bad terms because their children are quarrelling?' Dr Kissinger's question asked during the October war was quite revealing; American policy in the Middle-East conflict can be understood only against the background of détente and it is to this that we shall have to turn next. What were the basic conceptions of American policy makers when the Middle-East war broke out, and what, in particular, were their expectations with regard to the Soviet Union?

A Stable World Order

Dr Kissinger's appointment as secretary of state, confirmed by Congress in September 1973, was accompanied by a wave of publicity unprecedented in recent American history. Never before on similar occasions had there been such interest, so much comment, and it was probably also the first time that the future secretary of state had attracted several biographers even before he took up office. Dr Kissinger had, of course, played an important part for several years previously in the conduct of U.S. foreign policy; his name stood for secret missions, dramatic announcements, important new ventures. He was a friend of the media and a welcome guest at Washington parties. In the eyes of many observers his initiatives were the one redeeming feature of an otherwise disastrous administration. But the appointment provoked not only sympathetic editorials; there was a great deal of hostile comment as well. Some of it reflected envy; there must have been hundreds of political scientists firmly convinced that they would have been able to do as good, if not a better job than Henry.

There were attacks from left, right and centre. A writer in *Nation* was struck by the resemblance between Kissinger and Joachim von Ribbentrop, the Nazi foreign minister. Drawing a parallel between Nixon and Hitler there was the 'circumstance that they disdained to use the traditional channels of diplomacy to achieve their international successes, preferring instead the widely publicized services of colourful individuals, understood to be their personal agents.' A *National Review* commentator in an article headed 'A Foreign Policy without a Country' characterized Kissinger as an unassimilated outsider – 'a European by heritage and cultural choice, a cosmopolitan by circumstance, an American by deliberate (and hazardous) calculation'.* Mr W. Shannon of the *New York Times* referred to Kissinger as 'Nixon's congenial colleague and moral peer', whereas Anthony Lewis thought him little better than a trickster and con man. Whether Dr Kissinger was served any better by his friends is a moot point. In his book *Retreat of American Power*, Mr Henry Brandon tells us that 'Kissinger fell passionately in love with nineteenth-century nationalism,' while in the restrained prose of Mr Victor Zorza in the *Washington Post* Dr Kissinger 'is now working with his usual skill on a series of foreign policy initiatives as breathtaking and as interlaced as his earlier schemes'. Mr James Reston, re-reading Kissinger's Harvard thesis written almost a quarter of a century ago, quoted him: 'Life is Suffering, Birth involves Death, Transitoriness is the fate of Existence.' Profound observations, but of limited relevance to SALT II, let alone to the question of the recognition of Outer Mongolia and other such issues brought up by the Senate Foreign Affairs Committee in its hearings on Dr Kissinger.

The charges most frequently levelled at him were of being an 'intellectual elitist' and of practising 'deception'. As Senator Abourezk of South Dakota, who opposed the nomination, remarked, 'What has been wrong with our foreign policy since 1945 is that it has been conducted in secret by a few people.' In some ways Senator Abourezk's criticism did not go far enough, for had the situation been any different prior to 1945? Charles Beard apparently wrote all those books in vain about Roosevelt's perfidious foreign policy. Had the conduct of foreign policy not always and everywhere involved a measure of secrecy and deception? Perhaps the world would be a better place if foreign policy were abolished altogether.

* It continued 'When Kissinger ... opened his heart to the bitchy Italian journalist Oriana Fallaci and likened himself to a solitary cowboy hero ('Americans admire that enormously'), he revealed the derivative nature of his national identity in almost pathetic fashion. He cuts a dashing figure in chic drawing-rooms; ordinary Americans would never mistake him for John Wayne.'

More moderate critics stressed the need for a more open, non-partisan, middle-ground policy acceptable to the mass of the American people; a policy that would have the support not only of the president but also of Senator Fulbright and his friends, of 'globalists' and 'neo-isolationists', of those favouring an adequate defence programme, and the others demanding drastic cuts in military spending. Fully aware that a greater measure of public support was needed, Dr Kissinger countered by stressing the need for a new consensus ('which can give a new impetus and a new excitement to our foreign policy for the next decade or two'). Brave words these, but he must have known that the search for a consensus would be an uphill struggle. Outside the foreign affairs establishment and a small circle of experts, interest in world politics is strictly limited in America. Compared with Europe or Japan, the average American newspaper devotes very little space to foreign affairs; it is no secret that most senators and congressmen speak with infinitely more authority on domestic affairs than on foreign affairs. No remedy has been found to the problem of the narrow sphere of influence ('iron law of oligarchy') in foreign affairs. 'No foreign policy – no matter how ingenious – has any chance of success,' says Dr Kissinger, 'if it is born in the minds of a few and carried in the hearts of none.' Foreign policy, alas, is not usually carried in the hearts of men except in extreme cases, when they face a clear and present danger. Dr Kissinger would endeavour to gain wider support for his policy in Congress and among the media. It would still be an 'élitist foreign policy', but there might be fewer complaints.

One of the side effects of Dr Kissinger's rise to eminence was a sudden revival of interest in Castlereagh and Metternich, triggered off by his book *A World Restored*. Political commentators not previously known for their expertise in the intricacies of early nineteenth-century European diplomacy have been eagerly leafing through the pages of this book, expecting to find some useful leads – if not the master key – to Kissinger's grand design for the 1970s. Nowadays, no article seems complete without a quotation or two about the Metternichian system or Bismarck's *Realpolitik*. The purpose of these exercises is not readily obvious unless of course, one happens to believe in the universal applicability of certain 'lessons of history', the philosophers' stone of historians. The study of diplomacy does not necessarily produce great statesmen. Kissinger's great advantage over many of his colleagues was that he always saw his main concern in the real world rather than in theoretical abstractions, and, of course, his ability to express himself in clear language. Beyond this, the study of his intellectual development as revealed in his early writings was of limited relevance to the understanding of his more recent activities.

In the world of politics, as he saw it, one should be guided by a realistic approach rather than by ideological preconceptions, and certainly not by excessive expectations. Early on he accepted the fact that the number of options in any given situation was limited. Throughout the 'fifties and 'sixties he maintained a consistent and, on the whole, sensible criticism of the conduct of American foreign policy: not that it was basically wrong, but that it was insufficiently subtle and lacked initiative and an overall concept. Sometimes he was clearly wrong; for example, in his assumption that the West had missed a unique opportunity to negotiate with the Russians in the late 'forties, his excessive admiration for De Gaulle and his doctrine of limited nuclear war. About the Soviet Union and its willingness to work for a stable world order he had few illusions. When Harold Macmillan, then British Prime Minister, talked about the 'thrill of hope and expectation round the world' aroused by the Geneva meetings between the leaders of West and East, he called it a fatuous statement typical of the philosophy of personal diplomacy. He thought (rightly) that the 1960 summit meeting would not have accomplished much even if the U2 incident had never occurred. Twelve years later he was to express himself in similarly eulogistic terms about the 'revolutionary change' and the 'dramatic transformation' that had taken place in the world situation. The erstwhile sceptic now talked about historical missions and the beginning of a new era; he developed theories of how to establish common interests with the Soviet Union through a strategy of linkages creating a momentum of achievement. Such declarations were in obvious contrast to his previous thoughts on the subject, even discounting the exaggerations inherent in American political language. What were the changes in the world situation that had taken place to inspire such confidence?

Until July 1971 the full extent of Dr Kissinger's role in the conduct of U.S. foreign policy was not yet widely known. It was only when his meeting with Chou En-lai was first announced, and particularly after his visits to Moscow and his negotiations with the Vietcong, that the limelight was focused on him. He was subsequently acclaimed as the architect of détente who had put an end to the war in Vietnam, had negotiated SALT I, liquidated the remnants of the cold war, and laid the foundations for a new and constructive relationship with the U.S.S.R. and China. There was some criticism – Japan had been neglected and Europe not consulted – but on the whole there was much admiration for the vision, the persistence, the diplomatic skill and ingenuity which had been invested in what was widely acclaimed as a historic turn in world politics – not just a temporary improvement in the international climate such as had been witnessed many times since 1945.

There have been second thoughts on the extent and the significance of Dr Kissinger's achievements, and, *a fortiori*, on his prospects in the years to come. It was Bismarck who said in his old age that the true measure of the stature of a statesman was to ask whether a certain event would not have taken place but for his initiative. Seen in this light, Bismarck's achievement (the unification of Germany) was less of a surprise than Cavour's and Garibaldi's, for Bismarck had the Prussian Army behind him, whereas the Italians had no similar instrument of power. But for Lenin the Russian Revolution of 1917 would not have taken place; but for Weizmann there would have been no Balfour Declaration. It seems fairly certain that American involvement in Vietnam would have come to an end in any case – the pressures to end the war in Vietnam had become overwhelming by 1968. Unless American policy-makers were to be totally insensitive, the situation between the U.S.S.R. and China after the invasion of Czechoslovakia was such that both sides were looking for closer relations with Washington; a rapprochement with each was therefore predictable. It was Dr Kissinger's good fortune that he became the president's adviser at the very time when America, despite its Vietnam misfortunes, had acquired greater freedom of manoeuvre than at any time since the end of the Second World War.

Of all Dr Kissinger's achievements, his part in the negotiations to end the war in Vietnam must be rated highest, even conceding that the whole operation was no more than a rearguard action, and that in historical perspective it may appear devoid of significance to the fate of South-East Asia. The facts surrounding the negotiations in Paris are known only in part: given the violent domestic opposition to the war, it is difficult to imagine what more could have been achieved than a breathing spell of at best a few years for the South Vietnamese to enable them to stand on their own feet and to defend themselves – or to be overrun by the North. Again, the Sino-Soviet conflict helped in the last phase of the war, but Kissinger could have easily made a worse settlement.

No one would claim so much for SALT I, welcomed by Dr Kissinger at the time as an agreement 'without precedent in all relevant modern history'. This appraisal will no longer be shared by many people, and it is perhaps more than just coincidence that most of those who negotiated SALT I moved on, or were moved, to other assignments. It was argued at the time that the SALT I agreements ended the arms race; Soviet superiority with regard to missiles, throw weight and megatonage did not matter, since America had what the strategists called 'assured destruction'. But U.S. strategic forces had been at a stable level since 1968, whereas Russia had increased its armament at a very energetic rate which continues to this day. It is by no means certain that they could have built more I.C.B.M.s and submarine launchers than specified in SALT even if they had tried. True, numbers do not greatly matter so long as Soviet missiles are not very accurate, but with rapid technological improvement – and the application of M.I.R.V. (Multiple Independent Re-entry Vehicle) which erases the American advantage in warheads – the Soviet Union is moving from parity to potential superiority, while staying within the letter and spirit of the SALT agreement. Summarizing the SALT talks, John Newhouse wrote in his *Cold Dawn* that what had been achieved was neither reassuring nor disappointing but inconclusive, simply a modest interim agreement. He saw as most useful the fact that the two sides had engaged in a frank, open, non-polemical dialogue on the weapons most vital to their security. But even this judgment may be unduly optimistic, for while frank and open dialogues are always useful, what matters in the last resort is, of course, the outcome. In this case the bargain could not be regarded as successful from the point of view of either America or world peace, and might even be an obstacle to any further significant progress towards arms control. The Soviet strategists clearly did not share the American ideas about parity and assured destruction; if they did, they would hardly have engaged in a costly build-up of their strategic forces. Numbers do matter – politically and psychologically. Dr Kissinger has argued that if U.S. negotiators had insisted on equality, on including offensive as well as defensive weapons, anti-ballistic missiles (A.B.M.), agreement would certainly not have been achieved in 1971. But would this have been such a great loss, given the dubious character of the treaty? It is equally likely that if the Soviet leaders had been told unequivocally that America was firmly though regretfully resolved to match any Soviet strategic build-up, a more effective and wide-ranging agreement would have been reached two or three years later. All that can be said in defence of S A L T I is that the Soviet negotiators realized that the Americans had stopped building strategic weapons, that there was strong domestic resistance to matching the Soviet defence effort, and that the Nixon administration was under growing political pressure to reach an arms agreement on offensive weaponry; there was no inducement for the Russians to make greater concessions. The Soviet negotiators, in other words, were operating from a position of strength, whereas Dr Kissinger was batting, to use the English phrase, on a sticky wicket. These are mitigating circumstances; they do not make S A L T I a success.

S A L T I was the cornerstone of the co-existence declaration of May 1972 and the accord on avoiding atomic war signed in June 1973. The declarations published on these occasions stated that both sides proceeded from the common belief that in the nuclear age there was no alternative but to conduct their mutual relations on the basis of peaceful co-existence; that they wished to base their relationship on the principles of sovereignty, equality, non-interference in internal affairs and mutual advantage, and that they would always exercise restraint in their mutual relations. This was, of course, very good news, and if the agreements had stopped there, their impact would have been considerable. Unfortunately, it was deemed necessary to depreciate the value of the agreement by the inclusion of a great deal of ritual humbug ('Both sides will strive to strengthen the effectiveness of the U.N. on the basis of strict observance of the U.N. charter'), and promises which everyone knew were not meant seriously and would not be kept ('The two sides reaffirm their intention to deepen cultural ties with one another and to encourage fuller familiarization with each other's cultural values').

In the last resort, of course, it was not the wording but the spirit of the agreement which mattered, the relationship established between Nixon and Kissinger on the one hand and Brezhnev and his colleagues on the other. Nixon and Kissinger detected in Brezhnev a willingness to co-operate in establishing a structure of peace, an international system in which the participants would 'operate with a consciousness of stability and permanence'. As Mr Brezhnev told a group of American businessmen during his visit to Washington in June 1973: 'We have certainly been prisoners of those old tendencies, those old trends, and to this day we have not been able fully to break those fetters.' As Nixon and Kissinger saw it, Brezhnev and most, if not all, Soviet leaders wanted to enter history as the men who liquidated the cold war, normalized relations with the United States, and moved towards close and mutually advantageous co-operation in many fields. Mr Brezhnev's admission that both sides might have been 'prisoners of old tendencies' certainly contradicted the official Soviet version of the cold war. The cold war as defined by the *Soviet Diplomatic Dictionary* is 'the policy of the United States and their allies in the imperialist military blocs towards the Soviet Union and other Socialist States after the Second World War'.

About the price of détente and the durability of the 'significant landmarks' in the relations between the two countries few people worried in the first flush of rejoicing. Even the grain deal was held up at first as an example of mutually advantageous relations;* doubts about this and other deals began to creep in only later. In the general mood of goodwill it seemed tactless to ask to what extent

---

* 'The sales of grain to the Soviet Union have had, of course, beneficial effects on our balance of payments and have reduced the expense to the American taxpayer of storing surplus agricultural products.' (*United States Foreign Policy 1972. A report of the Secretary of State*, p. 314.

American and Soviet concepts of détente coincided, whether for the Soviet leaders, as for the Americans, détente was a concept making for 'generations of peace', stabilizing not just the arms race but the international order in general. Not to seek 'unilateral advantages at the expense of the other' as stated in the 'Basic Principles' of May 1972, was an admirable sentiment, but what did it mean in practice? Nixon and Kissinger probably had few illusions on this score. The ideological differences would, of course, persist and so would the ultimate aims of the other side. No one could reasonably expect the Soviet leaders to give up their basic beliefs overnight. But was there not at least a good chance that détente would develop a momentum of its own, that the development of common interests would eventually diminish the intensity and rigidity of Soviet doctrine? Was it not likely, in other words, that if the present situation lasted long enough, the Soviet Union, too, would become a status quo power – if it had not done so already?

It is not clear whether Nixon and Kissinger underrated the domestic consequences of their own declarations, the mood they were bound to engender in America. In a closed society such as Russia, the repercussions of détente could be easily controlled; if the mass media were instructed to tone down their attacks on American imperialism, the danger of ideological contamination by Western ideas was negligible; there was no reason to assume that the directors of Soviet banks and industries would rush to Washington to get their share of the American market. There was no risk that Soviet senators would demand drastic reductions in the defence budget, the dissolution of the Warsaw Pact, the closing of certain radio stations and other such relics of the cold war. By contrast the American architects of détente faced a very real dilemma: their actions, and even more their rhetoric, provided grist to the mill of those who had maintained all along (and who now had greater justification) that the military confrontation was over and that there was a powerful convergence of vital Soviet and American national interests. The obvious conclusion was that the ruinously expensive military and political apparatus inherited from a bygone period could be safely dismantled. Such arguments, needless to say, were undermining the détente policy of the administration, which knew only too well that the road to peace was long and arduous and that unilateral disarmament – military, political and moral – would not bring the goal any nearer.

The U.S. rapprochement with the Soviet Union was greatly aided by the Sino-Soviet conflict, but at the same time it presented a major obstacle to an improvement in relations with China. For Mao, Chou and their comrades, America, in contrast to Russia, was no longer a serious military and political danger, and for this reason they regarded with considerable misgivings a U.S. agreement likely to strengthen the Soviet Union and give it greater political and military freedom of manoeuvre. This fact was, of course, no secret to Dr Kissinger: 'I have no particular reason to suppose that they [the Chinese leaders] will necessarily approve a bilateral agreement between the U.S. and the Soviet Union whatever its consequences,' he said at a press conference on June 22nd, 1973. As the Chinese leaders saw it, American willingness to prop up the national economy of their adversary and to assist, directly or indirectly, in strengthening its military potential was highly suspicious, and the American tendency to ascribe to the Russians a real change of heart disturbing, to say the least. They would have preferred a deterioration in U.S.-Soviet relations which would have given China a decade or two, if not more, of protection from pressure, and, possibly, attack. But how could they have prevented an American-Soviet rapprochement short of offering the U.S. a political and military alliance directed against Russia? This would have been the natural course of action in a world free of ideology and nuclear weapons. When faced with two adversaries locked in bitter struggle, one's natural ally is the weaker of the two; even minor gangsters know these facts of life, not only those familiar with the writings of Machiavelli. But an explicit and formal alliance with the main bastion of Western imperialism would have presented the greatest difficulties in view of China's ideological commitment. And it was not at all clear what help America could have expected from such an ally if the *casus foederis* should ever arise. These difficulties were compounded by a far from stable domestic situation in China and by debates on its foreign political orientation, the course and results of which are not so far fully known in the West. The case for extending economic assistance to China was at least as strong as the case for granting long-term credits to the

Soviet Union: Sino-American trade expanded from almost nothing to $600 million in 1973.

Nixon's foreign policy was generally regarded as the most successful aspect of his presidency, and Kissinger's appointment as secretary of state and subsequent confirmation in September 1973 did not come as a great surprise to observers of the Washington scene. Shortly before, Kissinger had quoted Teddy Roosevelt in a speech ('Mighty things must be dared'), and when his nomination was made public he announced that he would try to 'solidify what had been started, to conclude the building of a structure that we can pass on to succeeding administrations'. But the number of rabbits on the international scene being limited, it was reasonable to assume that the days of pulling them out of hats were over and that the three years to come would be something of an anti-climax. The developments that had been taking place in world affairs – though dramatic in character – were bound to disappoint hopes for 'revolutionary change'; there is a world of difference between a normalization of relations and a structure of peace.

The issues facing Dr Kissinger were unglamorous, and partly – specifically, U.S. relations with Europe and the situation in the Middle East – also insoluble; the issues in the field of international trade were more manageable in the long run, but this is not the arena in which clear victories are won and great reputations made. The basic problem was still Europe's inability to make progress towards political and military co-operation. A strong and united Europe could collaborate with America as an equal, or alternatively follow a third-force, Gaullist policy. A disunited, impotent Europe could do neither and there was unfortunately reason to believe that no amount of persuasion would induce the Europeans in the foreseeable future to speak with one voice, let alone to act with one political will. The last annual report of the American State Department announced that in 1973 'we will be initiating new negotiations and developing new relationships which could determine the political-economic structure of the world for the remainder of this century'. This was followed on April 23rd by Kissinger's famous 'Year of Europe' speech, in which he called for a new approach to Atlantic problems, stressing that the political, military and economic issues in Atlantic relations were linked by reality, 'not by our choice, not for the tactical purpose of trading one off against the other'. The U.S., in other words, was not looking for unilateral concessions in trade and the reform of the world monetary system, but it expected the European members of N A T O both to accept a greater share in the defence of the Continent and to pay more for the maintenance of American troops in Europe to help reduce the permanent deficit in the U.S. balance of payments.

European reactions to the New Atlantic Charter were not even lukewarm. The grievances were many and by no means unjustified. America had virtually stopped consulting its European allies even on such a vital issue as M.B.F.R. (Mutual Balance Force Reductions); as Kissinger said in his speech there was the feeling that super-power diplomacy might necessitate the sacrifice of the interests of traditional allies. Nixon's proposed Trade Reform Act, it was feared, would enable the president to extract concessions from Europe by raising or lowering import barriers. It would be tedious and unprofitable to survey the whole list of European suspicions and American complaints, for even if some of them were removed in the coming talks, there would still be no Europe other than a loose customs union, able at best to produce a joint document evading specific commitments and merely expressing pious wishes. In the circumstances, given domestic pressures for the withdrawal of U.S. troops from Europe, Dr Kissinger in all likelihood will have to make concessions to the Russians despite the promises not to disengage from solemn commitments to allies and not to withdraw from Europe unilaterally. The only question is how many troops will be withdrawn, and when; how far the weakening of the American position in Europe will go. In all probability the drift will be slow and the consequences will not be readily apparent for several years.

The task ahead as far as Europe was concerned was not 'to match and dwarf the great accomplishments of the past decades', as the 'Year of Europe' speech proclaimed. It was far more modest: namely, to shore up provisionally the dilapidated Atlantic Alliance and to pray that Western Europe, disunited as it was, would somehow muddle through. Dr Kissinger had to fight a war on two fronts: against European inertia and against indifference and lack of support for the Atlantic Alliance at home. After a visit to London and Paris Senator Mansfield wrote in the summer of 1973 that it might be too late to salvage much more than a N A T O in mothballs and that the U.S. could ill afford to be deflected from the course of détente by the anxieties of the West Europeans. Such views found a great deal of support in Congress and they weakened the position of the secretary of state in his negotiations with Europe.

Second Thoughts on Détente

By autumn 1973 second thoughts were voiced in America about the benefits that had accrued so far, and that were likely to accrue to America in future. Searching questions about the price of détente were asked with regard to the treatment of political and intellectual dissent in the Soviet Union. Most Western students of Soviet affairs considered these questions and complaints a little naive, but among the public at large there had been a genuine belief that détente meant liberalization on the Soviet home front and the realization that this would not happen caused great disappointment. Dr Kissinger had little use for the moralists: 'We don't disagree about the human problem,' he said in the Senate hearings, 'but we have to ask ourselves whether it should be the principal goal of American foreign policy to transform the domestic structure of societies with which we deal.' This argument was unassailable as far as it went; Chancellor Brandt had put it even more strongly, and American leaders emphasized even at the height of the cold war that they had no desire to interfere in the internal affairs of the Soviet Union. ('We do not propose to subvert the Soviet Union. We shall not attempt to undermine Soviet independence,' Dean Acheson said in a famous speech in April 1950, defining his concept of containment.) However sad the fate of Soviet dissenters, however reprehensible the policy of internal repression, such considerations could not affect the overriding exigencies of peaceful co-existence. Even if Soviet repression were far harsher, even if there were not the slightest chance that the Soviet regime would ever mellow, the efforts to remove the danger of nuclear war would have to be pursued with undiminished vigour.

But this was merely stating the obvious and it left basic questions unanswered. For the détente policy, including the agreements scheduled to reduce and ultimately to remove the danger of nuclear war, had to be based to a large extent on trust. How could such trust be established in dealings with an isolated autocracy where there was no public opinion, no checks and balances, no right of free expression? This was not an abstract issue but involved very real practical problems; it was relatively easy to reach agreement in SALT I about the number of I.C.B.M.s, for the number of holes can be fairly reliably verified. But SALT I was only a prelude, and to make substantial progress there would have to be agreement on issues such as the limitation of M.I.R.V. and a ban on anti-submarine warfare (A.S.W.) which were the main de-stabilizing factors in the arms race. There were, however, no known means to verify whether such agreements concerning M.I.R.V. and A.S.W., if reached, were adhered to; the Soviet Union was unalterably opposed to on-the-spot inspection and the U.S. would have to take its assurances on trust. To provide another example: the Soviet Union proposed at one stage that all five nuclear powers should agree to cut their defence budgets by 10 per cent – an admirable suggestion if there ever was one. There is no secret about the American defence budget; it is specified each year in great detail down to the last dollar in dozens of volumes open to public inspection. But no one in the West, and only a handful of people in the Soviet Union, know the real size of the Soviet defence budget – whether it is 6 per cent of the G.N.P. or 16 per cent, leaving aside such technical questions as the purchasing power of a 'defence rouble' and a 'defence dollar', which are quite different. If, in other words, agreement were reached tomorrow to slash defence spending by 10 per cent, any attempt to cheat by the Americans could be easily detected, whereas the Soviet Union could easily increase its budget by 10 per cent or more instead of reducing it, and no one would be any the wiser.*

To give yet another illustration: it was difficult to envisage large-scale expansion of trade with the Soviet Union except on the basis

* It has been claimed that Western Intelligence, using the so called 'building block method', can make shrewd guesses concerning Soviet defence and space efforts. But this method can at best quantify in physical terms things visible and observable; it cannot say anything of relevance about the qualitative aspects such as research and development which, according to authoritative experts, account for one-fourth to one-third of the annual Soviet defence product. (Herbert Block in *Soviet Economic Prospect for*

of trust, for most of this trade would have to be based on long-term credits. The past record of the Soviet Union as a debtor was exemplary, but the loans in these cases had been small and short term. In 1959, for instance, Soviet scheduled repayments on Western credits were a paltry $12 million. The loans being discussed in 1973 were of a very different magnitude altogether. Soviet external indebtedness that year amounted to some $8 billion, a quarter of its hard currency sales, and it was estimated (by Michael Kaser) that this would rise to $31 billion in 1980. By that time, the Soviet Union will have to allocate half of its foreign exchange earnings to repaying its debts. Mr Brezhnev may still be in power then; rumours – which may be quite unfounded – say that he explained détente to fellow communist leaders as a temporary phase in Soviet foreign policy which would result in an all-round strengthening of Soviet power, so that at some future date it would be in a position to put the squeeze on the West. Mr Brezhnev may be replaced by others who feel that not repaying debts to capitalists does not necessarily involve a breach of Marxist ethics.

These were some of the question marks facing the West in its relations with the Soviet Union and they all pointed to an apparently insoluble dilemma: that the West must not interfere in Soviet domestic affairs, but that any separation between Soviet foreign and domestic policies was virtually impossible. This dilemma was not unknown to a long-time student of world affairs like Dr Kissinger. On more than one occasion he had written scathingly about Western diplomats who thought that all that was required was good faith and the willingness to come to an agreement when dealing with a power which does not accept the legitimacy of the existing international system but intends to replace it by a world order of its own. Nor had he shown much patience with those who explained Soviet policies by reference to their 'basic insecurity', and who put their hope in the progressive *embourgeoisement* of the Soviet Union which would make it easier to deal with. In a congressional briefing

the Seventies: a compendium of papers submitted to the Joint Economic Committee, Congress of the United States, 1973, p. 184) Thus, the 'building block method' may be of use in monitoring general trends in the Soviet defence effort, but it cannot provide the accuracy that would be needed to establish whether an arms control agreement is being adhered to.

after Nixon's return from the Moscow Summit in 1972 he declared that past experience had amply shown that 'much heralded changes in atmospherics, but not buttressed by concrete progress, will revert to previous patterns at the first subsequent clash of interests'. Signs of a reappraisal of the world situation on the part of Dr Kissinger could be found back in the late 'sixties when he wrote that 'the Soviet Union may not be willing indefinitely to use the Red Army primarily against allies as it has done three times in a decade and a half', and when he maintained that 'the Communist leaders *must* make sooner or later the choice whether to use détente as a device to lull the West or whether to move towards a resolution of the outstanding differences' (my italics).[1] This last statement bears re-reading for it contains at least three doubtful assumptions: that the Soviet Union was somehow bound to make a choice, that there was no third way between 'lulling' the West and the 'resolution of outstanding differences', and lastly the belief that the 'outstanding differences' could be resolved by agreement and were not, at least in part, inherent in the very character of two different political systems and their conflicting global interests.

One should perhaps not make too much of incautious formulations; what mattered in Dr Kissinger's eyes and what marked the essential difference between the international constellation in 1973 and on previous occasions were, above all, the advent of nuclear-strategic parity between the U.S. and the U.S.S.R., the Sino-Soviet conflict and the willingness of the Russian leaders, above all Mr Brezhnev, to engage in practical talks about the preservation of peace and mutually beneficial co-operation. Whatever the reasons which induced the Soviet leaders to decide on a new peace plan at their twenty-fourth Party Congress in March 1971, Kissinger knew as a student of history that no society is immune to the laws of change and that immobility, the lack of initiative, had been the main defect in American diplomacy in recent decades. What if the Soviet leaders regarded peaceful co-existence only as a tactical phase in their ultimate strategy of expanding their political power? Was it not possible that a lengthy period of peaceful co-existence and collaboration would trigger off irreversible internal changes in the Soviet system – not of course in a year or two, but in a perspective of several decades? Was it not true that the Soviet leadership had become largely bureaucratized, guided by *Realpolitik*, expediency and enlightened self-interest, and could not American leaders influence Soviet policy by strengthening the hands of the Soviet pragmatists against their doctrinaire rivals? Was not the age of super-powers drawing to an end, and with it the rigidity of military bipolarity which overshadowed more than two decades of post-war history; was not the emergence of a new 'pentagonal balance' making for new and dynamic relationships in a world in which power no longer translated automatically into influence, and in which smaller nations had an unprecedented scope for autonomous action? And even if it was only a manoeuvre, even if it did entail risks, was it not a worthwhile endeavour in view of the great stakes?

To analyse these arguments in detail is to write the post-war history of international relations with digressions into such topics as the balance of power and the changing character of international systems. Some of the arguments were at best only half valid: no 'pentagonal world system' is in sight; there is no symmetry – if America is retrenching, the other side is not; Finland has little scope for autonomous action – let alone Czechoslovakia. True, diplomacy should not be based on a pessimistic analysis but should act in accordance with the philosophy of the 'as if'. How could the overall objective be achieved, the creation of that climate of greater trust of which Brezhnev said that 'to live at peace, we must trust each other, and to trust each other, we must know each other better'. Leaving aside the question of whether greater familiarity necessarily results in greater trust, it seems clear that this required an opening up of Soviet society which could not be expected in the near future. However frequently businessmen, psychiatrists and oceanographers met, however friendly the atmosphere prevailing at their conferences, however cordial the toasts exchanged, the political impact was bound to be negligible: there could be no 'strategy of linkages' between a symposium on schizophrenia and M.B.F.R. The Soviet regime might become more liberal over several decades or perhaps even sooner, following some unforeseen developments, but the possibilities open to U.S. foreign policy to influence and accelerate this process were small. American pressure could achieve certain concessions with regard to the treatment of individual dissenters or the number of Jews permitted to leave the Soviet Union. But even if there had been no Sakharov, Solzhenitsyn or Jewish activists, the basic problem would still have been there. Western demands for greater human contacts, freedom of movement and ideas might be useful bargaining chips at conferences but there could be no illusions as to what could be achieved in this respect. There were limits beyond which the Soviet Union could not go for reasons of the basic structure of the regime. To make détente dependent on convergence, on basic changes such as the granting in the Soviet Union of elementary human rights as the West understands them, was asking for the impossible. In other words, it should have been clear that for years to come détente would have to be negotiated not on the basis of trust, but on the assumption that the political aims of the two sides were in some respects compatible and that in these fields it might be possible to co-operate.

One such field was the stabilization of strategic competition. The radical acceleration of S A L T had been suggested to reduce not only the overall number of weapons but to bring qualitative developments under control as well. About the desirability of this objective there could be no two views, but how to achieve it? For there was a possibility that in 1977, when the current S A L T agreement would end – or in the early 'eighties – a situation would arise in which American I.C.B.M.s would be vulnerable, whereas the Soviet I.C.B.M.s would not. The Soviet Union would then be able to argue that parity with the U.S. was no longer sufficient since it also faced another potential enemy on its eastern border. Soviet negotiators would be able to refer to those American commentators who have argued for a long time that the pursuit of strategic superiority is illusory and offers no real advantage. If so, a little asymmetry could not be regarded as an obstacle on the road to a more comprehensive arms agreement. Unfortunately, in the real world, in contrast to the games in which symmetrical country 'A' is poised against 'B', and in which strategic nuclear power is indeed ineffectual, military power is by no means outmoded. There still is that great arc of insecurity reaching from Scandinavia through the Middle East to Manchuria in which nations great and small are exposed to the intrusive political influence which Russian military power generates, a world in which economic power counts for little and in which the weak must conciliate the strong.

Such a scenario may be unduly pessimistic; for all one knows there may still be nuclear parity five and ten years hence. The Soviet leaders can perhaps be persuaded that a strategic equilibrium should be accepted indefinitely, preferably on a lower level of military preparedness than at present, an aim which S A L T I failed to achieve. But in that case conventional military forces would regain much of their importance and in this respect Dr Kissinger's position was weak, for his view that the number of American troops abroad should not be cut except by mutual agreement was no longer shared by a great and growing number of senators and congressmen. The Russians could wait; they were not subject to similar internal pressures. There was always the chance that America would finally lose patience with Europe and that there would at long last take place the 'agonizing reappraisal' in U.S. foreign policy mentioned by Dulles exactly twenty years ago; this was, of course, much more likely to occur during détente than at the height of the cold war.

Dr Kissinger, and to an even greater degree other U.S. spokesmen, attached considerable political significance to the expansion of commercial relations with the U.S.S.R. A recent Congressional study had listed three main benefits that would accrue to the United States:

1. Soviet reliance on the U.S. as a source of supply and expertise. Soviet dependence on U.S. agricultural products and advanced technology, for example, is a potential source of U.S. political leverage.

2. Encouragement to the Soviet Union to re-order its priorities between military and civilian programmes. Expanded commercial relations may serve to reinforce the arms control and other agreements between the two countries.

3. Encouragement of domestic change in the Soviet Union. The presence of many American citizens in the Soviet Union with some decision-making power and a wider exchange of ideas may in the long run help to moderate the Soviet political control system and command economy.[2]

Only six months later it emerged that most of those assumptions had been false, partly because of developments which were not foreseen at the time (for instance, that there would no longer be abundant agricultural surpluses). The optimism of 1972 was based on the belief, as expressed by Kissinger after the first summit, that the Soviet leaders regarded new strategic systems as both very costly and of modest benefit, and that therefore a re-ordering of priorities would take place in favour of civilian spending. But such a re-ordering has not occurred yet. Nor was it clear how the presence of American engineers in Russia would somehow 'moderate the Soviet political control system'.

Individual firms – from Mr Hammer's Occidental Oil to I.T.T. and I.B.M. – could of course substantially benefit from trading with the Soviet Union. It was less certain that what was good for Mr Hammer was also good for the nation. The study just quoted reached the conclusion that the volume of Soviet trade with the U.S. was not likely to represent a large share of U.S. foreign trade even in optimum conditions, and that the American balance of payments deficit might receive benefits which were 'at best, only marginal'. Which brings one back to the political considerations involved in the expansion of trade.

The M.F.N. (Most Favoured Nations) clause, while psychologically important, was not really decisive, because Soviet exports consist mainly of raw materials and primary products, which are largely unaffected by M.F.N. treatment. (The rates of duty in the U.S. tariff schedules rise in accordance with the degree of processing.) The real issue concerned long-term credits and major joint ventures in energy and raw material extraction. These programmes would require multi-billion dollar investment in exchange for energy supplies to be made some time in the 'eighties. This was more than swapping Pepsi Cola for vodka, it signified more than propping up the civilian sector of the economy of a country which was, after all, not yet an ally. It meant giving indirect help to the military sector both by the transfer of technology and by making it possible to release for military programmes resources which would otherwise be needed in the civilian sector. These fears were perhaps exaggerated. But once multi-billion dollar investments were made and Soviet control over U.S. investments had been established, American political leverage would certainly be very limited indeed.

Gradually it was understood that the removal of barriers to U.S.-

Soviet trade would not by itself bring about any radical change in the volume of trade. Expansion could take place either as a result of a re-orientation in Soviet priorities so that its exports conformed to the needs of the American market, or on the basis of massive long-term loans from America. As far as the Soviet Union was concerned, there was no other country that could replace the U.S. as a source of credit; fears frequently voiced in the U.S., that Japan or Western Europe would monopolize the Soviet market by default if the U.S. failed to seize the opportunities offered, were groundless. The kind of money needed by the Soviet Union was simply not available in Japan and Western Europe and, even if it were, European and Japanese businessmen would still be averse to taking risks beyond a certain modest level. During 1973 the Soviet Union had unsuccessfully tried to get $300 million in credits from Western Europe and Japan.

There was no doubt that such an infusion of capital and technology would greatly reinforce the development of the Soviet economy, speed up its modernization, and on occasion bring relief in critical situations. But it was clearly wrong to talk about 'desperate urgency' for the U.S.S.R. to co-operate with the U.S.; the Soviet Union had managed after all to survive in worse circumstances. True, massive American credits and the large-scale transfer of modern technology could conceivably buy years of détente. And this is apparently what President Nixon and Dr Kissinger meant when they spoke about 'mutually advantageous commercial deals'.

These then, very briefly, were the prospects facing Kissinger when he became secretary of state, a few weeks before the outbreak of war in the Middle East. He had three years ahead of him, a short time to achieve 'mighty things', long enough to burn his fingers. The last few years had been calm on the whole, but there were still plenty of latent danger zones: South-East Asia and the Persian Gulf, the Mediterranean and Latin America.

It seemed likely that the disastrous events (e.g. Watergate) on the domestic scene would act as a spur to the administration in its search for results in foreign policy. There was nothing wrong with this endeavour, except of course if it resulted in disadvantageous agreements or meaningless treaties. It appeared that the weakness of the administration, its greater dependence on a distrustful Congress, would make it impossible for Dr Kissinger to take great risks and thus prevent him from making mistakes. But it also narrowly circumscribed his freedom of action and precluded any major initiatives. His steps would be closely watched by Congress and by a public pressing for incompatible objectives: to negotiate neither from a position of strength – since the cold war and the political confrontation with the Russians were over and done with – nor from a position of weakness. To spend as little as possible on defence and on foreign aid, but also not to give up anything and to maintain American influence abroad. To be nice to the Russians and at the same time to induce them to make substantial concessions on issues on which they were particularly touchy. To withdraw American troops from various parts of the globe and to persuade America's allies that the U.S. was as strong as before and that it would stand by its commitments. To persuade (or press) Japan and Western Europe to help America to reduce its balance of payments deficit without necessarily reciprocating in kind.

The secretary of state could not hope to accommodate his critics even to a limited extent. All he could do was to display a great deal of activity and a new style in diplomacy, exude confidence, reassure and placate. With a little luck he could hope to prevent major disasters during the next three years, to continue the dialogue with friend and foe alike. But if circumstances were adverse and basic interests conflicting, no amount of travelling and discussing would bring about a basic reversal. He was to preside over America's de-commitment, to take care that the process was carried out as smoothly and as painlessly as possible. This could be described as a long overdue withdrawal from an exposed position, a realistic adjustment to a new world situation; it would be interpreted by Russians and Europeans, by Chinese and Japanese, as a retreat from power which made it imperative for them to re-consider their own positions. Dr Kissinger assured them that American policy aimed at a more stable world order, at greater security for all, at a world community based on shared aspirations. They said 'Amen', and began to adjust themselves to the fact that the old global game continued, but that the rules had changed – and not in America's favour.

With all that it seemed likely that détente would survive, even though in a lower key. It was in America's interests, because the Russians could cause a great deal of trouble if they decided to revert to cold war tactics. It was in the interests of the Soviet Union; even if Mr Brezhnev and his colleagues realized that they were likely to get fewer concessions from America than they might have thought at one stage, the fringe benefits, the negative achievements of détente, were considerable. It hastened the erosion of NATO, it prevented the emergence of another power bloc in Western Europe. It would have been foolish from Moscow's point of view to jeopardize these gains by reverting to cold war language and tactics, to threats and bullying. There was likely to be a little less warmth and crises were bound to occur. Brezhnev and his colleagues would find it easier to adjust themselves to these ups and downs, for the Russians had argued all along that the ideological-political struggle was bound to go on. On the other hand, Nixon's and Kissinger's rhetoric (whatever their private doubts) had helped to raise expectations among the American public about the extent and the prospects of détente which would have to be modified in future, something that would not be easy to accomplish.

Surveying the international scene at the beginning of October 1973, Dr Kissinger may well have thought back with some nostalgia to the happier days of 1971-2 when it was a blessing to be alive, when he was so often the carrier of good tidings, when so many new options seemed to open, when one could look ahead with optimism and confidence. On the other hand there was no reason to be unduly pessimistic. Détente was still fragile but the political barometer indicated no storm warning. Everything seemed to point to further normalization in West-East relations when Dr Kissinger suddenly found himself facing a major crisis threatening all his achievements in recent years.

America Surprised

When the Arabs attacked, Dr Kissinger was in his New York hotel, President Nixon at Cap Biscayne, Chancellor Brandt was visiting Prime Minister Heath at Chequers and the Soviet leaders were presumably in Moscow. At once there was a flurry of activity: after the meeting at Chequers a joint Anglo-German initiative at the United Nations was announced by British official spokesmen which was flatly denied by Chancellor Brandt after his return to Bonn: the Middle-Eastern situation had been discussed but there was no common initiative. Bonn announced its deep concern about the fact that the military conflict in the Middle East had assumed such proportions.[3] Unofficially it was said that Bonn's policy would be even-handed, strictly neutral. President Pompidou's advisers said that he would wait and see; the only French comment at that stage was an aside by M. Pierre Messmer, minister of defence, who said in Sarrebourg that an attacking army always had some advantages in the beginning.[4] This innocuous remark was interpreted by some of his colleagues as an unwarranted pro-Israeli declaration. Shortly after the outbreak of war a letter was received in Paris from Colonel Qadafi who complained about France's 'reserved attitude' – an unfair statement in view of France's pro-Arab policy since 1967 and the massive arms deliveries to countries such as Libya. In all East European capitals (except Bucharest) as well as in most Asian and African capitals Israel was sharply condemned for having launched a surprise attack against Egypt and Syria; the Egyptian foreign minister had meanwhile said on American T.V. that his country had struck first, but this admission was dismissed as irrelevant. In Western Europe there was a great deal of moaning and hand-wringing but little else. The Danish foreign minister, temporarily chairman of the committee of the Nine, announced that a meeting of the West European foreign ministers was not envisaged. There was nothing Europe could or wanted to do. There was no Europe.

What action there was took place in New York and Washington. Joseph Sisco, assistant secretary of state for Near-Eastern affairs, called Kissinger at 6 a.m. E.S.T. on October 6th at his New York hotel with the disturbing news that there were clear indications of military action on Israel's border. Half an hour later Kissinger spoke with President Nixon and was told to 'make a major diplomatic effort' to prevent fighting from breaking out. U.N. Secretary General Waldheim was informed, as was the Soviet ambassador in Washington. Cables were sent to King Faisal of Saudi Arabia and Husain of Jordan to use their good offices to urge restraint – but they had little if any influence as far as the main combatants were concerned. Kissinger was greatly surprised by these sudden events; he had seen Zayat, the Egyptian foreign minister, only the day before and there had been no indication whatsoever that Egypt would go to war. On the contrary, just a week earlier the Egyptian Government had signed a contract worth hundreds of millions of dollars with an American financial group to construct a major oil pipeline in Egypt. Kissinger had met Abba Eban, the Israeli foreign minister two days before, and it had been agreed that there should be new talks about a peace settlement in November, after the Israeli elections. As McCloskey, the State Department spokesman, subsequently said, 'We never had any indication there was military action intended . . .'[5] Whatever Mr Zayat told Kissinger that Saturday morning, it could not have given him much comfort and Eban could merely reaffirm what went without saying, that Israel would defend itself against any attack. The Syrian foreign minister could not be found. After two hours the news reached Washington that the Arab attack had actually started and American policy from now on was to urge restraint and a return to the ceasefire lines as soon as possible. At Cap Biscayne White House aides said that Mr Nixon was 'very, very concerned' and in Washington a Special Action Group was convened. It consisted of Kissinger, William E. Simon, chairman of the president's Oil Policy Committee, Deputy Secretary of State Kenneth Rush, Joseph Sisco, Defence Secretary James R. Schlesinger, C.I.A. Director William E. Colby and the Chairman of the Joint Chief of Staff, Admiral Thomas H. Moorer.

Contact was established with the Kremlin but Mr Brezhnev was very sorry, the news had just reached him, he could not do anything. Of course there would have to be concerted American-Soviet action, but perhaps one should wait a little until the dust settled? One should consider one's course of action very carefully, and this could not be done in a hurry. He did not agree with President Nixon's suggestion that the Security Council should be convened, unless one knew what one wanted it to do.

Meanwhile the Egyptians announced that they would call for a special meeting of the U.N. General Assembly 'to make an informative statement'; the Arabs could count on an overwhelming majority in the General Assembly in which moreover there was no veto. Also it would take a fairly long time to convoke the General Assembly with its 135 members; in the meantime the Egyptian and Syrian forces would be able to consolidate their gains. Sir Laurence

McIntyre of Australia, president of the Security Council, intended to issue a personal appeal for a ceasefire, but he needed the agreement of the powers as to the contents of such an appeal and this he could not obtain.

Thus on Sunday afternoon, some twenty-four hours after the outbreak of fighting, there was no progress at all and President Nixon directed Dr Kissinger to call for a special meeting of the Security Council. To be on the safe side it was also decided to dispatch a carrier task force of the American sixth fleet to take up a 'holding position' half a day's sailing from the Suez Canal. The force was headed by the 60,000-ton aircraft carrier *Independent* with three supporting destroyers; they had been stationed in Athens and left for an area south-east of Crete, a few hundred miles from the Egyptian coast.[6]

The Security Council met briefly on Monday, October 8th, adjourned without taking any action and met again the following day for a most unproductive session. John Scali, the U.S. representative on the council, had not formulated a specific draft resolution but simply called for an immediate ceasefire, demanding a return to the lines before October 6th. The Egyptian foreign minister, who had the support of the Soviet and Chinese representatives as well as most other members of the council, declared that this was totally unacceptable. Just before the meeting started news about Israeli air raids on Damascus had reached New York. Jakov Malik, the Soviet representative, maintained that six, perhaps thirty, Soviet citizens had been killed in these bloody acts of Israeli aggression. (It was later announced that the report had been unfounded.) He called Mr Tekoah, the chief Israeli delegate, 'a representative of murderous gangsters', spoke about the filthy hands and the barbarism of the Israeli leaders and walked out of the meeting hall to the applause of delegates and spectators when Tekoah said that responsibility had to be put where it belonged – namely the Russians with their encouragement of fanatical barbarism and hatred of Israel. Without the Soviet Union the Middle East could now have been at peace, he said.[7] Israel was totally isolated; the Security Council wanted war, not peace; Israeli diplomats later said that they felt as if they were at a lynching party. On this constructive note the Security Council dispersed and the initiative passed back into the hands of the super-powers, or, to be precise, into the hands of Washington. The Soviet Union and the others believed that time was working for the Arabs, at least for the moment. During the next few days there were more speeches in the U.N. General Assembly including one by Abba Eban; various Arab and Israeli spokesmen gave press conferences and appeared on American television but all this had not the slightest impact on the course of events.

Washington's first reaction was one of extreme caution. In a speech on Monday evening Kissinger said that détente could not survive irresponsibility in any area, including the Middle East. President Nixon, in a meeting with Houphouet Boigny of the Ivory Coast, urged an end to the fighting which was going on at such terrible cost to both sides. There was no blame for Egypt and Syria for having launched the attack. On Tuesday when news reached Washington about a Soviet airlift of supplies into Egypt and Syria, American comment became a little more outspoken. The State Department spokesman said that if the airlift became 'massive' such an operation would tend to put a 'new face on the situation' and could imperil détente.[8] A Pentagon spokesman appearing on the same day had no doubt about the extent of the airlift: 'very big tonnages' of military material were involved. In a meeting with Congressional leaders on Wednesday President Nixon said that the U.S. sought to play a responsible role in a dangerous situation and to be 'very fair to both sides'. The Senate, upon the initiative of the leaders of both parties, had already adopted a resolution demanding the return of the Egyptian and Syrian forces to the old armistice lines. In the House of Representatives legislation had been introduced to step up shipment of war supplies to Israel in reply to the Soviet airlift.

Nevertheless, as the first week of fighting drew to its close it was still American policy to play down the extent of Soviet supplies to the Arabs and to criticize neither the Arabs nor the Soviet Union. Nor did America want to get involved in the war; open support of Israel would endanger American interests in Saudi Arabia and other parts of the Middle East. Any outspoken criticism of Soviet behaviour would jeopardize détente. The policy representing the majority view at the State Department, a minority faction in the

Pentagon and some legislators such as Fulbright and Mansfield, was that the U.S. should limit military aid to Israel in such a way as to promote a stand-off in Sinai. As a Pentagon official said, 'The Arabs have gotten some of their honour back, and we don't want the Israelis to take it away. It's time to settle.'[9] Egypt was the key to peace and should not be humiliated; these circles were much less worried about the possibility of an Israeli victory on the Golan Heights. As they saw it the military stand-off would be formally turned into a ceasefire *in situ*, and ultimately into the demilitarization of the Sinai Peninsula, including the complete withdrawal of both Egyptian and Israeli forces. This was, *grosso modo*, also Kissinger's line in a press conference on Friday, October 12th, which, as correspondents saw it, 'offered little comfort to Israel'.[10] There was no criticism of the Arab offensive. Kissinger did admit that the Soviet Union had not been 'entirely helpful' in urging other Arab states to support Egypt and Syria; while America had a traditional friendship with Israel, the Russians had a relationship with some Arab states. But he did not 'as yet consider that Soviet statements and actions threaten the stability of the détente'. As he saw it Soviet behaviour was less provocative, less incendiary and less geared to military threats than in the crisis of 1967. There were discussions with Israel but no final decision had been taken about a big American arms supply to Israel to replace its losses in aircraft and tanks. Nor did he insist any longer on the return by both sides to the old ceasefire lines. Hostilities should cease as quickly as possible in a manner which would promote a solution in the Middle East. True, there were some veiled warnings: a prolonged war was dangerous because there was a high possibility of great power involvement and this could affect the entire international atmosphere. And again: 'A war of this nature had a possibility of escalating.' But he also stressed that up to now the U.S. and the Soviet Union had attempted to behave within limits that would prevent a confrontation between them. The Soviet airlift was not helpful, but détente was not yet threatened: 'When this point is reached we will in this crisis, as we have in other crises, not hesitate to take a firm stand. We are still attempting to moderate the conflict. As of this moment we have to weigh against the actions which we disapprove, and quite strongly, the relative restraint that has been shown in public media in the Soviet Union and in the conduct of their representations in the Security Council.'[11]

Senator Mansfield, the Senate majority leader, who was in frequent contact with Kissinger throughout the crisis, told the Senate that Kissinger had made overtures to the Kremlin to find a diplomatic solution 'based on no arms shipments to either side'. We have it on the authority of Melvin Laird (special adviser to President Nixon) that Kissinger waited four days for signs that the Soviets were restraining re-supply before acting.[12]

Kissinger's policy was based on several assumptions. One was the alleged Soviet willingness to show restraint, and this despite the fact that when he gave his press conference on Friday, October 12th, 3,000 tons of Soviet war material had already been shipped to Syria and Egypt, not counting the convoy of Soviet transport ships. By Monday evening (October 15th) Cyprus Air Traffic Control reported Russian Antonov planes overflying at the rate of eighteen an hour. Western observers in Beirut said that they feared an escalation of the war because the Americans would now have no alternative but to restore the balance at least to some extent. If it had been thought at first in Washington that the Soviet Union would support only a limited Arab offensive, the strategic analysts had now to revise their estimates. The Soviet Mediterranean fleet had been strengthened; 10-15 additional ships had joined it and it now numbered 70 surface vessels, more than ever before.

There were other reasons for a gradual stiffening in the American position: at 7 a.m. on Saturday, October 13th, the Middle-Eastern battlefield was surveyed from a height of fifteen miles by American SR 71A planes, the successors of the U2. By late afternoon the films had been analysed and they showed that the Egyptians were about to pour many hundreds of tanks into what might be the decisive offensive. Western Europe refused to deliver supplies to Israel even though in some cases (for example Britain) there existed contractual obligations. (Having announced an embargo Britain continued to supply arms to Arab countries during the conflict but only on a small scale.) France continued to supply arms to Libya and Saudi Arabia; this war material would eventually end up in the hands of the Egyptians and the Syrians. The situation was critical and Congressional pressure on Kissinger, who had hitherto refused to supply Phantoms and tanks to Israel, was growing.

On Saturday morning, having given a breakfast for Senator Fulbright, Kissinger saw Eban and explained that he was not happy about recent Israeli declarations concerning 'devastating blows' which would be dealt to the Arabs; he was concerned about the Israeli drive towards Damascus because this was bound to make the Russians very angry indeed. Kissinger would have preferred a ceasefire *in situ* at this stage leaving the Egyptians in possession of both sides of the Suez Canal. According to Dobrynin the Soviet Union would agree to an armistice on these lines but it could do little (he claimed) because the Russians had no leverage in Cairo and Damascus. A return to the old ceasefire lines was opposed not only by the Soviets but also by Britain and France. Meanwhile on Saturday a personal message from Mrs Meir had been delivered to President Nixon; according to Israeli sources it was no more than a friendly message to the effect that a little more American help would be greatly appreciated. According to others it was considerably more urgent and pointed to certain acute Israeli shortages.[13] There was still no consensus in Washington as to how much help to give to Israel and how to treat the Russians. Melvin Laird did not share Kissinger's optimism and said that the Russians had behaved as if détente did not exist and that the U.S. was at present engaged in some kind of confrontation. A visitor to the State Department on the other hand felt himself 'on a different planet':[14] there was praise for President Sadat's moderation and a belief that the Russians were acting quite responsibly. Kissinger would have preferred at this stage to have given Israel enough war material – air-to-air missiles, some electronic equipment and ammunition on a small scale – to defend itself successfully against further Arab offensives. Meanwhile Jordan had entered the war and it was not clear to what extent this would expose the Israelis to fighting on a third front. On Saturday night the special task force met, discussed the level of fighting, Israeli losses and the scale of Soviet shipments. The next morning Kissinger reported to the President who had to take the final decision. He confirmed the recommendation to send F-4 (Phantom) fighter bombers to Israel at once and to start an air bridge matching, more or less, Soviet supplies.

Kissinger's main aim was to stabilize the military situation, his main fear a long war which was bound to have a detrimental effect on détente. According to some reports the delivery of American military supplies was made conditional on Israeli acceptance of the ceasefire *in situ* with the Egyptians firmly entrenched on the East Bank of the Suez Canal.[15]

Within a day or two 7-800 tons of war material were being shipped to Israel daily; cargo aircraft – mostly C-5 Galaxies, the biggest such planes in the world – were reported landing and refuelling at the U.S. base in the Azores.* Moreover, 20 Phantoms had been flown to Israel by October 17th, and 8 more were soon to be sent to replace the 25 believed to have been destroyed by Egyptian and Syrian air defences. Altogether the United States authorized shipments to Israel valued at $825 million, including transportation during this stage of the operations. Israel mainly owed its good fortune to the fact that while paying lip service to the cause of détente the Soviet leaders ignored American appeals for co-ordinated action until about the twelfth day of fighting. Only after they had realized that the Americans meant business, and that the Israelis after all were likely to win, did a sudden change take place in the Soviet attitude. It is difficult to establish which had the greater impact on this shift – the fact that the tide of the battle in the Middle East had turned in Israel's favour or the news received from Washington that détente was in serious danger. It cannot have escaped Dobrynin's attention that more than two-thirds of the members of the Senate signed a resolution to send Israel Phantom jets and all other equipment 'needed to repel the aggression'. A resolution of this kind was perhaps not unwelcome to Kissinger at this stage; it strengthened his hand in the talks with Dobrynin.[16] Dobrynin talked several times daily to Kissinger and he must have realized that Armand Hammer, Fulbright and Pepsi Cola alone would not be able to save détente

* Kissinger was opposed to the idea of using American aircraft and the Israelis were requested to hire transport planes and to take care of the shipment of war material. Only after this had proved to be impossible and following another message from Mrs Meir to President Nixon stressing the urgency of the Israeli requests the decision was taken to use American cargo aircraft and American bases. The first Galaxy arrived in Israel on October 14th.

if the war was permitted to drag on much longer.

Whatever the reason for the gradual Soviet change of mind, on October 18th Prime Minister Kosygin was in Cairo and after that date Soviet diplomacy slowly got into motion. The same day Kissinger declared that the crisis tested both diplomacy and the real meaning of détente. On the 19th President Nixon asked Congress for $2.2 billion in immediate military aid for Israel 'to maintain a balance of forces and thus achieve stability'. He expressed hope that there would be some progress soon towards ending the conflict, but said prudent planning was also required to prepare for a long struggle. The administration did not want to assure another spectacular Israeli victory, it aimed at a military stalemate which would lead to a diplomatic compromise. Washington, as James Reston put it, wanted to persuade Israel that even if it was winning the tank battle in Sinai the strategic problem had changed fundamentally. It was not just up against Cairo and Damascus but against Moscow and Washington: 'These big powers disagree about many things, but agree that Israel must pull back from Suez and begin negotiating and compromising and giving up much of the territory it captured in the 1967 war. Nixon and Kissinger don't say this publicly, but they are pressing privately, not for an Israeli victory, but for an Israeli compromise.'[17] This line of reasoning was not devoid of logic, but it was bound to encounter much opposition in Congress: why were the Russians to be rewarded for double-crossing their partner? Furthermore there was no certainty that the Russians would be able to induce the Arabs to accept a settlement on these lines, and even if they did, what guarantee was there that an Israeli withdrawal would bring about a more stable situation? What if after a few years Israel would again be attacked and American intervention would become necessary?

On October 17th, the foreign ministers of four Arab countries (Algeria, Morocco, Saudi Arabia and Kuwait) had two meetings with Kissinger and in between saw President Nixon for one hour. Their spokesman on this occasion was not Bontefliqa of Algeria, the best known of them (he had boycotted the Kissinger luncheon shortly before the outbreak of the war), but Saudi Foreign Minister Umar al Saqaf who said afterwards that they had been received well and had a fruitful talk. President Nixon concurred; it had been 'a very good talk', there were certain differences of opinion but a fair, just and peaceful solution seemed reachable.[18] Yet despite the good talk eleven Arab oil-producing countries decided the very same day to reduce production by 5 per cent every month until Israel withdrew from occupied Arab territories and restored the rights of the Palestinians. On the 18th Saudi Arabia announced it would cut production by 10 per cent, and Libya stopped oil exports to the U.S. altogether, to be followed on the 20th by Saudi Arabia and soon after by all other Arab oil producers.

International Reactions

While the diplomatic efforts in Washington continued, the rest of the world watched more or less passively the military events in the Middle East. There was no lack of comment, and none were more extreme than those emanating from Peking. The Israeli aggressors had undertaken a surprise attack much to the indignation of the Chinese people. American imperialism had made this attack possible by providing massive arms supply to Israel. But Soviet 'social imperialism' was at least equally responsible by permitting many Russian Jews to emigrate to Israel and by contemplating renewal of diplomatic relations with Israel. True, the Soviet leadership had also given some (sic) arms to the Arabs but it prevented them from achieving all their aims by merely insisting on the restoration of the pre-1967 borders. It was tying the Arabs' hands, there was a secret understanding between Moscow and Washington and this made it impossible to find a lasting solution.[19] Chu Peng-fei, the Chinese foreign minister, made an official declaration in the same vein on behalf of the Chinese Government, condemning 'the large-scale military attack' in the sharpest possible way; it had been planned by the Israelis in every detail but the people of the Arab countries and of Palestine would resist the aggression and carry their just war to final victory.[20] Such statements apart there was however a marked difference between the Chinese reactions in 1967 and in 1973; this time no help was offered, no mass protest demonstrations were organized, and the Chinese media did not devote much time or space to the war.

There was unanimous support for the Arab cause in non-communist Asia, and many expressions of solidarity. Mrs Indira Gandhi declared that Indian support for the Arab countries in no way affected the neutral stand of her country. Mujibur Rahman of Bangla Desh offered Sadat the help of 50,000 guerrillas willing to leave at a few minutes' notice. After a few days he modified his offer and sent instead 50,000 pounds of Bengal tea. In Islamabad, President Bhutto asked his compatriots to pray for an Arab victory; unfortunately there was no more they could do.

The Iranian Government, too, backed the Arabs. The foreign minister declared soon after the outbreak of the war that the Arabs were the aggrieved party, having been attacked in 1967 and virtually told to forget the territories they had lost at that time. But Tehran also advised the Arabs that they should not refuse to talk to Israel directly. The super-powers should stop the blood-letting, for it did not really matter who won the current round – the whole world would lose from it.[21] Iran was concerned in particular about the Muslim character of Jerusalem, but it had no excessive sympathy with radical Arab nationalism, which after all regarded Iran, too, as a potential enemy.

In Africa Israel fared very badly indeed. In 1972-3 Uganda, Chad, Mali, Nigeria, Congo-Brazzaville, Burundi and Togo had broken off relations. Zaire and Rwanda followed a few days before hostilities started. During the war diplomatic links were cut by Tanzania, the Malagasy Republic, Dahomey, Upper Volta, Cameroun, Equatorial Guinea, Ethiopia and Nigeria. Israeli relations had been close with many of these countries; thousands of Africans had received professional or military training in Israel; Idi Amin and Mobutu who became passionately anti-Israeli later on had been enthusiastic supporters of the Jewish State only a few years before. But many African countries had sizeable Muslim minorities, others needed Arab political support in the United Nations and elsewhere. A persuasive argument in most cases was oil money paid to African leaders; Colonel Qadafi was not far wrong when he claimed after the war that he, single-handed, had defeated Israel in Africa. (It was not altogether fair to the Saudis and Kuwaitis who had also made substantial contributions.) Jomo Kenyatta, always inclined to call a spade by its right name, watched the stampede into the Libyan camp with some misgivings: *'We* do not want to become prostitutes,' he declared pointedly.[22] Two weeks later he, too, broke off relations with Israel. Some observers regarded the *baksheesh* handed out by the Libyans and the Saudis as a welcome form of economic assistance to underdeveloped countries. The African leaders had been paid for breaking relations with Israel; would Colonel Qadafi and King Faisal continue to pay them in future? What if the price of oil went up? For the time being, however, many African countries were solidly behind the Arabs, so much so that Idi Amin later on bitterly attacked Sadat for accepting the 'treacherous Security Council resolution' calling for a ceasefire: 'I have been deeply disappointed by the demoralizing decision of my brother, President Sadat,' he stated in a message to Haile Selassie.[23]

European Attitudes or $9 \times 0 = 0$

Public opinion in Europe was in favour of Israel; according to the polls some 45-50 per cent sympathized with the Jewish State in Britain and France (57 per cent in West Germany); only 6 per cent in Britain were for the Arabs, 8 per cent in West Germany, 16 per cent in France. But public opinion had no influence on the conduct of foreign affairs,* a fact which was perhaps most palpably felt in France. From 1967 on, following the lead given by De Gaulle, the French Government had made it quite clear that it was in France's interests to be on the Arab side in the conflict; apart from the economic question, there was the argument that the Soviet Union should not be the sole influence in the Arab world. France voted fairly regularly against Israel in the United Nations, and the arms embargo against Israel imposed in 1967 was never lifted. Soon after the war broke out, M. Jobert, the foreign minister, uttered his famous 'petite phrase' (*'Est-ce que tenter remettre les pieds chez soi constitue forcément une aggression imprévue?'*: 'Can you call it unexpected aggression for someone to try to repossess his own land?') which stirred up much controversy. The overwhelming majority of Frenchmen wanted a balanced approach,

---

* As a Belgian diplomat told a group of journalists in Brussels: 'Eight European countries have observed strict neutrality. The ninth has followed public opinion. It is only normal that it should suffer the consequences.' (*L'Express*, November 5th, 1973)

Raymond Aron wrote, whereas M. Jobert was scarcely concealing beneath his coolness and boredom a conscious and resolute partiality.[24] This was not, however, the end of the tribulations of M. Jobert, who had a difficult time defending his government's policy in parliament; not a brilliant speaker at the best of times, the Paris newspaper *Combat* unfavourably compared his performance on this occasion with Buster Keaton. He announced that Israel was not going to disappear. But what about the Mirage aircraft supplied to Libya which were now used by the Egyptians? There was no proof, the minister replied. What about the Libyan pilots who had been trained in France and who had been in fact Egyptians? Well, how could one know the difference between a Libyan and an Egyptian, asked M. Jobert. He claimed that the war was really the fault of the super-powers who had sent so much armament to their clients. He also offered his services as an honest broker. If the war caused some uneasiness to the government, the opposition was also split. The Communists followed the Soviet line, whereas leading Socialists such as Mitterand and Deferre expressed solidarity with Israel. The Communists and the Trotskyites were furious and the Algerians bitterly denounced 'these anti-Arab ultras'.

British support for the Arabs was at first somewhat less outspoken. The government decision to refuse Israel spare parts for British-made Centurion tanks was criticized by Tory and Labour members of parliament alike. Sir Alec Douglas-Home, foreign secretary, had a difficult time in the House of Commons: he claimed that the embargo had halted combat arms, spare parts and ammunition of far greater value to the Arabs than to Israel.[25] The Arabs did not however agree with Sir Alec and warmly praised him for his stand. Should the existence of Israel be at stake (Sir Alec said) the government would reconsider its embargo.* A Labour back bencher enquired whether this was not the same undertaking that had been given to the Czechoslovaks in 1938 (when Douglas-Home had been parliamentary private secretary to Neville Chamberlain). 'No, this time it is meant,' replied Sir

* According to newspaper reports Lord Cromer, British ambassador in Washington, told Kissinger that Britain would stay neutral even if Israel's existence were at stake. (*L'Express*, November 5th, 1973)

Alec, implying that it had not been meant in 1938. A few minutes later, realizing the unfortunate implications of his answer he said, 'I withdraw the remark.' The Labour Party advised its members to vote against the government embargo, but 15 of its members voted with the government, whereas 17 Conservatives voted against it, with sizeable abstentions on both sides. Mr Harold Wilson said in a radio interview that the Foreign Office was a traditional strong-hold of the Arabists and that a strong prime minister and foreign secretary were needed to counterbalance their influence. But he also had some good things to say about the Palestinian Arabs, the real victims of 1948, who had to get at long last a state of their own. Meanwhile in the City of London a major loan was considered for Abu Dhabi, whose sheikh had promised Sadat financial assistance so that the Egyptians could pay the Russians, who reportedly, were asking for payment in cash for some of their deliveries.

In West Germany there was much comment on the wider implications of the war but little about the events in the Middle East – except in the most cryptic way. ('While we are neutral, we are not indifferent': W. Brandt.) The spokesman of the Christian Democratic opposition said that it was difficult to see how the government could still regard détente as a panacea in view of Soviet policy in the Middle East. But Chancellor Brandt did not agree: the Arab-Israeli conflict would have no effect on détente or his own policy of reducing tension and improving relations with the East. Arab ambassadors in Bonn were carefully watching the German scene; when Dr Schuetz, the mayor of Berlin, participated in a rally expressing solidarity with Israel, there was an immediate official protest. The Arabs threatened that they would not support West German rights in West Berlin (which they had never done anyway) if German politicians took an anti-Arab line. After that there were few manifestations of solidarity with Israel except on the part of some back benchers in the Bundestag.

When war material from U.S. bases in West Germany was shipped to Israel by way of Bremerhaven, the American ambassador was called to the German Foreign Ministry and sternly rebuked: the German Government was firmly resolved not to be drawn into the Middle-East conflict. Germany's policy was one of strict neutrality.[26] It sounded eminently reasonable; the Arabs received all the arms they needed, whereas only one country was willing to give active support to Israel. If the countries of Europe had had their way, this support would not have reached Israel. As a Pentagon official said after the war, 'We feel there wasn't one country in Western Europe that, if pushed to the wall, wouldn't have let Israel go under.'[27]

The German attitude caused much resentment in Washington. James Schlesinger, secretary of defence, said at a press conference that 'we maintain forces in West Germany because it provides us with enhanced readiness. But the reactions of the West German Foreign Ministry leads us to question whether they consider readiness what we consider it to be.'[28] Schlesinger said that America would have to reflect on that matter. Now it was the turn of the Germans to express their surprise; it had not been a rebuke, merely a 'political request'. The opposition criticized Chancellor Brandt's handling of the affair which had resulted in a crisis in U.S.-German relations. German policy in 1967 had been quite different, but much water had flown down the Rhine since then; there was the *Ostpolitik* to consider – early on during the war there had been a letter from Brezhnev to Brandt. Above all, there was Germany's dependence on Arab oil, and the feeling that if America could afford to defy the Arabs, Germany could not.

It would be tedious to analyse in detail the attitudes, official and unofficial, of the various countries in Western Europe towards Israel and the Arabs during the war. There was no NATO solidarity; Turkey let the Soviet air bridge violate its air space for many days without a protest; but it did not permit America to use U.S. bases in its territory for the airlift. Greece, West Germany, Italy and Spain did the same. Britain privately made it clear that any American request would be rebuffed. In the end only a single NATO country, Portugal, was willing to let the Americans use their military bases on its territory for shipping arms to Israel.

European attitudes were curiously ambiguous. On the one hand it was argued that the war in the Middle East had shown that Europe could be defended only with American help. A well-known expert noted that NATO was in the same position in Europe as Israel on October 6th. The Russians could easily concentrate 15,000 tanks in Central Europe. In view of the massive Soviet air defence,

Europe had a military chance of survival only if the American air force brought in its most recent electronic equipment. The idea that Europe could defend itself without American help was an illusion.[29] But at the same time European politicians saw no danger in refusing to comply with American requests whenever they saw fit, nor did they think that a major effort on their part was needed to reinforce Europe's defences. Denmark was about to halve its army, Belgium, Holland, Italy and West Germany either had reduced conscription or were about to do so: 'With the exception of France and Great Britain, both of whom had pared their forces to an absolute minimum in the early 'sixties, there is not one European NATO member that is not contemplating – or already implementing – plans to reduce or restructure its armed forces.'[30]

Western Europe desperately needed America and it took American help for granted; the idea that any alliance involves reciprocity seems not to have occurred to these governments. Seen from the capitals of Western Europe, American help for Israel was a major nuisance; it was sentimental in character, based on the special status of Israel in American opinion rather than America's vital global interests. This was of course true, but equally it could be asked whether any vital American interests were involved in West Berlin or whether, if by some catastrophe Britain disappeared, America would be any less secure than before? The Europeans' thinking was curiously parochial. Not that they were greatly enamoured of the Arabs and wanted Israel to disappear; but for the threat of the Arab oil embargo they might even have provided a little help. But given West Europe's dependence on Arab oil they reached the conclusion that they could not afford to antagonize those who had the oil. If this could be done without sacrificing Israel, well and good; it is unlikely however that Sir Alec Douglas-Home or M. Jobert would have spent many sleepless nights if European neutrality had caused the destruction of the Jewish State. But this seemed a remote possibility, for there was always America to support Israel in an emergency.

These European attitudes were dangerous inasmuch as they were bound to undermine America's trust in its European allies. The European governments behaved as if they wanted to provide support to the American critics of U.S. military involvement in

Europe, such as Senator Mansfield. Europe was an ally that could not be trusted in an emergency; it trembled when the Sheikh of Abu Dhabi spoke. Would it not collapse utterly if Mr Brezhnev one day decided to raise his voice?*

True, the existence of Israel was not an issue of vital importance for Western Europe. But would these governments have acted any differently if one of their own had been in danger? How reliable was Europe as an ally? Would it resist an attack? European dependence on Arab oil was certainly a problem, but – Israel or no Israel – there was a serious issue involved when a whole continent could be blackmailed. Would cringing before the oil sheikhs be an effective answer in the long run? Or was solidarity needed, a united stand and a forceful policy? Some of these questions were answered as the oil crisis broke; we shall have to return to the subject in a different context.

The collapse of Europe in face of the Middle-Eastern crisis was bound to sharpen all the doubts that had existed in Washington for a long time. When Kissinger flew to Moscow on October 20th, America's European allies had not been consulted and it is easy to see why.

* It appeared subsequently that, whereas all of America's European allies had publicly dissociated themselves from U.S. policy, some had in fact facilitated American arms shipments to Israel. But they were all afraid to show open solidarity with the United States.

Chapter Five   Confrontation

On Saturday, October 20th, 1973, Kissinger suddenly flew to Moscow. The announcement was a total surprise: there had been a personal appeal by Brezhnev to come immediately. The talks started less than two hours after Kissinger's air-force plane had touched down at Vnukovo airport. Why the sudden hurry on the part of the Soviet leaders after two weeks of masterly inactivity? The short answer is, of course, that until about October 18th the Russians had thought that their side was winning; not a total victory, needless to say, but gaining the ascendancy so that at the end of the war they could negotiate from a position of strength when armistice talks started, perhaps a month or two hence. The Israeli offensive into Syria had been halted and it was believed that in the great battle for Sinai the Egyptians grew stronger and the Israelis weaker with each day that passed. It will be recalled that on October 13th, the previous Saturday, the National Security Council had reached the conclusion that the Russians had no interest in either an immediate ceasefire, or any plan to stop arms supplies.

Soviet diplomacy was not entirely inactive but it proceeded at a leisurely pace. On Tuesday, October 16th, Alexei Kosygin, the Soviet prime minister, went to Cairo for two days of talks. He was told that the military situation was excellent, there was no reason to hurry. There were three meetings between Kosygin and Sadat about which not too much is known. Sir Alec Douglas-Home, the British foreign secretary, had been told, presumably by the Soviet ambassador, that Kosygin was in Cairo on a 'mission of peace' which was probably true to the extent that Egypt's peace terms were discussed. In these talks, according to a Yugoslav source, Kosygin favoured an Israeli withdrawal and minor Egyptian concessions on its borders with Israel; the new borders were to be guaranteed and to be policed by the U.S. and the U.S.S.R. The Egyptians turned down these suggestions; they would not give up a single inch of Egyptian territory.[1] While Kosygin had his talks the Israeli 'raiding unit' continued its activities west of the canal;

according to the Egyptians this was a mere propaganda manoeuvre. It took the Egyptian high command more than three days to realize the full extent and the implications of this operation: by the time it had woken up to the gravity of the situation, it was too late to do anything about it. The Russians were probably somewhat better informed, but it seems that a reappraisal of the military situation took place in Moscow only on the day of Kosygin's return, October 19th. On this day the Soviet press reported for the first time that Israeli units were operating on the west side of the canal. This, in briefest outline, was the background for Brezhnev's sudden decision and the great urgency of the invitation.

The request reached Washington in the afternoon. Kissinger was about to leave for a dinner with Chinese diplomats in Washington's Mayflower Hotel in preparation for his visit to Peking which was scheduled for October 26th. After the dinner Kissinger had a hurried meeting with Congressional leaders, but he could not give them any details about his impending visit; 'I am not certain Dr Kissinger had all the details,' Senator Mansfield said afterwards.[2] What Kissinger could not tell Mansfield was briefly this: the day before, Dobrynin had made a new offer on behalf of the Kremlin, demanding an immediate ceasefire and an Israeli withdrawal in stages to the pre-1967 borders. (Previously he had demanded an immediate Israeli retreat.) The American Government apparently showed insufficient interest in the Soviet proposal, whereupon the next day Brezhnev invoked the U.S.-Soviet accords of 1971-2, in which a certain procedure for crisis control had been established: both sides promised to enter into talks within forty-eight hours if one of them regarded the world situation as sufficiently dangerous to warrant immediate high-level talks. Brezhnev said in his invitation that the Soviet Government was very concerned about the situation in the Middle East and wanted consultations before decisions of grave import were adopted in Moscow.

Kissinger was accompanied on this trip by Joseph Sisco, Sisco's deputy Atherton, Helmut Sonnenfeldt, his chief adviser on European and Soviet affairs, Winston Lord, head of the State Department policy planning section, and some fifteen other aides. Following the initial meeting, soon after their arrival, there was a four-hour session on Sunday morning. Both sides agreed on the necessity for an immediate ceasefire. The American representatives were reportedly reluctant to accept Soviet proposals to link the ceasefire with immediate negotiations for a settlement, naming a time and place for negotiations. Brezhnev was accompanied by Podgorny, the Soviet president, and Gromyko, the foreign minister, as well as several foreign-policy experts; Kosygin was absent. A few details about the meeting became known only later; at the time only a three-line Tass statement was issued, according to which, 'The present situation in the Middle East was examined in detail and possible ways of establishing peace in that area.'[3] The Moscow meeting resulted in the convocation of the Security Council, within a matter of hours, which adopted the U.S.-Soviet call for a cease-fire. Never within living memory had so many diplomats acted so quickly.

On his return Kissinger briefly visited Tel Aviv, whereas Kosygin again went on a short visit to the Middle East, meeting the Iraqi and Syrian heads of state. The Moscow talks, it seemed, were eminently successful, everyone breathed a sigh of relief for a day or two. But in fact they were merely the prelude to a major confrontation which no longer involved Israel and Egypt. Nixon and Kissinger called it the most serious crisis since Cuba. Only yesterday peace had seemed within reach, only a month earlier détente had been all the rage. To understand the sudden change for the worse, we have to take a second, closer and somewhat harder look at Soviet policies before and during the Middle-East crisis.

Russia between Détente and Confrontation

Mention has already been made of the general trend of Soviet policy towards the United States and the Arab world before the outbreak of the war. But Soviet policy was not monolithic in the sense that it had been under Stalin, and, to a lesser degree, under Krushchev. There was a broad consensus about its aims but there were also tactical differences among those shaping Soviet foreign policy. Some members of the Politburo were a little more in favour of détente, some were more hawkish and suggested greater risk-taking. This appears quite clearly from an analysis of speeches and articles in the Soviet Union before and during the crisis, just as it can be established without difficulty that the attitudes of the

Polish and Hungarian governments were slightly more moderate than those of Czechoslovakia, Bulgaria, and above all East Germany, which put out the shrillest anti-Israeli propaganda. It is not very rewarding to try to establish with any degree of accuracy the identity of 'hawks' and 'doves' in the Soviet leadership; the dividing lines were usually not rigid, and some Soviet leaders from time to time modified their views. What does matter is the fact that there were differences of opinion, that debates on the tactics to be followed vis-à-vis the war and the United States did go on at the highest level and that there were unavoidable inconsistencies in Soviet policy because it wanted to make gains in the Middle East while preserving détente.

In August 1973, in a speech in Alma Ata, Brezhnev stressed that 'Détente should spread to the entire world and that political détente should be supplemented with military détente.' An editorial in *Pravda* at the time reiterated these points, and congratulated the Western powers for the realism they were showing. There were polite and even warm messages during August and early September, such as a dispatch on Kissinger's appointment as secretary of state and Podgorny's congratulations to Nixon on the Skylab mission.[4] But only a little later certain reservations about peaceful co-existence were voiced: *Izvestia* in September not only hailed wars of 'national liberation' but noted that there was 'bound' to be a conflict of interests between East and West.[5] While the Brezhnevites in the Politburo said that too much reliance should not be put on military power as a means of guaranteeing peace, and stressed the importance of diplomacy and peaceful co-operation,[6] the hawks were saying that imperialism had after all not changed its character, nuclear weapons had not been banned and that as long as the 'aggressive forces of imperialism' existed there would be a need to be ready to wage war by any means of armed struggle.[7]

Such debates about the role of the military at a time of détente were not entirely theoretical; soon in the Middle East Soviet policy had to face the issue head-on. The Soviet advocates of détente had never claimed that they were always and under any circumstances for peaceful co-existence. When the conference of so-called non-aligned countries in Algeria (September 1973) aligned itself quite strongly with the Soviet Union (with the notable exception of

Qadafi), Brezhnev warmly praised their stand against 'imperialism'. When the Arab oil-producers decided at their meeting in October 1973 to use the oil weapon, *Pravda* encouraged them and expressed hope that oil warfare would escalate.[8] Only a few months before, Brezhnev had signed the much publicized declaration of intent to ease tension in the world and it had been the general tendency in Washington to accept this at face value. While many American policy-makers dimly realized that their concept of détente and the easing of tensions was not quite identical with Soviet views on the subject, few were fully aware of the extent to which they differed. The dilemma facing the Soviet leadership was not, as already stated, whether to support the war, but how to do it without causing irreparable harm to détente.

When the news about the impending Arab attack reached Moscow some time during the second half of September the general consensus in the Politburo, according to the evidence available, was that a limited Arab campaign should be supported. Some of the hawks may have preferred something more ambitious because this would have done away with what they considered 'unhealthy tendencies' in international relations; it would have resulted in a sharper anti-American line, and greater allocations for the Soviet armed forces. For Brezhnev, Kosygin and their group this would have been a major set-back; for they were, after all, personally identified with détente policy. True, they had been dissatisfied of late with the progress of U.S. relations – for instance, American disillusionment with détente, such as manifested in the great support for the Jackson Amendment. But they were reasonably sure that these impediments would be overcome, just as the American architects of détente were inclined to regard the resistance of the Soviet hawks and the talk about ideological struggle and wars of national liberation as of no great consequence.

When Sadat and the Syrians officially informed Moscow about their intention to attack this was no doubt presented as a mere prelude to a political solution: the Arabs did not want to destroy Israel, nor were they in a position to do so; they simply wanted to break the deadlock which had lasted for a very long time and which had become intolerable. Without some shock treatment neither the Israelis nor the Americans would be willing to move.

163

Such a presentation almost certainly met with Soviet approval. Soviet leaders had very often stressed the necessity of a political solution to the conflict. In his Alma Ata speech Brezhnev included the following among the most urgent tasks the U.S.S.R. had to discuss with friends: 'The achievement of a political settlement in the Middle East on the basis of the decisions of the U.N. Security Council and General Assembly which provide for the withdrawal of Israeli troops from all occupied Arab lands.'[9] This was the party line and the statement was reiterated in many speeches and articles up to the outbreak of the war. Soviet leaders repeatedly said that it was inadmissible to acquire territory by force – unless of course the country in question happened to be a super-power like the Soviet Union. When Prime Minister Tanaka of Japan went to Moscow in October 1973 to ask for the restoration of several islands seized by the Soviet Union in 1945 he could have made use of this argument, but being a tactful man he refrained from doing so. During August and September Soviet policy became somewhat more anti-Israeli in tenor, even though it had not been particularly friendly before. In mid-August Yasir Arafat was accorded more or less official recognition in Moscow, he had an interview published in the Soviet press and was invited to the Soviet capital in connection with the world students' games.[10] The Israelis, on the other hand, were denounced in the Soviet press as gangsters, international bandits and even Nazis. There were many cartoons depicting horrible creatures with pronounced Jewish features; somehow the cartoonists could not make up their minds whether Dayan wore his patch over the left or the right eye but it was clear that they did not like him – or anything he stood for. Israeli Zionist agents were said to have attempted to commit sabotage in the U.S.S.R. Israel was described as the enemy of the national liberation movements and the 'spearhead of Israeli's aggressive policy was directed primarily against the international communist and workers' movement'. Sometimes comment was a little far-fetched even by Soviet standards; one writer referred to 'Peking's connivance with the Israeli aggressors' and the 'Maoist-Israeli duet of anti-Sovietism'.[11] Foreign Minister Gromyko, speaking in the U.N. General Assembly on September 25th, made it clear that the Soviet Union wanted no compromise with regard to the territories; the Soviet position was clear: 'The situation in the Middle East should be settled on the basis of the complete, I repeat complete, withdrawal of Israeli troops from occupied Arab territories ...'

There was support for the Arabs, but the decision to assist them in the coming war left some major questions open: how could it be assured that a limited military operation would not turn into something bigger and more dangerous? The Politburo assumed no doubt that if things should get out of hand Moscow and Washington would get together at short notice and impose a ceasefire, as indeed they eventually did, though only after certain complications had occurred. But relations with the Arab countries were not as close as they should have been and there was no full control. The Soviet press repeatedly and pointedly praised the late Gamal Abdel Nasser and his achievements – implying criticism of Sadat. There were some difficulties with the Syrians too: in September there was a clampdown on the movements of the 3,000-odd Soviet military advisers in Syria. There is some evidence to the effect that while Sadat and Asad were disappointed by Brezhnev's détente policy they were not unaware of the existence of dissenting voices in the Kremlin. There may not have been a full understanding between the Arabs and the Soviet hawks, but they assumed that once war broke out they would be able to count on the support of the military in Moscow. According to some evidence, the constellation in May 1967 had not been dissimilar.

On the eve of the war some little-noticed and apparently unconnected events took place in the Soviet Union: on October 3rd the unprecedented number of nine spy satellites was put into orbit (another one was to follow on the 6th); *Pravda* carried a warning that 'Tel Aviv's aggressive course is threatening peace not only in the Middle East'[12] – the full meaning of this became clear only a few days later. The correspondents of *Pravda* and *Izvestia* who had regularly reported from the Middle East suddenly fell silent. There was, however, one astonishing news agency statement which was totally ignored, perhaps because it emanated from an unlikely place – Sofia. On October 2nd, the Bulgarian Telegraphic Agency carried a report from Beirut which stated, *expressis verbis*, that the Arab armies were about to attack Israel:

Insistent rumours are circulating in the Lebanese capital about imminent military operations between the Arab states and Israel ... During his visit to the Syrian capital of Damascus yesterday the B.T.A. correspondent in Beirut learned from a number of his Syrian colleagues that in Syria there are in fact serious preparations made for such operations. All hospitals in Homs and Damascus have been evacuated and are ready to admit casualties, all private lorries and even motor cars are mobilized. According to numerous Syrian journalists, quoting people who have arrived from Cairo in the Syrian capital, in Egypt there was also much talk about the resumption of military operations and preparations were in progress.[13]

In a fit of absentmindedness, or because instructions had not been sufficiently clear, the Bulgarian censor had passed this revealing cable; fortunately for him, not a single newspaper picked it up.

On October 6th, the Soviet media announced that Israel had treacherously attacked Syria; one report even claimed that Israel had perfidiously attacked Syria, Egypt and Lebanon. Ermakov, one of *Pravda*'s star reporters, wrote that, 'after careful preparation and mobilization of reserves Israeli troops have attacked Egypt and Syria';[14] he apparently wanted to rub salt in the wounds of the Israeli high command. Marshal Grechko, now a full member of the Politburo, left the question open as to who had attacked: 'The peoples of the Arab countries have had to take up arms to defend their national independence in a just struggle.'[15] On Sunday, October 7th, there was the first official reaction in a Soviet Government statement which did not commit itself either as to who had fired the first shot: 'As a result of the absence of a political settlement, military actions have again broken out in the Middle East ... For several years now Israel, enjoying the support and patronage of imperialist circles, has by its reckless aggressive actions constantly fomented tension in the Middle East ... The responsibility for the present development of events in the Middle East and their consequences rests wholly and completely with Israel and those outside reactionary circles who constantly encourage Israel in its aggressive aspirations.' The statement reiterated the Soviet demand for the complete liberation of all Arab territories occupied by Israel and the ensuring of the legitimate rights of the Arab people of Palestine and ended with a warning: 'If the government of Israel should remain deaf to the voice of reason this might cost dear the people of Israel. The leaders of the government of Israel will bear full responsibility for the consequences of such a reckless course.' The statement avoided direct accusations against the United States but implied that it bore the responsibility. Interesting also was the threat to the people of Israel, not just its rulers.

During the next few days Soviet leaders stressed on many occasions that all their sympathies were on the side of the victims of aggression (meaning the Arabs). On October 9th, messages went out to Boumediene and other Arab and African leaders to give full support to Egypt and Syria, but these appeals were not published in the Soviet media. On the same day the Soviet air bridge to Egypt and Syria (likewise not mentioned in the press) went into top gear; some Soviet planes were landing at airstrips near the Israeli northern and southern front lines. The heavy cruiser *Admiral Ushakov* and other warships were heading rapidly for the Mediterranean. Soviet newspapers stressed the 'serious consequences of the war for the whole international situation' and Grechko made a rather bellicose speech addressing Polish generals in Warsaw: 'The most important task is further to improve and consolidate our combat alliance and raise the political vigilance and combat readiness of the armed forces.' On Saturday, October 13th, the Soviet Army newspaper *Krasnaia Zvesda* for the first time published enthusiastic reports about the effect of the modern Soviet weapons successfully used against Israel on the battlefield.

It will be recalled that at this time the American arms lift to Israel had not yet started and that Kissinger was waiting for some encouraging signs from Moscow. But there was little comfort for him: true, Brezhnev still talked about the 'turn from the cold war to détente and co-operation', and Kosygin said at a dinner for the prime minister of Denmark that the opponents of détente were trying to use the Middle-East situation to arouse distrust in the policy of peaceful co-existence. He added, with excessive modesty, 'The Soviet Union seeks nothing for itself in this region.'[16] But Kissinger was no longer so sure, and furthermore there were other ominous developments. Marshal Grechko participated in talks with

Boumediene in Moscow; the statement published after the meeting said that the sides confirmed their resolve to promote in every way the liberation of all Israeli-occupied territories. What did 'in every way' mean? And how had they defined 'Israeli-occupied territories'? According to Boumediene the Soviet leaders had told him that the Arabs need not stop at Israel's pre-1967 borders.[17] If so – what about a just peace and the guaranteed borders which the Soviet leaders had always stressed? Shelepin, one of the more hawkish Soviet leaders, made a speech in Varna (Bulgaria) which carried the attack against America a little further: 'The nature and character of imperialism remain the same' – no nonsense about détente as far as he was concerned. *Pravda*, in an editorial on October 17th, presented a curious blend of hawks' and doves' arguments – the relaxation of international tension should be made irreversible, but since the forces of aggression and reaction had by no means laid down their arms the peace-loving peoples had to rally their ranks still closer. Another leading Moscow newspaper called on the Arabs to make full use of the oil blockade and also suggested that they withdrew their multi-billion-dollar deposits in Western banks, for this could play an 'important if not decisive role'. Israel had no chance of winning because America had become weaker during the recent years: 'The present balance of power in the world arena has undergone substantial changes since the Six Day War, by no means in favour of the capitalist world.' There was a fierce struggle going on in America between hawks and doves, the paper said, but the voices urging restraint were growing; the wiser people in America had obviously understood that their country was no longer the leading military power.[18] *Krasnaia Zvesda* published an article on October 20th by Colonel Leontiev which was read by some observers as a hint that the existence of Israel could no longer be taken for granted, though he stopped short of spelling it out in so many words. Israel, he said, was facing a completely new, more powerful and skilful foe. With the first-class Soviet equipment which the Arab fighting men used so proficiently the myth of Israeli invincibility had been broken: 'The Arab countries will never reconcile themselves to aggression ... Israel's aggressive policy is fraught with serious consequences for the entire international situation. It is dangerous for Israel itself. The chase after an illusory "victory" can lead it only to catastrophe.' When Colonel Leontiev and his colleagues spoke about the 'most serious consequences' and 'catastrophes' they cannot have had the defeat of Israel by the Arab armies in mind for about the military outcome of the war the Soviet experts had no illusions. Thus Bovin, *Izvestia*'s star commentator, in a reply to the Chinese, who had urged the Arabs to fight on, wrote: 'An analysis of the situation which has arisen shows that a continuation of the war would merely increase the number of casualties.'

Thus, by the second half of October, the local war had become something considerably bigger and more dangerous. The climate of peace, of goodwill and relaxation of tensions had grown much chillier; Soviet editorials now proclaimed, 'The military actions of the imperialist states are forcing the countries of socialism to undertake measures further to strengthen their defence capability.'[19] Détente had taken a great fall; would Brezhnev, Kissinger, their horses and men be able to put it together again?

Def Con Three

When we lost sight of Dr Kissinger he was in the Kremlin, and the date was October 21st. In Israel it was generally assumed at the time that the Moscow talks were merely exploratory in character. As the Israelis saw it there was no sense of particular urgency on the part of the Americans; no dramatic new developments were likely to emerge from the Kissinger-Brezhnev talks until after the return to Washington of the secretary of state.[20] Much to the Israelis' surprise, events were moving much faster than they had anticipated: on October 21st the Israeli ambassador to Washington was urgently asked to call upon General Haig, President Nixon's chief of staff, who showed the ambassador the text of the three-point agreement just signed in Moscow. The message was sent posthaste to Tel Aviv, whereupon the Israeli Government was convened for a meeting; while it was still in session, around midnight, a personal message from President Nixon to Mrs Meir arrived. The president asked the Israelis cordially but very firmly to accept the agreement, which, it was said, reflected the American point of view on all the essential points. Israel, the president argued, would accept the agreement from a position of strength; furthermore, the Soviets

169

had agreed for the first time that there should be direct negotiations between the two sides, something they had always rejected in the past. And, lastly, the American arms shipments to Israel would continue, *after* Israel had signed the armistice agreement.[21]

The formula worked out in Moscow and subsequently submitted to the Security Council read as follows:

The Security Council (1) calls upon all parties to the present fighting to cease all firing and to terminate all military activity immediately, no later than 12 hours after the moment of the adoption of this decision, in the positions they now occupy; (2) calls upon the parties concerned to start immediately after the cease-fire the implementation of Security Council Resolution 242 in all of its parts; (3) decides that immediately and concurrently with the cease-fire, negotiations start between the parties concerned under appropriate auspices aimed at establishing a just and durable peace in the Middle East.

The only hard fact was the ceasefire; the reference to Resolution 242 was ambiguous and there was furthermore a certain contradiction between the second and third points in the new resolution (Resolution 338). The form of negotiations was left open; there was no specific provision for supervising the truce, nor was the prisoner-of-war issue mentioned. It appeared that Kissinger had tried to reach an agreement in Moscow about arms supplies but had failed.

Kissinger commented twice on his talks with the Soviet leaders; before leaving Moscow for Tel Aviv, he said that the talks had been intense, constructive and fruitful, they were held in a warm and cordial atmosphere. They would facilitate the restoration of peace and a new improvement in Soviet-American relations.[22] Three days later in his press conference at the height of the international crisis he was somewhat less sanguine. On the basis of his talks with Brezhnev there was every reason to expect that Soviet and American interests were not congruent. But a 'certain parallelism' could perhaps develop in the direction of establishing permanent peace.[23] There was at the time a great deal of speculation about far-reaching agreements which had allegedly been concluded in the Moscow talks; this was denied in Washington and a few days later it did indeed appear as if all the essential questions had been left open.[24] The vagueness made it possible for Israelis and Egyptians to accept the plan without much delay, but it was at the same time the source of more friction. The resolution had been passed in the Security Council by 14 to 0, with China abstaining; the Chinese denounced the resolution as yet another imperialist plot but they did not veto it. The Chinese position throughout the crisis was curiously inconsistent; verbal extremism went hand in hand with great caution. This was after all a case of military aggression and perhaps the Chinese were a little afraid that the bells would be tolling for them next time. It was therefore imprudent to obstruct totally an international procedure, which, for all they knew, they would need themselves one day.

The first to accept the resolution – unanimously – was the Israeli Government, on October 22nd; in its announcement it stressed that it regarded it as an American proposal rather than a Security Council resolution. The government further requested President Nixon to ask Kissinger to visit Tel Aviv on his way home, but it is important to note that it did not make its acceptance of the resolution conditional on further explanations. Egypt accepted the resolution in the early afternoon. President Sadat praised his armed forces for 'breaking the deadlock' and 'changing the political map of the Middle East'; Sadat made it known that he had received assurances from Brezhnev on October 21st, after he had been in contact with a number of Arab capitals directly involved. Iraq and Libya rejected the Egyptian decision. Jordan said it would abide by it and Syria ignored it. Syria's acceptance came only on October 24th when the Damascus government in a cable to U.N. Secretary General Waldheim announced that it accepted Resolution 338 on the understanding that it was based on the 'complete withdrawal of Israeli forces from all territories occupied in June 1967 and after'.[25] This, of course, was quite unacceptable to the Israelis. Asad later admitted that the resolution came as a surprise 'and was contrary to our course and to the picture we had in mind'.[26] He accepted it because Sadat had assured him that he had received a guarantee from the Soviet leaders that the Israelis would completely withdraw from all the Arab territories. Still he was unhappy: he had in mind a long war, and the ultimate objective of the battle was no doubt something more ambitious than complete Israeli withdrawal. He said he would like to talk about this point, but 'more explanations and details could benefit the enemy'.[27] In Israel, too, there was considerable opposition to the ceasefire: the executive of Likud, the national opposition, said that the implementation of this resolution would not bring peace but would permanently jeopardize the security of Israel and its people.[28] The Israeli generals were unhappy about the ceasefire; Dayan noted that Israel had neither asked for it nor needed it.

The issue came up in the talks between Kissinger and Mrs Meir and other Israeli representatives near Tel Aviv on October 22nd. No announcement was made at the end of the talks but it transpired that Kissinger explained to the Israelis that the president had reached the conclusion that if the war in the Middle East was allowed to drag on much longer, irreparable damage could be caused to détente and that he had therefore made use of the Soviet initiative and acted so quickly.[29] American military experts assumed that the Israeli Army needed more than a day or two of 'mop-up' operations for a decisive victory; for this reason did it really matter that much to the Israelis whether the ceasefire agreement came into force on October 22nd or two days later? But this consideration quite apart, a decisive Israeli victory would not have been in the American interests as Kissinger saw it, for it would have made the Israelis unwilling to make any concessions at all. He reassured his Israeli interlocutors that there were no secret clauses in the Moscow agreement. The second paragraph in the agreement – Resolution 242 – was connected with the third – direct negotiations – and the Israelis had no reason to fear it.

If the Moscow conference had ended in ambiguity, the results of the Tel Aviv meeting were also somewhat nebulous. The Israelis thought that while they would eventually have to accept the ceasefire, this did not necessarily preclude a little push here or there; after all, the armistice in Vietnam had not been complete from the very first moment either. As for the more distant future, everything was open to discussion; as Mrs Meir said a few days later in the

Knesset, the Americans, to the best of her knowledge, did not have a detailed peace plan. Israel would not be compelled to accept borders that were not defensible. She quoted an exchange of documents with Washington affirming that as long as a peace settlement was not achieved, Israel would maintain its stand in Jerusalem and in the territories as established in the ceasefire. Kissinger did, however, tell the Israelis that Resolution 242 was part of the agreement and that an armistice must come into force. Everyone was happy, at least for forty-eight hours.

On October 23rd fighting broke out again on the southern Suez front. Israeli forces broke through on various sectors, seized three airfields, cut off the main Ismalia-Cairo road, and completely encircled the third army. There was near panic in Cairo, all men between 21 and 35 were called up for active service and there were frantic messages to enlist Soviet help, whereupon the Soviet Union threatened Israel with the 'most serious consequences,' said that Israeli acceptance of the U.N. ceasefire appeal had been 'pure falsehood', and ordered Israel to withdraw immediately to the lines held on Monday.[30] Unfortunately no one could say with any certainty where the Monday lines had been. Ambassador Keating made 'serious representations' in Tel Aviv and the Security Council met on October 23rd and issued another ceasefire call; the proceedings had to be interrupted for ten minutes for Mr Malik and the Chinese representative were shouting and waving their arms at each other. Chiao Kuan-hua protested at the 'malicious practice' of using the Security Council as a tool to be juggled by the two super-powers at will. But again there was no Chinese veto. This second ceasefire worked better than the first, there were some minor violations but on the whole fighting died down. But the real crisis was yet to start.

It began, innocently enough, with notes from President Sadat to Nixon and Brezhnev asking them to send forces to the Middle East to see that Israel abided by the ceasefire.[31] A White House spokesman said that President Nixon had not yet received such a request, that the U.S. had no intention of sending troops and hoped that no other outside power would do so.[32] Then, all of a sudden, at 12.10 a.m. on October 25th, Defence Secretary Schlesinger ordered 'Def Con Three' – a world-wide state of alert of American military forces.* Troops, planes and ships were ordered to take positions. No one understood what it was all about, no one that is except the members of the National Security Council. A great many people in the United States were firmly convinced that it was just one of Nixon's tricks to distract attention from the Watergate scandal. The president was in deep trouble, having a few days before dismissed Professor Cox, the special investigator, which had led to the resignation of Elliot Richardson, the attorney-general, and William Ruckelshaus, his deputy. Cox had rejected Nixon's 'compromise proposals', according to which a digest of the famous tapes should be supplied subject to verification only by one man, Senator John Stennis: this was the most recent in a seemingly unending series of scandals. On the evening of October 25th President Nixon was to appear on television and explain his course of action which had attracted so much criticism. As some critics saw it, Def Con Three was just a red herring, there was no crisis; they regarded the whole Middle-East war as a nuisance inasmuch as it distracted the public from the really important domestic issues.

Def Con Three was declared following a series of unusual happenings. On the evening of Tuesday, October 23rd, there was a sharp decline in the previously heavy Soviet airlift of supplies into Egypt and Syria. This had been noticed by the Pentagon, whose spokesman Jerry Friedheim had reported it; at first it was apparently interpreted as a sign of belated Soviet willingness to come to an agreement with the U.S. with regard to a limitation of the arms supplies.[33] This interpretation was discarded when U.S. intelligence began to pick up indications that Soviet army and transport units had been placed on alert.[34] There was news about the concentration of seven Soviet parachutist divisions, altogether about 50,000 men. On Wednesday there were more alerts involving Soviet air force units; 6,000 Soviet naval infantry men had been dispatched to the *Eskadra* in the Mediterranean and a fleet of Antonov 22 air-

* America has five different defence-readiness conditions. Def Con Five is normal peacetime readiness, Def Con One is 'maximum force readiness'. The last time Def Con Three was declared was after the assassination of President Kennedy in 1963. According to some reports it had not been intended to give publicity to the alert on October 25th.

craft was redirected to Hungary and other East European countries. Six more ships were added to the Soviet Mediterranean fleet. There were reports about the transfer of S C U D missiles with atomic warheads to Egypt.[35] On Wednesday Kissinger had discussed with Dobrynin the site, date and participants in the coming peace conference; Geneva was mentioned and a date in December. But on Wednesday evening Dobrynin again appeared with a message from Brezhnev to Nixon which the president later said left very little to the imagination. Senator Fulbright regarded it as 'urgent', Senator Jackson called it 'brutal, rough'.[36] President Nixon also termed it as rough. It was reportedly harshly worded, repeated the warning about the 'gravest consequences' for Israel and announced that Soviet troops would be sent unilaterally if necessary to enforce the ceasefire.

What were the reasons for the sudden Soviet concern? It will be recalled that from the Arab point of view the ceasefire had come a few days too late; their pride and the unwillingness to accept realities on the front had made them hesitate. Their position was less advantageous on October 22nd than a week before, and it deteriorated even further as the result of Israeli advances between the first and second ceasefire. The third army was effectively cut off; unless it could be resupplied within a few days, it would have to surrender because it had no food, water or ammunition. The war had ended inconclusively, despite certain Israeli gains. If the third army had surrendered this would have been a major disaster. The Soviet leaders were alarmed both because their protégés were about to undergo another defeat and because they thought Kissinger had cheated, giving the Israelis a free hand for a day or two after the armistice; they had of course done exactly the same at the end of the war of attrition in August 1970. Russian anger with Israel had been mounting for a long time and they would have dearly loved the opportunity to teach the Jews a lesson they would not easily forget; this was, no doubt, what the Tass statement about 'gravest consequences' implied. They could provoke a collision with Israel by offering to supply the third army with their own planes and personnel. If the Israelis had had the audacity to shoot at the Russians, they would have brought in more troops and perhaps also their fleet. Any such course of action was however dependent on what America would do; but would the Americans have come to Israel's aid on Egyptian soil?

To mete out punishment to Israel substantial forces were needed; it is unlikely that Israeli soldiers would have fainted at the sight of one Soviet division, or even two, consisting of soldiers who had never seen battle and who would have to fight in unfamiliar conditions. Deeply engraved in Soviet military doctrine is the lesson of the winter war against Finland – never to under-rate the enemy, to attack only if considerable numerical superiority is assured. This would have involved the dispatch of five divisions or more, including heavy equipment; it would no longer have been a little local punitive action, but military intervention on a massive scale. Such an operation, needless to say, could be contemplated only if American intervention was ruled out, and it would seem therefore that the Soviet manoeuvre was meant to be a test for America. It could not possibly do much harm and it would impress on the Americans very forcefully that Moscow took a grave view of the situation and that the Israelis should not be permitted to make any further advance. It was, in all probability, the Soviet equivalent of 'Operation Spark', an effort to force a political decision. The American alert was meant to be a psychological warning sign; if Washington had been convinced that the Russians were about to attack, Def Con Three would have been insufficient. Soviet actions and communications were ambiguous, as Kissinger said, and even if there was only a remote possibility of Soviet military action, America did not want to find itself unprepared; the Israelis' surprise on October 6th acted as a deterrent. When Nixon's motives were doubted by some of the correspondents, Kissinger made it known that all senior advisers and the whole of the National Security Council had unanimously recommended this course of action as the result of deliberations in which the president himself did not participate.[37] For Kissinger these imputations were no doubt doubly hurtful, for not only did he again find the whole edifice of détente in jeopardy but by implication he found his own motives questioned – as if the chief architect of détente had not the most to lose by being needlessly tough to the Russians. Kissinger said at his press conference:

It is inconceivable that the forces of the great powers should be introduced in the numbers that would be necessary to over-power both of the participants. It is inconceivable that we should transplant the great power rivalry into the Middle East, or alternatively, that we should impose a military con-dominium by the United States and the Soviet Union. The United States is even more opposed to the unilateral introduc-tion by any great power, especially by any nuclear power, of military forces into the Middle East, in whatever guise those forces should be introduced.

And further on:

The United States and the Soviet Union are, of course ideological and, to some extent, political adversaries. But the United States and the Soviet Union also have a very special responsibility. We possess, each of us, nuclear arsenals capable of annihilating humanity.[38]

Speaking the next day, President Nixon in his press conference, which had been postponed several times, said that America had received information that the Russians were planning to send 'very substantial forces into the Middle East' and that this was the reason that he had ordered a precautionary alert. He had ex-changed messages with Brezhnev at the height of the crisis, insist-ing that all major powers should stay out of the troubled area. He regarded the outcome of the crisis as a 'victory for détente'. Both Russia and the U.S. now realized that they had a far more important stake in détente: 'Without détente we might have had a major confrontation in the Middle East, but with détente we have avoided it.'[39] He also claimed that the chance for permanent peace was better than it had been for twenty years. A third comment on the crisis came from James Schlesinger, secretary of defence, who mentioned three main military reasons for the alert. These were: the doubling in size of the Soviet Mediterranean fleet, the alert of about 50,000 Soviet paratroops, and the preparation of huge Soviet transport planes for troop transport. But the main reason for the alert was, according to Schlesinger, diplomatic. A world-wide alert of American forces seemed the only credible means of making sure that the Russians would not dispatch forces.[40]

When the details of the crisis, which had exploded without notice on an unprepared public, became known, almost all Congressional leaders supported Nixon. Senator Edward Kennedy, speaking in Brussels, said that the first flush of euphoria about détente was over and warned the Soviet Union not to under-estimate American internal strength; similar declarations were made by Senator Muskie and other critics of Nixon. The only major exception was Senator Fulbright, who said, 'From what I know the message was not threatening.' But would Fulbright have considered any Soviet action threatening, short perhaps of the occupation of the State of Arkansas? On October 26th the U.S. world-wide alert was partially lifted following a new agreement reached by Washington and Moscow. The Security Council approved with hardly any debate a resolution sponsored by eight 'non-aligned' members of the council to bar the five permanent members from participation in a peace-keeping force; the voting was again 14 to 0, with China abstaining. True, Brezhnev announced the same day that the U.S.S.R. would independently send 'representatives' to observe the ceasefire, but this was to be a limited number of senior officers, a far cry from military intervention. America announced that it was also ready to send a small number of observers but only if requested to do so by Dr Waldheim. And so the 'most difficult crisis we have had since the Cuban confrontation in 1962' (Nixon) vanished as suddenly as it had come.

The crisis left a great many questions open.[41] What made President Nixon believe that the chances for a real peace settlement were better now than at any time in the past? Did he really think that but for détente there would have been a nuclear war? There had in the past been other crises at least as serious – from Berlin to Cuba – which had been settled without the benefit of détente. There were certain internal inconsistencies in the official American accounts of the crisis: for instance, the behaviour in the Security Council of Mr Malik, who justified the dispatch of Soviet forces to the area of conflict. But Malik's declaration was made well after the American alert had come into force. The intelligence reports about Soviet movements were inconclusive and partly contradictory.

The air bridge had slowed down several days before, and the Soviet parachutists had been on alert since October 18th. If the Russians had reinforced their forces in the Mediterranean the Americans had done the same. It is not clear what induced President Sadat to ask for Soviet and American troops; perhaps this action had been concerted with the Russians. The presence of several Soviet divisions on Egyptian soil would have hardly given him much joy; it was, after all, only a little more than a year since thousands of Soviet advisers had been asked to leave Egypt. Sadat probably had an undertaking from the Russians that they would come in only together with the Americans – or not at all. Or could he have been desperate enough to ask the Russians in unconditionally? One could think of many sound reasons why America should reject the idea of sending troops to the Middle East; but only two weeks after the October 25th crisis, Mr Kissinger began to discuss an international, presumably U.S.-Soviet, guarantee for Israel's border, and this, needless to say, would involve sending troops to the Middle East at a time of crisis.

Nevertheless, one does not have to look too hard for hidden moves or motives to explain American action during the crisis. One does not know what the Soviet leaders said in their private communications but there was enough in their public statements to give cause for concern. If the U.S. Government had published a solemn warning to Bulgaria or Syria that these countries faced the 'gravest consequences', the Soviet Union would no doubt have expected some action to follow up these words; the Kremlin would have regarded it as a threat not just to Bulgaria or Syria but also to their patron. It might have been sufficient for the U.S. to counter the Soviet move by some firm warning, but this might not have been sufficient to prevent a further escalation of the conflict. It will be impossible for a long time to say with any degree of certainty whether the United States acted as they did because there was a breakdown in communications. If the president and the National Security Council over-reacted, this was perhaps connected with the exaggerated expectations about Soviet behaviour at a time of crisis. Most probably the Soviet Union was engaging in a dangerous game which could easily have got out of hand.

On the day President Nixon gave his press conference, Brezhnev addressed a Soviet sponsored 'World Peace Congress' in Moscow and stated that some 'urgent and decisive' Soviet measures had been necessary to stop Israel from flouting the Security Council resolutions. He did not make it clear what kind of measures the Soviet authorities had prepared but instead accused 'certain circles in NATO countries' – meaning the U.S. – of having 'artificially intensified Middle Eastern tension' and having reacted irresponsibly by circulating 'fantastic rumours' about Soviet intentions.[42] He castigated Israel several times in his long speech and said that outside patronage had apparently something to do with the Israeli attacks. Without denying that the Soviet Union had made military preparations, he criticized Washington: 'A more responsible, honest and constructive approach would have been more proper.' The same theme was taken up two days later in a special Tass statement: Tass was authorized, it said, to declare that the actions of the Soviet Union were aimed solely at promoting the implementation of the decisions of the Security Council on a ceasefire. The American action was 'absurd', it did not promote détente but was obviously taken in an attempt to intimidate the Soviet Union: 'But those who are behind this step should be told that they have chosen the wrong address.'[43] According to Western observers in Moscow, the authorization had come from Brezhnev himself, who had apparently felt piqued by the fact that Nixon had alluded to their correspondence during the crisis. The only obvious conclusion that could be drawn from the Soviet reaction was that the understanding reached in the Brezhnev-Kissinger talks a few days previously had been both limited and fragile. The Soviet leaders were obviously worried by the military situation in Egypt, assuming that a few more days of fighting could result in complete defeat for their protégés. On the other hand, they did not wish to pursue their polemic with Washington any further; after all, both Nixon and Kissinger had been most restrained even at the height of the crisis. Mutual recriminations would have damaged U.S.-Soviet relations, and the Russians decided therefore not to engage in any further criticism; there were no more attacks and only a week later the Soviet press with apparent approval quoted at some length a Republican spokesman who had said that impeachment of Nixon would be both unfair and wrong.

The crisis between the United States and its N A T O allies was not so easily settled. On October 26th Robert McCloskey, the State Department spokesman, had some very harsh things to say about the Europeans. America had gone through a very critical period which also affected its European allies. It would have appreciated support, but instead some of its allies had gone to some lengths to dissociate themselves publicly from the U.S. President Nixon referred to this statement in his press conference ('Our European friends have not been as co-operative as they might have been'), and Schlesinger, singling out West Germany, said that the West German protest (against arms shipments to Israel from American bases in Germany) might force the United States to review its commitments to the Bonn government.[44] Kissinger, in an aside a few days later, was reported to have said that he was so disgusted by the behaviour of the Europeans that he did not care what happened to N A T O in future – a statement duly denied by a State Department spokesman.[45]* But Kissinger's comment, real or apocryphal, was fairly typical of general feeling in Washington. Some noted in sorrow, others in anger, that the Europeans would never help America unless it was to their own immediate benefit. When Sir Christopher Soames, the E.E.C. Commissioner for External Affairs, came to Washington on October 29th he had to listen to some very 'sharp nagging'; other European visitors underwent the same treatment. Kissinger told a delegation of visiting European parliamentarians that he failed to understand why the allies had behaved for two weeks as if the alliance did not exist. They seemed to be more interested in gaining marginal individual advantages than in co-operating on united action.[46] It transpired that during the crisis the United States had given briefings to the N A T O Council on three separate occasions on action to stop the fighting but there had been no support from the Europeans because they feared that the Arabs would cut off their oil supplies if they co-operated with America.[47]

Furthermore, Donald Rumsfeld, permanent U.S. representative

* Dr Kissinger in conversation with the author emphatically denied that he had ever made this comment.

to N A T O, had informed the Europeans about the American alert within three hours. Washington was particularly angry with the British Government which had promised early on during the war to co-sponsor a resolution calling for an armistice, only to withdraw it after Arab diplomats had told the British that the fighting should go on. The Americans had not expected any help from the French, but when M. Jobert had been in Washington not long before, he had promised Kissinger full support, only to engage in unending anti-American tirades a few days later. Herr Scheel, the German foreign minister, offered a curious argument to explain his action; after all, his country had banned further arms deliveries only after the Middle-East ceasefire had come into force. While the fighting was in progress Bonn had shown understanding for American policy to keep the balance in the Middle East. Such an explanation annoyed the Americans and certainly did not placate the Arabs. There was a pained outcry in Europe; the Americans had failed to consult them all along, which was an outrage, and now they dared to complain that Europe had dissociated itself from America's suicidal policy.* Technically, the Europeans were right, they had merely been informed, not consulted. But how does one consult with someone in an acute state of fear and collapse? In the words of a leading European weekly, the crisis had shown 'Europe trying to shut its eyes to what was at issue, and then running around in frightened circles because the problem would not go away. It managed to combine the behaviour of the ostrich and the hen.' [48] This belief was not, of course, shared by European statesmen who, on the contrary, believed that they had shown calm, foresight and responsibility. The British foreign secretary declared that there was no evidence that the Soviet Union was seriously considering moving troops into the Middle East; an assertion which was no doubt technically correct. It is unlikely that Sir Alec had received an official communication about Soviet preparations from the Soviet ambassador to the Court of St James.

* With equal justice the Americans could argue that the Europeans had not consulted them. When Dr Kissinger was in Cairo he was greatly surprised by the Brussels Declaration of the Nine; there had been no advance information to the State Department. Statements made by British and French diplomats in Arab capitals during and after the war were clearly anti-American in both tenor and content.

Various backbenchers said or implied in parliament that Nixon was insane.

The most the European political establishment was willing to admit was that both sides, meaning Europeans and Americans, had valid reasons for acting as they did but that neither side had come out with much credit from the whole affair.[49] Bonn was particularly apprehensive about the American rebuke for it knew only too well that it needed American protection, whereas the United States could easily exist without West German help. The West German opposition criticized the government for mishandling the crisis. The place of West Germany was with its main ally; Bonn had made a shambles out of U.S.-German relations.[50] Chancellor Brandt sent a private message to President Nixon to explain the German stand; the Italians and the smaller European states had preferred a very low profile during the crisis and were neither heard nor seen. Official French reaction came from President Pompidou, who exhorted his fellow Europeans to take some 'positive common stand' on the Middle East. He called for a Common Market summit meeting before the end of the year; the well-known writer M. F. Revel remarked dryly that this meeting, he understood, would be attended by historians. But Pompidou's move was of some importance for it preceded the Brussels statement of the E.E.C. representatives on November 6th which was adopted on French initiative. This curious document called on Israel to give up all the territory occupied since 1967 – but those who had signed later claimed that it really did not mean what it said. It also stated that the legitimate rights of the Palestinians should be taken into account, and that all countries engaged in the war should have the right to secure boundaries.[51] The declaration was hailed by M. Jobert as proof that the Europeans could take common action, if necessary; others were less sanguine about the outcome – 'E.E.C. gives in to Arabs', 'E.E.C. Nine issue statement designed to placate Arabs' were typical newspaper headlines.

The document was interesting for a number of reasons; the E.E.C. meeting had been called to discuss the oil situation and the problem of helping Holland but there was no allusion to either oil or Holland in the common declaration; perhaps they had forgotten why the meeting had been convened. The statement went beyond

Resolution 242 inasmuch as it demanded Israeli withdrawal from all territories; the Germans, the Danes and others made it known subsequently that they were not altogether happy with the Brussels Resolution. They had to shelve their reservations, for otherwise there would have been no common decision at all. Its authors regarded it as a masterly balancing act, but they had a bad press. *The Times*, for instance, said that it made a strong impression of insincerity; the obvious intention behind it was not to help the cause of peace in the Middle East but to get preferential treatment from the Arab oil-producers. But would the Arabs be so easily appeased?[52] There was a flood of cartoons about the signatories of the Brussels Resolution, all of them unflattering, there was talk about Munich, sycophancy, abject surrender to blackmail and appeasement.[53] This irritated the governments – who claimed that their critics were acting irresponsibly – but it did not induce them to change their tune. Perhaps their action was undignified; it certainly was insincere; but in the last resort oil was needed even if it involved concessions. As M. Daniel Mayer put it so inelegantly, 'One sells Jews for oil.' *

After a week of recriminations attempts were made by both Washington and the West European capitals to heal the rift. The crisis had come at a most inconvenient time for the conference in Vienna on Mutual Balance Force Reductions (M.B.F.R.) was about to begin. The West European countries were vitally interested that the Americans should not unilaterally withdraw their forces from the Continent and they had always stressed the need for Western solidarity. But when Washington had asked them during the Middle-East crisis to chill temporarily their relations with the Soviet Union so as to put some political pressure on Moscow, they had flatly refused to do so.[54] These 'misunderstandings' had to be removed; Secretary of Defence Schlesinger went to Brussels and returned outwardly satisfied. The strains were easing, there was mutual agreement that the U.S. would in future consult more fully with its allies on foreign policy whenever time allowed these

* Some leading newspapers defended government policies, notably *Le Monde* and R. Augstein, editor of *Der Spiegel*; the editor of *Die Zeit* argued that West German support for Israel would result in Neo-Nazi victories in the next elections.

communications to take place.[55] Assistant Secretary of State Joseph Sisco went to several European capitals to report on the Middle-East situation, Walter Stoessel and Helmut Sonnenfeldt paid another visit to Brussels in an attempt to save something out of the ruins of 'the Year of Europe'. The immediate aim was to draft a common declaration of principles, a kind of new Atlantic Charter which had been high on Kissinger's agenda before the Middle-East war broke out.

Among the Europeans there was also a sudden flurry of activity. Once the crisis was over, everyone talked bravely and resolutely, there were clarion calls for greater European unity. Chancellor Brandt rejected the subordination of Europe's role with the U.S. and said that the E.E.C. should be treated as an equal partner – 'Europe has become self-confident and independent enough to regard itself as an equal partner.'[56] Prime Minister Heath made a speech in a similar vein at the Lord Mayor's banquet and the unfortunate M. Jobert announced that the Soviet Union and the United States wanted to dominate the world and that a united Europe – under France's leadership – was needed to counteract these trends, for France was the most European of all nations.

Events in Europe have been reviewed in some detail despite the fact that it did not really matter very much what Europe did, or failed to do – it would not affect the situation in the Middle East one way or another. The whole tenor of the Brussels Resolution was a little ridiculous. The Middle East 'must' do this and that, as if any European country could impose its will, as if any had an army comparable to Egypt's, let alone Israel's. For Europe the October crisis was a totally unexpected hour of truth: observers had been pointing out for a long time that beneath the façade of stability, prosperity and impressive statistics, the real Europe was in a state of decay. But for the crisis this façade would not have been shattered perhaps for another five or ten years. The crisis showed the real Europe: self-confidence sapped by two world wars, national egotism time and time again being proved stronger than the tendency towards unity.

Furthermore there was deep internal unrest paralysing much of the Continent. American observers had always found it difficult to accept that a continent with 250 million inhabitants, the biggest foreign trade in the world and a most impressive G.N.P. should be politically and militarily impotent. But this was the sad truth; Europe could not defend itself and it had given up any attempts in this direction. In these conditions, the angry complaints of Messrs Heath, Pompidou and Brandt, the demands to be treated as an equal were, of course, quite ridiculous. How could there be equality between non-equals? The Europeans could have established common political institutions and a common army, but this course of action had been rejected.

The crisis could have been the 'great federator', the challenge which united Europe. But shock treatment, unfortunately, is not a panacea; sometimes it causes a deterioration in the state of the patient, and Europe, alas, was in too weak a state to benefit from shock treatment. Brandt maintained that it was wrong to seize territories but what had *Ostpolitik* been all about? It was a sad spectacle: the patent insincerity and the empty phrases – 'We are bound by the same ideals as the Americans' – as if the governments of Europe were still guided by ideals. It was sad because many had hoped that Europe would behave with a little more dignity than the medieval peasants praying to St Florian: 'God and Father, if thy thunder strikes, let it be my neighbour's house, not mine.' The issue was not in the last resort the Arab-Israeli conflict. The crisis showed that Europeans would not help one of their own who had quite arbitrarily been singled out by the oil sheikhs for a boycott. It showed the French Government appearing as the oil-producers' chief agent in Europe, hoping to achieve this way what had eluded them so far – the leadership of Western Europe.

Europe's policy was opportunistic, and any such policy has to be measured by its results. The results were a crisis in relations with America, and an acute oil shortage. Nor were the long-term perspectives encouraging; giving in to blackmail almost invariably means inviting further blackmail. But the oil sheikhs would not last forever and Europe's behaviour must have taught the Soviet Union a very important lesson: that by gaining control of the Persian Gulf they could gain control over Europe. It was surely not beyond the resources of a super-power to depose the rulers of some mini-states. Not much imagination was needed to figure out what this could mean for Europe. These then were the short-term results and the long-term perspectives of Europe's 'constructive' policy, which its architects compared with considerable pride with America's impetuosity and bungling.

For American policy-makers Europe's behaviour during the crisis was a shock which would not be easily forgotten. Europe in its present state was not only weak – it could not be trusted in an emergency whatever the issue at stake. The alliance had of course to be patched up. For years to come the diplomats would make their speeches about common sentiments and heritage. But beyond the empty talk there was the stark fact that Europe suffered from paralysis of the political will, that the alliance would survive if the going were calm in the years ahead but that Europe would again collapse if it had to face a real danger.

Kissinger the Mediator

The second truce in Egypt was holding, but for how long? The line was so complicated, with so many pockets and enclaves, that it was almost certain that the ceasefire would break down unless some more permanent arrangement was made soon.

There had been important developments, adding urgency on the diplomatic front. The Soviet Union had told Washington on October 26th that it would supply the besieged third army with its own forces and if the Israeli forces would hinder their movements they would have to bear the consequences. Whereupon an urgent message was sent by Kissinger to Mrs Meir, which was received in the early hours of the morning of Saturday, October 27th, stating that if the Israelis would not allow supplies to go through, they would be fighting the Russians on their own.[57] Official spokesmen in Washington denied that there was any pressure on Israel; Mr McCloskey said that the U.S. felt it would be useless for outside powers to insist on a return to positions held by the two parties on October 22nd, the day of the first ceasefire call. But in fact there was a great deal of pressure which caused much uneasiness in Jerusalem and as a result on October 30th Mrs Meir decided to go to Washington for talks with Nixon and Kissinger. The Israeli Government had already decided to accept the American demand, there was no alternative, as Dayan said in a speech in the Knesset. When challenged by Begin, the leader of the opposition, Dayan noted dryly that those who complained that Israel was making unnecessary concessions were apparently not aware that the shells fired that day had not been in Israel's possession a week previously. Israel had sometimes to swallow bitter pills, but it would not give in to every American demand.[58] But Mrs Meir was perturbed; in contrast to Egypt Israel had not even been consulted about the ceasefire, now there was a second peremptory American demand within a week; would this be the shape of things to come? She was concerned both by the immediate problems facing Israel and the long-term perspectives; American spokesmen had always maintained that they wanted a strong Israel, but did this tally with the demand for an almost total retreat, without peace, without any substantial concessions? Was the Rogers Plan shelved or was it still American policy? What were the Americans going to tell Ismail Fahmy, the new Egyptian foreign minister who had suddenly shown up in Washington? To find out more about U.S. intentions and to obtain American support, Mrs Meir went to Washington on October 31st accompanied by Major-General Yariv who had played a central role in the negotiations with the Egyptians. It was significant that Abba Eban was not asked by Mrs Meir to accompany her in her meetings; at a time of crisis she wanted to be her own foreign minister.

In Washington Kissinger had meanwhile announced that he would visit Cairo and other Arab capitals on his way to China; in a meeting with the Senate Foreign Relations Committee he had echoed Nixon's optimism: 'I believe we are under way to establish the ceasefire firmly and to move from the ceasefire to a durable peace.' (It was the same meeting in which he had allegedly made his disparaging remarks about NATO.) On November 1st, when Mrs Meir met first Kissinger and later on Nixon, the State Department spokesman announced that the U.S. favoured a permanent corridor through Israeli lines to provide non-military supplies to the third army. True, this was just one of several possibilities: 'We are not attempting to impose a solution. If a solution is to be reached it will have to be by the will of the parties.' Mrs Meir's talk with the president went well, which was not surprising because the conversation with him dealt with general topics. But the negotiations with Kissinger were exceedingly difficult; the secretary of state firmly demanded greater Israeli willingness to co-operate and to help create an atmosphere which would make peace talks possible. If Israel insisted on making difficulties with the third army, the ceasefire would not hold and the Russians might intervene. Kissinger said that if the Israelis withdrew to the October 22nd line, Sadat would start releasing the prisoners, an issue which was topmost in Mrs Meir's mind. She did not however accept Kissinger's arguments: Egyptian and Soviet promises could not be believed. Kissinger did not insist on the demand for a corridor, there were perhaps other ways and means of supplying the third army. But he warned Mrs Meir repeatedly that the Russians might intervene and, if so, America would be unable to protect Israel. The Russians could ask for a convention of the Security Council in which there would be an absolute majority for a resolution demanding an Israeli retreat to the lines of October 22nd; America could not possibly veto such a resolution because he, Kissinger, had agreed with Brezhnev on this point. Once there was a Security Council resolution Soviet intervention would no longer be unilateral in character but would simply enforce a United Nations' resolution.[59]

It is by no means certain that Kissinger was really so frightened by the possibility of a Soviet intervention; it was not very likely. On the other hand Kissinger needed a few trumps for his coming talks with Sadat; without some Israeli concessions he must have feared that his mission would be doomed from the outset. His talks in Washington with Ismail Fahmy had been encouraging; the new Egyptian foreign minister had the reputation, rightly or wrongly, of being pro-American; the Russians apparently mistrusted him. Fahmy made it clear that Cairo wanted an improvement in relations with the U.S. and this, of course, was the opening Kissinger had hoped for. It was Kissinger's policy at this stage to dangle incentives before the Egyptians and visions of catastrophe before Israel. In the words of one well-informed Washington observer, Kissinger told the Arabs that renewed war would mean the destruction of the third, and, possibly, also the second army.[60] Defeat would erase Sadat's war gains and endanger his regime. The Syrians could not help him, because the winter mud on the Golan favoured the Israelis. Mrs Meir on the other hand was told that the destruction of the third army would settle nothing. Israel would be totally isolated, oil pressure would turn the whole world against her, and it was not certain whether America could in the long run continue its arms supplies to Israel. (By November 14th, when the air bridge was discontinued, some 22,000 tons of war material had been shipped to Israel.)

Still Mrs Meir would not give in; there was a limit to Israeli concessions. She displayed all the intransigence which had made her a tower of strength in time of war and had obstructed progress to a settlement in days of relative peace. While accepting in principle the idea of an Israeli retreat, she insisted that the agreed line should be drawn by the military representatives of the two sides. Food, water and medicine would be supplied to the third army if the Egyptians returned the prisoners and also agreed to lift the blockade at Bab el Mandeb. Alternatively she suggested that both Israel and Egypt should withdraw ten miles from the canal, but this proposal had already been rejected by Sadat and Kissinger could not possibly accept it as a basis for discussions in Cairo. Long-term perspectives were only briefly touched upon: Mrs Meir said that Israel would insist on secure borders. She hinted, allegedly, that she would resign rather than accept any settlement which would invite further military attacks on Israel. Kissinger, who had found the going rough enough as far as the immediate problems were concerned, said that this was not the time to deal with long-term policies. Mrs Meir stayed in Washington a day longer than originally intended but even her last talk with the secretary of state on November 3rd did not affect the outcome which was, on the whole, disappointing. When Mrs Meir landed in Lod she expressed full confidence that U.S.-Israeli friendship remained as firm as ever; Kissinger said in Washington that the talks had been constructive. But in fact neither side had budged and the latent crisis in U.S.-Israeli relations had by no means been overcome. This, very briefly, was the state of affairs as Kissinger left on November 5th for Rabat, the first stage on his trip to China.

The mood in Cairo was rather pessimistic: Heykal wrote that if Kissinger could not force the Israelis back to the lines of October 22nd how could he ever push them back to the lines of 1967? On the eve of his visit the Egyptian media tried hard to create the impression that the situation was highly explosive: that it was more than likely that war would break out again any moment. If Dr Kissinger failed to prepare a political settlement this would not only affect his prestige but also have repercussions in such areas as Vietnam and Korea.[61] How failure in Cairo would influence the situation in Korea was not readily obvious, but it reflected Egyptian belief that Kissinger would not bring strong pressure on the Israelis unless he himself was subjected to considerable pressure.

Dr Kissinger was the third American secretary of state to visit Cairo; Dulles had been there in 1953, and Rogers in May 1971; neither visit had been a great success. Yet if some pessimists in the Arab world called Kissinger's visit 'Mission Impossible' there was in fact a considerable improvement in the mood in Cairo during the forty-eight hours preceding his arrival. Ismail Fahmy, who had returned to the Egyptian capital on Monday night, November 5th, had told reporters that Golda Meir had been quite unsuccessful in Washington. His original dispatches from America had been far more pessimistic; perhaps there were at last signs that America would see the light?[62] Kissinger himself showed confidence; before his departure he told assistants that the U.S. had an unusual chance to mediate since it was the only one of the super-powers which had direct contacts with all the warring parties. Developments within the next few days seemed to bear out such optimism: Kissinger arrived at midnight on November 7th and already in the morning after a three-hour talk with Sadat it was announced that the two countries would renew relations, broken off in June 1969, and that ambassadors would be exchanged soon.[63] The talks had been 'quite tough', according to reporters accompanying Kissinger, but in some ways 'better than we had expected'. When the two emerged from their meeting Kissinger said, 'I think we are moving towards peace', whereupon Sadat added, 'I agree with him.' A journalist asked, 'How rapidly?' Sadat, 'For myself let it be immediately.'[64] Cairo radio voiced some doubts: quoting Kissinger's words it said that Egypt had come close to peace many times before, but Israeli intransigence and arrogance had always frustrated it. The Israeli military establishment had said 'No' to Rogers, it could not be ruled out that it would say 'No' to Kissinger.[65]

Details of the Cairo talks became known when Joseph Sisco, accompanied by Harold Saunders of the White House staff, immediately flew from Cairo to Israel in a surprise move indicating that a breakthrough had been achieved. According to their report, Israel was to permit continuous supplies to the besieged Egyptian Army, there were to be talks between military commanders on the cease-fire lines about the return to October 22nd lines, the Israeli check-points on the Cairo-Suez road were to be replaced by U.N. checkpoints. Following this there would be an exchange of prisoners of war beginning with the wounded. According to first Israeli reports, Egypt undertook also to lift the Bad el Mandeb blockade, but the Egyptians denied this.[66] According to unconfirmed reports Israel was subsequently to withdraw its troops to a line some 13 miles east of the canal, retaining the Mitla and Gidi passes. Egypt would then withdraw its forces from the east bank; finally the third stage would provide for peace talks some time in December in Geneva or Nicosia under U.S. and Soviet or U.N. auspices.

This arrangement was in some ways closer to the Israeli point of view than what had been offered by Kissinger to Mrs Meir in Washington, but observers thought that there had been a *quid pro quo*: Kissinger had promised Sadat U.S. support for the implementation of Resolution 242, meaning an Israeli withdrawal to the pre-1967 borders with only minor rectifications. Sadat had shown greater flexibility than the Israelis in the hope, which was probably not unfounded, of far more substantial gains later on. Israel announced on the same day that it would accept the U.S. plan (which the Egyptians referred to as the 'U.N. document') but there were last-minute hitches and several cables to Kissinger, who had meanwhile reached Riyadh, the capital of Saudi Arabia. Israel sought further clarification about the check-points on the Cairo-Suez road, the linking of the return to the October 22nd positions to the broader issue of disengagement and separation of forces and the lifting of the naval blockade. The final text of the six points as announced in Jerusalem, Washington and Cairo read as follows:

Egypt and Israel agree to observe scrupulously the ceasefire called for by the U.N. Security Council.

Both sides agree that discussion between them begin immediately to settle the question of the return to the October 22nd positions in the framework of agreement on the disengagement and separation of forces under the auspices of the U.N.

The town of Suez will receive daily supplies of food, water and medicine. All wounded civilians in the town of Suez will be evacuated.

There shall be no impediment to the movement of non-military supplies to the east bank.

The Israeli checkpoints on the Cairo-Suez road will be replaced by the U.N. checkpoints. At the Suez end of the road Israeli officers can participate with the U.N. to supervise the non-military nature of the cargo at the bank of the canal.

As soon as the U.N. checkpoints are established on the Cairo-Suez road there will be an exchange of all prisoners of war, including the wounded.[67]

On Sunday, November 11th, at 3 p.m. the agreement was signed in a drab army tent pitched in the desert at Kilometre 101 of the Cairo-Suez road by General Aharon Yariv for Israel and General Mohamed Gamazy for Egypt. The meeting was presided over by the commander of the United Nations forces, General Ensio Siilasvuo. Each side signed three copies, handed them over to the other, and signed their three. The officers exchanged salutes but there were no handshakes.

Meanwhile the secretary of state on his whirlwind tour was finding the going rough in Saudi Arabia. There was a long handshake, but King Faisal was adamant, the oil supply would not be renewed unless and until all demands were fulfilled. There were rumours that the Saudis had made overtures to their arch enemies, the Russians; the monarch was old and ailing, perhaps the idea of suicide was no longer frightening.

The Russians were very quiet while Kissinger was engaged in his peace moves. Their only major initiative was an invitation extended to the leaders of the Palestinian organizations. All the factions were to be included, from the Fatah 'moderates' like Arafat to the leaders of the various wings of the Popular Front, Dr Habash and Hawatmeh. The Russians reportedly impressed on them that they had to bury their differences and submit a constructive programme, involving the recognition of Israel, albeit a very much smaller Jewish State. If they refused to participate in the peace talks King Husain and his supporters would represent the Palestinian Arab people, which was about the last thing the Russians wanted. Such advice was very much in contrast to the 'all or nothing' attitude counselled by the guerrillas' main backers, Libya and Iraq.[68] But for some guerrillas the idea of a state of their own was very tempting; it remained to be seen whether this chequered coalition of opposed forces would last, once they had to face problems transcending the fight against the Zionist invader. The Russians had an obvious interest in getting a strong foothold in a Palestinian Arab State; apart from pre-empting the Chinese, always an important consideration in Soviet policy, it would mean having yet another iron in the Middle-East fire. If there were peace one day between Israel and Egypt, and if Sadat should veer too much towards the West the Russians would be able, if at all necessary, to stoke the fire so as to perpetuate Arab dependence on the Soviet Union.

Meanwhile in Peking Kissinger was musing on the pros and cons of a security treaty with Israel. If Israel gave up the territories this would pose a very serious problem and the question of guarantees would arise; 'we have to ask the question – what sort of guarantees: unilateral, several countries and so forth.'[69] The idea had been voiced several years earlier by Senator Fulbright and it was now studied in Washington 'at the very highest level'. How much a Soviet guarantee would appeal to Israel, how much a European guarantee would be worth, could easily be imagined. But there was also the gravest doubt with regard to an American guarantee; if Senator Fulbright and his friends had their way would America still have the military power actively to intervene – assuming there was the will to do so? Kissinger himself had said, admittedly in private conversation, that 'nobody was convinced anymore that any kind of U.S. guarantee is any good. It is plain to the world that the U.S. does not keep the promises it makes.'[70] Would Israel not share the sentiment expressed by Chou En-lai to French visitors: *'La bombe atomique c'est la paix'*?

But these were questions for the more distant future. The accord signed on November 11th could be the first step on the long road to peace if the Egyptians were able to resist those forces in the Arab world who demanded a struggle to the end, and if the Israelis showed sufficient wisdom to give up temporary, limited advantages in an attempt to reach a wider and perhaps lasting settlement. No one in Jerusalem, Cairo or that tent in the desert expected a rapid settlement; hostility and distrust were too deeply engrained and the forces who had a vested interest in the perpetuation of the conflict were very strong indeed. There were at best protracted negotiations ahead, very probably also breakdowns in the talks, further crises and perhaps a renewal of the fighting. The situation in Vietnam had shown how little an armistice could mean. Peace was anything but assured and if there was a spark of hope it had to do with the fact that the alternative to a settlement would lead both sides further on to the road to destruction.

Chapter Six   The Oil Weapon

Oil, it has been said, seems to bring out the worst in nations.[1] Oil has no more magic qualities than other minerals or raw materials; it simply happens to be essential at present for the functioning of modern industrial society, and it will remain vital for some time to come. Oil is unequally distributed among the nations of the world, and some leading industrial countries have none at all. Thus it was bound to become the object of rivalry and conflict and temporarily to bestow on some of the owners of the oilfields power and influence quite out of proportion to the size of the country, its population, its general importance in the world and its military strength.

The idea of using oil as a political weapon against 'imperialism' and Israel was not born in October 1973. Radical Arab spokesmen had advocated such a course of action for many years, Soviet commentators had for an even longer period advised the Arabs to use the oil weapon against the West. In 1956 and again in 1967 Arab oil-producing countries had temporarily cut their supplies to Western Europe, causing some disruption but no lasting damage. Yet when in 1973 the Arab oil-producing states decided to cut production and stop supplies to certain countries altogether their decision had an enormous impact on West European policy and it affected America's course of action to a much greater extent than ever before. In order to understand what caused this reversal and what it implies for the future we have to examine briefly the peculiar nature of the international oil business, as well as the politics of the oil-producing countries themselves.

In theory, the three dimensions of the international oil business – economic, fiscal and political – should intersect, but if they ever do, they rarely seem to produce a coherent result. Usually they simply do not add up. This is why one reputable oil economist, Professor M. A. Adelman of M.I.T., could proclaim in 1973 before the outbreak of the war that there was no oil shortage in sight but rather a vast surplus that would continue to 1985 and beyond, a surplus that should ensure virtual price stability; while an equally

196

reputable expert, Walter J. Levy, could express great alarm about the price of future oil supplies and indeed about their absolute availability. Both were arguing from roughly the same set of facts, but each was looking at a different dimension of the oil business.

According to textbook economics, the size of fully proven oil reserves in the Persian Gulf, 367 billion barrels, should indeed, as Professor Adelman claimed, result in a buyers' market with plentiful supplies. For even by 1985, worldwide imports from the Gulf are unlikely to exceed 15.5 billion barrels a year, including just under 4 billion barrels a year for the United States. In other words, even if it is assumed that not one additional barrel of reserves will be added to the *proven* fields in Saudi Arabia, Iran, Kuwait, Iraq, and the sheikhdoms, Persian Gulf oil would suffice for $23\frac{1}{2}$ years of world demand at 1985 rates of consumption. Moreover, every oilman with experience of the area believes that the 367-billion-barrel reserve figure is much too low an estimate.

In physical and economic terms, then, Professor Adelman was clearly right: there *is* plenty of oil; and since operating costs amount to about 5 per cent of the sale price, or at most 10 per cent in the less prolific fields, the price of oil should not increase even if there were a 400 per cent growth in demand. Indeed, the price of oil could even go down – if, that is, the owners of the different oilfields were to compete with each other to capture greater shares of the market.

Walter J. Levy's projection of world-wide demand for Middle-East oil was somewhat higher than Adelman's, but it was not over the data that they disagreed. Levy simply believed that economic facts would not matter. Having observed the oil business since the 'thirties, Levy saw no reason to think that the restrictive 'cartel' structure of the industry would change. The only difference would be that, instead of a company cartel, the industry would become a 'host-country' cartel (to use a term which is now obsolescent, since the 'hosts' are getting rid of their guests, and going into the production end of the business on their own or at least taking the profits). And, Levy argued, if the Organization of Petroleum Exporting Countries (O.P.E.C.)* does indeed continue to function as an

* O.P.E.C. is made up of Abu Dhabi, Algeria, Indonesia, Iran, Iraq, Kuwait, Libya, Nigeria, Qatar, Saudi Arabia and Venezuela.

effective cartel, the physical surplus of oil will be irrelevant, since the 'host' countries will restrict supplies and charge whatever the market will bear.

All but two of the Persian Gulf producers (Iran and Iraq) do not even *need* the additional cash flow that more abundant oil sales would generate. Thus, Levy pointed out, there may be no way of inducing them to produce additional oil, and certainly they will have no incentive to lower prices in order to sell more oil. For the Sheikh of Abu Dhabi, or even for the Saudis, an ever-greater cash surplus would simply make them more attractive targets for insurrection or external attack; in the Saudi case, spending money for large-scale economic and social development would create a new class of detribalized ex-Bedouins who would no longer tolerate a monarchy that is still alien to most Arabians two generations after the Saudi conquest. As it is, much of the money paid to these countries by the oil companies has been deposited at very low interest rates in Swiss franc-Deutschmark accounts, or invested in depreciating dollar bonds.

According to Adelman, it was the U.S. State Department that had supported the 'majors', or, as their critics like to call them, 'the seven sisters' (B.P., Shell, Jersey or Exxon, Stancal or Chevron, Texaco, Gulf and Mobil) in their appeasement of O.P.E.C. And it was the State Department that had persistently discouraged any talk of meeting blackmail with sanctions. Adelman's solution was to induce the 'majors' to give up the production end of the business. This would turn them into marketing companies, which would have every incentive to buy oil at the cheapest possible price in order to maximize their 'downstream' profits. Adelman asserted that this would weaken O.P.E.C.'s 'host-country' cartel, and that the latter could even break up as its members began to underbid each other in order to sell their oil.

Levy, however, foresaw precisely the opposite happening. He pointed out that with the short-sighted unilateralism that is also painfully evident in East-West relations, the developed nations of the world were competing with each other in courting the favour of the tinpot dictators, kings, emirs, sheikhs and self-appointed presidents of the Persian Gulf. Thus the Japanese had chosen to advertise the fact that they would never support any use of military force or *even political pressure* on the oil-producers, and most European powers agreed. This meant that the internally fragile and quite defenceless mini-states of the Gulf would be allowed to wage what would amount to economic warfare against the West (to which Japan belongs in this context) while the West in turn would abide by a self-denying ordinance that would deprive it of any means of exerting countervailing pressure. Levy thought that in the absence of an adequate incentive – and mere money would not suffice – only a *political* entente among the consumer nations could bring the energy economy of the West into balance by posing the ultimate threat of force.

Neither Levy nor Adelman nor any other reputable energy economist believed that there was a substantial alternative to O.P.E.C. oil over the next decade, or indeed into the 1990s. To look at one example of a much-advertised alternative, fuel extracted from the tar sands of Canada: it would take a capital cost of the order of $60 billion – with many more billions needed for feeder lines, storage systems and trunk pipelines, not to mention environmental damage – to supply all projected U.S. import needs for 1985. In the Middle East the comparable costs would be less than one-tenth as much, and with no environmental damage to speak of – even if it mattered in the wastes of Arabia.

The *long-term* prospects of atomic energy, on the other hand, are now considerably brighter than even a few years ago. Until recently all reactor systems planned were based on the use of nuclear fission, which is not very efficient, requires a great deal of uranium, and also involves the major problem of radioactive waste disposal. The process of nuclear fusion, in contrast, could provide a literally unlimited supply of heat for conversion into electricity; and deuterium, on which the process will ultimately be based, provides an inexhaustible fuel supply, and avoids the problem of the disposal of nuclear waste. But major *scientific* as well as technological problems remain to be solved. Progress since the middle 'sixties has been impressive and the speed of *technological* advance will largely depend on the financial allocations made; but the scientific factors are unknown, and more research money could simply be wasted. At present the Atomic Energy Commission's fusion research budget is only $90 million annually.

Significantly, some leading oil companies, including Gulf and Shell, have gone nuclear in recent years. Hardly anyone expects that nuclear energy will contribute more than 15 per cent of total U.S. energy supply by 1985 or much more than twice that at the end of the century – though much depends on the priority assigned to energy self-sufficiency. At the cost of one year's growth in the G.N.P. even present technology could supply all the general energy and all the synthetic fuel needed.

As for the 'realistic' self-sufficiency programme for the U.S. now being promoted by the 'major'-supported National Petroleum Council (N.P.C.), which calls for 90 per cent self-sufficiency by 1985, this is both expensive and environmentally undesirable. Among other things, this programme entails the construction of 435 nuclear (fission) plants (of one million kilowatts each) as well as 70 assorted shale-extraction, coal-gasification, coal-liquefaction and geothermal plants. The programme assumes, moreover, a 37 per cent increase in domestic natural-gas and oil production, in addition to a 176 per cent increase in coal output – all by 1985. Even if one is disenchanted with the environmentalist lobby and its professional alarmism, it is obvious that the N.P.C. programme would result in serious environmental damage – not to mention a substantial increase in energy prices to the consumer.

Obviously, if the oil business were like any other industry – dominated, that is, by *economic* considerations of profits and costs – the currently projected energy needs of Europe and Japan (which the N.P.C. programme would not help to satisfy), and those of the United States, would cause no alarm, any more than the projected need for imports of luxury automobiles and Scandinavian 'hostesses' into the Persian Gulf causes alarm to the O.P.E.C. nations. But while there is no Organization of Automobile Exporting Countries and no international cartel for blondes, there is an Organization of Petroleum Exporting Countries, and one that is fortified both by the solidarity of shared victories and the well-founded expectations of still greater successes in the future.

When O.P.E.C. was founded thirteen years ago, few observers expected that this timid alliance of conservative states would become the Frankenstein monster of the oil world. Like any bona-fide international body, O.P.E.C. acquired a headquarters building, a (Venezuelan) secretary-general, a well-paid staff of consultants ready to turn out elegantly bound reports at a moment's notice. But unlike many other similarly equipped organizations, O.P.E.C. also had a clear purpose, in fact only *one* purpose: 'Price stability,' or in other words, high oil prices.

Being a cartel, O.P.E.C. would be no stronger than the weakest of its members, and its membership included – as it still does – some of the most fragile states of the world: Kuwait was still a British protectorate, Iran and Saudi Arabia were submissive clients of the U.S. and all but one, Iraq, were effectively dominated by the production consortia established on their soil. Even the fairly erratic Iraqis were careful not to go too far, and for all their bombast they refrained from nationalizing the production acreage of the Iraq Petroleum Company. In fact, O.P.E.C. was so fragile a creature that it only survived because the 'majors' adopted towards it the policy they still pursue, of mild public opposition and strong private support. For once they had absorbed the shock of seeing the natives joining in a common front – as they themselves had been doing for decades – the 'majors' realized that O.P.E.C. could be used as a decisive weapon in their fight to keep prices high in the face of aggressive competition from the 'independents', the 'nationals' (such as E.N.I. of Italy and Petrobas of Brazil) and the Russians.

The one thing the 'majors' did not anticipate in O.P.E.C.'s early years – when it could have been easily destroyed – was that some power other than themselves could make use of the organization. Nor, in fairness, did anyone else anticipate the emergence of the once-complaisant Shah of Iran as the aggressive leader of O.P.E.C. Qadafi has made more noise, but it is generally recognized that it was the Shah's persistent and finally successful attempt to achieve a quantum jump in his oil revenues that transformed O.P.E.C. into the powerful cartel of today.

Engaged in a large-scale programme of economic development and land reform, with a prudently commensurate expansion of his army/police repressive base, the Shah began to press the Iranian consortium for a rapid increase in output and hence in his own tax revenues. But the interlocking ownership structure of Gulf oil meant that the partners in the Iranian consortium had no incentive to lift more oil there at the expense of growth elsewhere in the Gulf. The leading company in Iran, B.P., whose share of the output amounted to 40 per cent, was already 'long' on crude and did not want more in Iran. It preferred to 'offtake' more in Kuwait, where its share was 50 per cent, or in Abu Dhabi where its share was only 23.75 per cent, but where its profit per barrel was also higher. Jersey (Exxon) was in a similar position. Its share of Iranian output was only 6 per cent while it had 30 per cent of Aramco liftings in Saudi Arabia, and Aramco rules penalized partners who did not take their full share of a production increase.

After toying with an 'economic' solution (i.e. a tax cut), the Shah tried the political highroad: he threatened retaliation unless the consortium agreed to lift much more oil at a rapid and specified rate. At the same time he skilfully diffused opposition from other Gulf producers (whose own production growth would thereby be curtailed) by propounding a new criterion, based on Iran's large population and vast developmental needs and, more to the point, by promising the political support and security assistance of a strong Iran to the weak states on the Arab side of the Gulf.

In this first confrontation, the pattern of events that followed all the way to expropriation was set: the U.S. State Department strongly urged the 'majors' to be conciliatory; the French announced their willingness to help Iran if the consortium should show a fight. From Italy to Japan the irresolution and disarray of the consumer nations were made very evident. That the Libyans went on to limit output (1970), raise taxes (repeatedly), and finally expropriate B.P. (in 1972) and its U.S. 'independent' partner, Hunt (in 1973), surprised no one.

Like the 'majors', O.P.E.C. believed in maximizing profits per barrel, instead of maximizing revenues on expanded sales – as many naive entrepreneurs persist in doing outside the oil business.

It was for all these reasons that Walter J. Levy, hitherto a consistent supporter of accommodation with the 'host' countries, declared at the March 1973 Euro-American Amsterdam Conference that the world energy equation could not be balanced if the sanction of force were removed. So far, however, no form of genuine co-operation among the consumer nations has materialized, while the prospect of *forceful* co-operation remains very remote.

Oil and Political Power

Because the oil industry is not dominated by economic considerations, the countries which have most of the proven reserves and the extra capacity to supply oil – Saudi Arabia, Iran and the Persian Gulf emirates – have become very important in any consideration of what the future holds. There is every reason to assume that by the end of the decade all oilfields and installations will be nationalized, or that there will be something like 100 per cent participation on the part of the producer countries. In any case, the local governments will be in effective control of operations, and the question of who will be in power in Riyadh, Tehran, Kuwait and Abu Dhabi is therefore crucial.

It was widely believed until recently that the Arabs (to put it crudely) would have to sell their oil anyway, since they could not drink it. This is true to the extent that the more populous countries such as Iraq need all the money they can get for their ambitious domestic development plans. But it is only partly true of Saudi Arabia, which was able to make use of only 60 per cent of its oil income in 1973. To the mini-states like Kuwait, which has already put aside some $6 billion in investments, a billion dollars more or less does not really matter. Colonel Qadafi or the Kuwaitis rightly argue that since oil prices constantly rise, a barrel of oil in the ground is worth more than a barrel on the market. Libya's present production is only about half of what it was in 1970. As for the smaller countries like Abu Dhabi (population 55,000) which a few years hence will produce as much oil as Kuwait does at present, it is difficult to think of any convincing Western argument that expansion of output to match Western demand will be worth their while. If they cannot drink oil, they cannot eat gold either. Once they have collected their first few billion dollars, the smaller Middle-Eastern countries can cut production or stop it altogether for a lengthy period without suffering major harm.

Nature has certainly been most unjust in distributing the oilfields of the Middle East; they should have been located in poor countries like Egypt which desperately need capital. But they are not, and these vagaries of nature will almost certainly have far-reaching political consequences. For however great the riches these small or thinly populated countries amass, they will remain weak and hence exposed to danger. In less enlightened ages, these states would have been taken over by their more powerful neighbours, or at least held to ransom, just as rich medieval cities had to pay tribute to robber knights and highwaymen. In our day more subtle methods are applied, such as take-over by proxy. This does not entirely rule out direct super-power intervention, should the situation in the Middle East get out of control altogether; it would not be the first time the Middle East has been divided into spheres of influence. Such high-handed action could even be justified in Marxist-Leninist terms. For if monopolies are not tolerated any longer in any advanced country, and if the super-rich are heavily taxed or even expropriated, there is no valid reason to accept super-rich mini-states monopolizing the oil supply, provided adequate compensation is paid to the former owners and the oil is made accessible at cheap prices to all countries.

Among the oil-producing states in this area, Iran is the strongest and most stable, but the vacuum created by Britain's withdrawal from most positions east of Suez has had immediate repercussions on Persian policy. Iran's defence budget has increased twenty-fold since 1968, and the Shah's shopping list during his visit to Washington in 1973 included one of the biggest helicopter fleets in the world and F-14 aircraft; elsewhere the Persians are acquiring Chieftain tanks and missile-firing ships. Five years ago Iran felt reasonably secure, maintaining excellent relations with the Soviet bloc, the West, and most of its neighbours. Today it feels threatened from several directions: the break-up of Pakistan, the coup in Afghanistan, Indian designs in the Persian Gulf, Iraqi intrigues and aggression, have all contributed to this change.

Not all of these dangers are immediate or constitute an overwhelming threat to Iran's security. India, that colossus on feet of clay, is much too absorbed in internal affairs to pursue an active foreign policy, far away from its own borders. Iraq, Iran's main foe, will go exactly as far as the Russians permit; and the Russians do not seem eager at the moment to risk a major crisis in the Gulf. But this may change, and the Shah has mended his fences with the Saudis and the smaller oil-producing states in the Gulf. Nevertheless, there remains a good deal of traditional suspicion between

Persians and Arabs: the Arabs know that while the Shah has been making sympathetic noises regarding their grievances against Israel, they can count on his active help about as much as on Venezuela's.

There is no doubt about Iran's progress in recent years nor its prospects for further advance. But such progress on its own does not guarantee political stability. The extreme Left and extreme Right continue to oppose the Shah's policy, and there are separatist tendencies in Khuzistan (fostered by the Iraqis from across the border) and in other parts of the country. Manifestations of open hostility to the regime are restricted on the whole to Persian students in America and Western Europe; with a few exceptions SAVAK, the political police, has been able to prevent the emergence of terrorist gangs on the Turkish pattern. Yet if there is no strong opposition to the regime, there is no widespread organized support either, simply because political activity on the domestic scene has been discouraged. The danger to the present regime is a military coup on the Arab pattern.

Of Kuwait's 700,000 inhabitants, the majority are not locals but Palestinians, Iraqis and others, without whose technical and administrative skills the city-state would soon collapse. Kuwait has a little army of some 8,000 men on whose expansion no less than $500 million are spent; it has bought Phantoms from the United States and three squadrons of fighters from Britain. It pays some $200 million yearly to Egypt, Jordan, and al-Fatah as a way of expressing sympathy with the cause of Arabism, and, incidentally, to assure its survival. But it remains highly vulnerable. The native Kuwaitis have become rich (one-family apartments for $300,0000 are no longer a rarity), whereas the foreigners who do the work are treated like servants. A threat of attack from outside coupled with a rising from within would find the country quite defenceless. Kuwaiti oil revenues are at present about $2 billion, making it the country with the highest standard of living in the world, with the exception of Abu Dhabi – in theory at least. By the end of the decade revenues will be at least three times as high, making the attraction for a would-be invader well nigh overwhelming.

Kuwait has survived so far owing to the delicate balance of power in the Persian Gulf with Iran, Iraq and Saudi Arabia directly involved and the big powers discreetly in the background. The same goes *a fortiori* for the mini-mini-states like Abu Dhabi, Dubai, the Sultanate of Oman (population 750,000) and Qatar with 115,000 inhabitants. They are all 'nice little oligarchies' (to quote a recent writer) governed by ruling families with countless cousins, nephews, and especially uncles, who among them occupy all key positions; coups are of course frequent.

Saudi Arabia is now the biggest oil-producer in the Middle East and it also has the largest reserves. When Lee Dinsmore, former U.S. Consul General at Dahran, appeared at the House of Representatives hearings on U.S. interests in the Persian Gulf in 1972, the first question he was asked by the chairman, Lee Hamilton (D. Ind.), was, 'Mr Dinsmore, how stable is the Saudi Arabian Government today?' Mr Dinsmore, tongue in cheek, 'The regime of Saudi Arabia is as stable as it has ever been.' Hamilton, 'Are there sources of discontent in the country?' Mr Dinsmore, 'If there are sources of discontent in the country, they did not talk to American diplomats.'

This seems to be a very fair description of the prevailing state of affairs, even though it is not very enlightening. Following Egypt's eclipse, Saudi Arabia's importance in Arab affairs has increased. But the political base of the regime is as narrow as it ever was. While King Faisal is a great improvement over Saud, his predecessor, the country is still run by the royal family as if it were its private property, with an inner core of some 500 princes of varying importance; together with their retainers they may number 5,000. The oil industry employs altogether 15,000 people out of a population of 5 million. But there are 700,000 foreigners, including many Yemenites, Egyptians and Palestinians. Reluctant concessions to the modern world have not so far transformed the Saudi Arabian desert into the paradise promised by Ahmed Zaki Yamani, the influential oil minister. Newspapers, the two local universities and social clubs are under strictest supervision; in comparison with Saudi Arabia, autocratic Kuwait is a permissive society, an anarchist's utopia. But strict controls have not been sufficient to quench the spirit of rebellion. There have been five attempted coups in recent years, mainly involving the Saudi air force.

The remaining two major oil-producers in the Middle East are Libya and Iraq; their politics have been discussed elsewhere in this study.

Oil Embargo 1973

The oil embargo imposed by the Arab states in 1973 was far more successful than any similar attempt in the past, because the dependence of the industrial countries on the oil supply had risen sharply during the preceding years. So much has been written on the energy gap that only the essential facts will be reiterated in the following. The yearly increase in world demand in 1973 was 21 billion barrels, which mainly came from the Middle East. Western Europe imported almost 85 per cent of the oil it needed from the Middle East, Japan about 90 per cent and even U.S. imports had risen from 3 per cent in 1971 to more than 5 per cent in 1973. According to reliable forecasts total U.S. demand ten years hence was likely to be 29 million barrels a day of which more than half would have to be imported. It was predicted that total world demand in 1985 would be 40 billion barrels; while it was thought that Middle-East output could perhaps be doubled from its 1973 level (8 billion barrels), many experts thought it was unlikely that even in ideal conditions – disregarding both politics and finance – Middle-Eastern oil could possibly provide all the oil that would be needed. Some observers thought that even by 1978 production would no longer be able to meet the increase in demand.[2] The experts urged radical rethinking and new planning to meet the coming crisis; some even maintained that an interruption in Western oil supplies in the near future 'would be in our long-run best interest'. For it would provide a shock, compelling the consumer countries to take decisions which would have otherwise been postponed with perhaps fatal consequences.

Appeals to use the 'oil weapon' were voiced almost immediately after the war had broken out. The Palestine Liberation Organization announced that 'Arab oil must become a weapon for the Arabs – let the flow be stopped immediately. The Arab countries on the Red Sea are duty bound to stop and prevent all the oil tankers and ships proceeding to Israel.'[3] Kuwait was prodding neighbouring Iraq with which it had a long account to settle: why was Iraq not taking a more positive stand towards the battle, instead of playing up its ideological reservations?[4] But Iraq was not idle; the Baghdad government almost immediately nationalized the holdings of American companies in the Basra Petroleum Company. A few days later it nationalized the Dutch shares, because Holland had allegedly taken a pro-Israeli stand; in fact Holland supported Resolution 242 of the Security Council. The Iraqi Government newspaper *Al Thawra*, calling the 'masses' to strike at the American interests, wrote, 'Our enemy is using our oil as a weapon to fight us.'[5] Kuwait could not lag behind and its council of ministers took the initiative, asking the other Arab oil-producing countries to hold an urgent meeting to deliberate on the role of oil in the war – suggesting Kuwait as the place where the meeting should take place.[6] Iraq, not to be left behind, issued a similar invitation: 'What are we waiting for? Our oil is our sharpest weapon. The Arab masses demand the suspension of the flow of oil ...'[7]

The Arab oil-producers met at the Kuwait Sheraton Hotel on October 17th under the chairmanship of the Algerian oil minister and decided 'to make the United States aware of the exorbitant price the great industrial states are paying as a result of the blind and limitless support for Israel.'[8] They agreed to reduce production immediately by not less than 5 per cent. This was to continue until Israel withdrew from the occupied Arab territories and the rights of the Palestinian people were restored. Present were Abu Dhabi, Algeria, Bahrein, Dubai, Egypt, Iraq, Kuwait, Libya, Qatar, Saudi Arabia and Syria. Next a competition began as to who would make the sharpest increase in the price of oil. There had been several price increases during the previous months but they were relatively small. Libya announced on October 19th that its oil would cost 28 per cent more quite irrespective of the war and Israel's misdeeds. This may have been in answer to the Saudi decision the day before to cut production by 10 rather than 5 per cent. The same day Abu Dhabi announced that it would halt oil exports to the United States altogether. Iraq proclaimed that the price of its oil would go up by 70 per cent, 'a basic turning point in the history of the oil industry'.[9] And so the escalation continued: Saudi Arabia and the other oil-producers stopped oil to America altogether; Algeria and Kuwait also included Holland in their boycott. The general feeling was that something had to be done; the fact that less than 5 per cent of the Arab oil went to the United States was thought to be of no importance, and that the under-developed countries of Asia and Africa (such as India) would suffer infinitely more was not taken into consideration either. Given the highly complicated nature of the oil industry it was virtually impossible to enforce a total boycott against any country; it was quite possible that Arab oil would even end up in Israel. But on the other hand the oil-producers assumed quite correctly that it would be easy to intimidate Europe and Japan, and that these countries would exert great pressure on the United States to make Israel retreat and to restore the flow of oil.

The United States was facing a serious energy crisis; energy consumption between 1950 and 1970 had doubled, and it was expected to double again between 1970 and 1985. In 1972 two-thirds of the U.S. balance of payments deficit, about $4 billion, resulted from energy imports, mostly oil. It was calculated that this deficit would rise to some $7 billion in 1973 and $10 billion or more by 1975. These calculations did not even take into account the enormous price increases announced by the Arab producers quite irrespective of the war in the Middle East. According to authoritative projections the oil earnings of the producers would amount to between $50 and $150 billion, as much as the world's combined reserves of gold and foreign exchanges in 1973. All other problems apart this raised the question of how the United States (and, *a fortiori*, the other industrialized nations) would be able to pay for the oil imports. Pressure was mounting for a massive research and development programme, something on the scale of the Space Programme, to make America self-sufficient in the 'eighties. Senator Jackson, a key Congressional figure, suggested that a ten-year, $20 billion programme could have this effect. There was growing support for these schemes, for in addition to all other considerations growing American dependence on Arab oil would have had the gravest consequences for U.S. financial stability and national security. Thus, seen in a wider perspective, the 'declaration of war' by Arab oil-producers was indeed a blessing in disguise; it could have had the most serious consequences had it come four or five years later. At an O.P.E.C. oil meeting in Vienna during the first week of the war a delegate told an American friend, 'We are helping you to find new sources quickly.'[10] As the producers were talking about pushing the price of Persian Gulf oil up from $3 to $5 a barrel, an American commentator noted that it would be as economical in this case for the American companies to extract oil from shale in Wyoming as to buy it from Aramco.[11] Meanwhile there would be shortages, especially on the East coast of the United States, and Melvin Laird was widely quoted: 'Buy a sweater, it may get a little cold...'[12]

The main hope of the Arab oil-producers – neither Iran nor Nigeria or Venezuela participated in the embargo – was to cause disruption in Western Europe, which was most exposed to their pressure. Britain and Norway were in the long run least vulnerable in view of the North Sea findings, but there were no major oilfields on the Continent, and furthermore there had been in Western Europe the same lackadaisical attitude towards energy as towards defence. Thus the countries of Europe reacted to the imposition of the oil embargo like a bunch of scared rabbits. This is not to say that these countries did not face a serious crisis, but panic is hardly ever a good counsellor. Even in Britain, whose electrical power supply depended only to some 20 per cent on oil, there was talk about an additional burden of £1 billion to the balance of payments. The French reacted by raising oil prices, Italy and Belgium cut exports of kerosene and gasolene, and most other European countries gradually introduced controls. Holland was hardest hit because it became subject to a total boycott, and though the president of the E.E.C. promised that it would be helped, it was soon to appear that European solidarity was but skin deep and that in an emergency every country would put its own interests first. Economic growth was jeopardized and further dissension caused between Europe and the U.S. The Americans argued that they had helped Europe during the 1956-7 crisis when there had been an Arab oil embargo, and it was now Europe's turn to be generous and share its oil supplies.[13] But the Europeans had not the slightest intention of being generous; they argued that America would have to restrict its consumption, it was not fair that 6 per cent of the world's population should consume one-third of its energy. Thus within a mere three weeks Europe was in a state of total disarray.

What were the oil-producers' terms for lifting the oil ban? The

Libyans, as usual, were the most extreme: Qadafi spoke about 'ruining Europe's industry' and suggested in passing the conversion of Europe to Islam; after all Europe was only the geographical extension of Africa and the Middle East. One would assume that a declaration of this kind would be received with something less than enthusiasm in the Vatican, but this was not so. Monsigneur Alessandrini, an official spokesman of the Vatican, praised the 'unifying power' of oil and said that the Arabs were quite entitled to use the oil weapon; after all the Jews had mobilized high finance for such a long time. It was later announced, to prevent any misunderstandings, that this declaration should not be construed as a renewed expression of traditional church anti-semitism.[14] Colonel Jalloud, Qadafi's deputy, said in an interview that the Arabs, or at any rate his country, would renew the delivery of oil only if they received certain weapons (including strategic weapons) which had been refused to them previously. The future belonged to the third world – Europe had to obey or to go under.[15] The Saudis were more moderate, they merely wanted to put pressure on the U.S. to reduce support for Israel. The Saudi oil minister told a visiting American congressman, 'This winter, when there is a shortage of fuel in the United States and your people begin to suffer – the change will begin. Americans are not used to being uncomfortable.'[16] The Iraqis, usually the most radical among the producers, boycotted the U.S., Holland and Israel, but otherwise maintained and even increased production; they argued that it was stupid and counterproductive not to supply oil to Europe, which had shown a friendly attitude towards the Arab cause.

The oil producers were of course aware that tactics and targets would have to vary from country to country. From Japan one could safely demand the severance of relations with Israel, from Europe that they should stop trading with Israel, whereas from the United States less could be expected. Japan, the biggest customer of Saudi Arabia and Abu Dhabi, was particularly exposed to the threat; as an Arab spokesman put it, 'Either they break off diplomatic and trade relations with Israel or we break their balls.'[17] With regard to Western Europe various categories of priorities of 'most favoured nations', 'favoured nations' and 'unfriendly nations' were established with apparently several degrees in between. Countries were upgraded and demoted according to undertakings and promises made by their governments. The existence of these undertakings was indignantly denied by European diplomats; thus Sir Alec Douglas-Home: 'There has been a great deal of talk recently about submission to Arab blackmail. This is nonsense. The Arabs have made no demand on us and we have offered no price.'[18] But Nadim Pachachi, former head of O.P.E.C., revealed that Britain, France and Spain *had* given certain undertakings (for instance that they would participate in the boycott of Holland) and as a result they had been included in the list of the most favoured nations. The British press was a little more outspoken than the foreign secretary: 'Britain's oil is safe – if we behave ourselves.'[19] Such treatment, needless to say, was unfair to West Germany and the other European governments which had signed the anti-Israeli declaration together with Britain and France, without getting any *quid pro quo*. The German Government also denied that it had been threatened in any way; but in fact Qadafi had put an ultimatum to Chancellor Brandt to make a 'satisfactory declaration' not later than November 6th about Germany's policy in the Middle-East conflict.[20] Daghely, the Libyan ambassador in Bonn, said in an interview that if the Germans regarded the boycott as blackmail, he would not quarrel with them.[21] It was not readily obvious why European politicians continued to deny that they were subjected to heavy political pressure or that they had acceded to most demands at a time when the threats and the oral understandings were common knowledge.

Europe had been warned a long time ago. In January 1970 the American representative had informed the Europeans at a confidential meeting of O.E.C.D. that after 1975 they could not count on American supplies in the case of an embargo; such supplies, it will be recalled, had reached Europe during the war of 1956 and again in 1967. In the event, it appeared that as a result of the strong increase in world demand even this warning had been over-optimistic. Half-hearted attempts to work out a common European energy policy failed in 1971-2 because national egotism again prevented any long-term planning in the common interest. France, as so often, was the chief offender; the French argued that they would not accept rules with regard to the import of oil unless a market organization was established beforehand. When the war broke out the European countries were obliged to have a reserve for 65 days; it had been envisaged that this reserve would be extended to 90 days by 1975. The results of the oil embargo are known: the lights went out in Washington and London, and even the Greeks, who should have qualified for 'most favoured nation' status, had to stop flood-lighting the Acropolis. That Queen Juliana of Holland was seen riding a bicycle came as no surprise, but Mrs Indira Gandhi, too, took to riding in a two-wheeled horse-drawn gig. (Indian policy had been consistently pro-Arab, but according to the polls 80 per cent of the Indian public supported the Israelis; the oil-producers no doubt wanted to re-educate the Indian public.) The price of petrol went up all over the world, rationing was introduced, there were speed limitations and driving was banned on certain days.

The total ban on oil supply to Holland was the test of faith for Europe. Holland had been strictly neutral during the war; Israeli ships which had called at Dutch ports on October 7th had not been permitted to load arms. With equal justice the Arab oil-producers could have singled out other European countries such as Germany, Denmark and even Britain, because leading politicians had made pro-Israeli statements. But imposing a ban on Holland had the double advantage of hitting a country which had traditional sympathies for Israel, and putting the squeeze at the same time indirectly on other European countries. Europe received 17 per cent of its oil imports through Rotterdam. The Dutch almost immediately invoked Article 34 of the Treaty of Rome, according to which export licensing systems must not be used within the E.E.C. and commodities must circulate freely. Sr Ortoli, the President of E.E.C., assured the Dutch that they could count on the help of the community, but the initial scepticism of the Dutch about European solidarity was only too justified: the French, with the connivance of the British Government, declared their readiness to join in the Arab blockade of Holland, 'clearly a contradiction of the spirit as well as the practice of the European community'.[22]

The French answer to the Dutch call for help was brutally frank, the British more hypocritical. Messmer, the French prime minister, said in a speech at Le Creusot that the oil-producers were perfectly entitled to sell their commodity to anyone they chose, and since France wanted to establish with them 'a confident, balanced and lasting relationship', it was in no position to extend any help to the Dutch. Other French leaders blamed the Dutch for having brought their misfortune upon themselves; why did they have to be nice to the Israelis? As long as there was no common European foreign policy there could be no effective co-operation in an economic emergency. It should be noted in passing that France wanted to use the opportunity for a little blackmail of its own; for a long time it had wanted to deflect part or all of the Rotterdam oil trade to French ports such as Lorient, and this, of course, seemed a good opportunity. The French also, more legitimately, wanted to use the occasion to remind their European colleagues that they had long been pressing their neighbours to establish a joint European plant for enriched uranium for use in nuclear power stations – but they had found little enthusiasm for their scheme. Sir Alec Douglas-Home, expressing the British point of view, said that no hasty resolution should be passed, that one needed to keep cool; the Nine should concentrate on the main political problem, namely bringing pressure on Israel. This, after all, was the essence of the problem; it was no good dealing with the consequences rather than the core of the problem. Denmark and West Germany were the only countries to express support for the Dutch. But they, too, retreated when the Libyans uttered some threats. It was decided not to call a state of crisis in the E.E.C., because this would have meant implementation of the oil-sharing system used on two previous occasions in 1956 and 1967, which would have brought Britain and France into Arab disfavour; instead, the anti-Israel resolution was passed in Brussels by all Nine, including the Dutch, in the hope that this would induce the Arab oil-producers to modify their stand. Previously the Dutch had sent diplomatic envoys to Riyadh, Kuwait and other oil capitals explaining that they had been neutral throughout the conflict, but these missions were quite unsuccessful; finally the Dutch asked the French to intervene on their behalf. But to jeopardize their special relationship with the blackmailers was about the last thing Paris wanted. In the end the Dutch were given to understand that if they behaved in future, the integrated oil companies would somehow, in some devious, under-the-counter movements, see Holland through the crisis.[23]

Following the British and French initiative, the Nine hoped they would somehow succeed in appeasing the Arabs and preventing the collapse of the E.E.C. But this was not the only immediate problem facing them. Italy was promised oil by the producers on condition that it did not use any part of it to supply fuel to the American Sixth Fleet. The same presumably applied to West Germany and other European countries; they were to withhold oil supplies to the United States on whose military protection they relied. Thus as a result of the policy advocated by France and Britain the rift within NATO was likely to deepen even further. Pompidou and Heath knowingly pursued a Gaullist line; when the Americans suggested that they might retaliate and put their national interest first there was a great commotion in Paris and London. This they had not expected of the Atlantic partner; without American help Europe could not be defended. America *must* defend Europe because of its vast investments, said the *Guardian*. A look at the statistics showed that American investments in Europe were less than 5 per cent of its yearly Gross National Product, hardly sufficient reason to keep several hundred thousand men in Europe year after year, with all the risks involved.

The European Dilemma

With the outbreak of the oil war the industrialized countries, particularly Western Europe and Japan, were faced with a danger not just to their economic well-being but to their national security and thus their very existence. It was quite immaterial whether this war would be over in a week, a month or a year; for their dependence on the oil sheikhs would continue and the tap could be turned off at any time. The danger should of course have been known: the assumption that cheap oil in unlimited quantities would be available for a long time to come was totally unfounded. The many warning signs had been ignored and the first reaction to the oil embargo was not to adopt a common policy but a scramble to get better conditions from the producers by making greater political concessions. There was concerted action, but only in a negative sense: the Europeans co-ordinated their retreat, but they would not agree on a forward-looking policy to make their oil supply more secure in the years to come.

It was not an easy situation for it compelled the Europeans to face a dilemma which has beset politicians since time immemorial: how to face blackmail? To give in to blackmail is always dishonourable but there are instances, albeit not many, in which there is no alternative but to surrender, the aim being to gain time and to enable the victim to make a more resolute stand against blackmail at some future date. On such grounds, if the Western powers had used the time gained for rearming, it would have been possible, for instance, to justify the British and French policy of appeasement between 1936 and 1939. In the event Britain and France were not much better prepared for war in 1939 than three years earlier; on the contrary, Nazi Germany benefited from the delay much more than they did. If there was a certain logic in Neville Chamberlain's policy, it is difficult to find any consistency and thought in Europe's policy vis-à-vis the Arab boycott. It had no chance of success. It could have been argued that it was pointless to make a common stand on Holland's behalf for this would have caused great damage to the whole community and also would not have helped Holland. But this was not even the rationale behind a Western policy which genuinely thought (as Messmer had said) that it would be possible to reach an agreement with the Arab oil-producers which would ensure the oil supply for many years to come. Whatever way one analyses these assumptions, it is impossible to find extenuating circumstances for such folly.

To the extent that there were rational considerations behind the European policy they can be summarized briefly as follows: but for the Arab-Israeli conflict there would have been no energy crisis. Hence the need to find a solution to the conflict which would satisfy the Arabs so as to restore the flow of oil at the earliest possible date. In a similar vein certain circles in America had argued in the 'fifties that (as one observer put it) but for the existence of Israel the oilmen would get their concessions in Arab lands, the generals their bases and the missionaries their converts. This line of argument had ignored the fact that not only the Arabs could shut the oil tap; if driven hard Israel too had the means of disrupting oil supplies from the Arab world. To do so would not make the Israelis more popular in the industrialized world, but if driven against the wall, they might not care about their popularity which was at low ebb anyway. But this was not the only, nor the main flaw in this train of thought. For, assuming that the Arab-Israeli conflict could somehow be solved according to the Arabs' demand and assuming furthermore that the Western countries would make an all-out effort to lessen their dependence on Middle-Eastern oil in coming years, there were still two major problems to which the West had no answer. There were the exorbitant financial demands of the oil-producers; as Zaki Yamani, Saudi Arabia's oil minister, said in Washington, the price of oil 'will be beyond your imagination in 1974.'[24] Or, in the more restrained language of Abder Rahman Khane, the secretary general of O.P.E.C. and a former Algerian Cabinet minister, while the decision by O.A.P.E.C. (the Arab exporting countries) had political overtones, there would be 'economic consequences'.[25] The price squeeze, in other words, would outlive the war. The *Petroleum Press Service*, the leading professional journal, not known for making rash and extremist statements or voicing anti-Arab attitudes, summarized the situation as follows:

The O.P.E.C. governments did more last month [October 1973] than tear up contractual agreements, line their own pockets and indulge in political blackmail. They forced upon the rest of the free world the urgent question whether it is tolerable that the energy supplies which are indispensable to modern ways of life should in future be subject to the will of a small group of exporting countries.[26]

Governments' oil revenues in the Middle East had more than tripled between 1963 and 1972 in Kuwait, they had grown six-fold in Saudi Arabia, eight-fold in Iran, and fifteen-fold in Libya. There was every reason to assume that they would again double, treble or even quadruple between 1972 and 1975. Expressed in per capita income this meant that the income of citizens of Abu Dhabi and Kuwait – ignoring temporary residents – was at least eight times and three times as high as that of the richest industrial country. Per capita income in Libya and Saudi Arabia (for that part of the population which had benefited and was likely to benefit in future from the oil boom) was also considerably in excess of the U.S., Sweden or West Germany. But the real problem was not, of course, that a small number of individuals in the Arab world could amass incredible fortunes; no one would have begrudged them their wealth. The crux of the matter was that the industrialized countries would simply not be able to pay the sums demanded by the producers, and that within several years these few would have a stranglehold on the world monetary system.

European policy-makers no doubt assumed that the oil-producers would show wisdom and restraint and lower their financial demands to a point that would be acceptable to the Western industrialized nations. After all, they had an interest in not pricing themselves out of the market, and they would not wish to cause too much damage to the world financial system; for as a result their holdings, too, would be adversely affected. This assumption was unwarranted, for it ignored the crucial, political dimension. It was apparently taken for granted that ten or fifteen years hence Saudi Arabia would still be ruled by King Faisal or a like-minded successor, Iran by the Shah, and Kuwait and Abu Dhabi by their emirs and sheikhs. It is possible that in some of these countries rulers with moderate ambitions will still be in power, but in most of them it was highly unlikely, precisely because European and Japanese behaviour during the crisis had shown that Arab oil offered an unlimited potential for economic and political blackmail. Whoever ruled the oilfields potentially ruled Europe and Japan. It is unlikely that this lesson will be lost on ambitious, Nasser- or Qadafi-type officers in Saudi Arabia and Iran, let alone in the Persian Gulf mini-states in which power could be seized without undue difficulty by a handful of adventurers. It is even more unlikely that the lesson will be lost on the Soviet Union. Even Brezhnev, the great proponent of détente, congratulated the Arabs on their use of the oil weapon against the West and Japan;[27] was it not likely that other, more aggressive Soviet leaders would sooner or later draw the obvious conclusion that their aims could be attained more quickly, cheaply and effectively by gaining control of the Persian Gulf than by going through the motions of détente which would, at best, give them much more limited gains at some future date?* They would

* This does not, of course, necessarily imply physical occupation of some or all of the oil-producing countries. It would be sufficient to install more or less pro-Soviet regimes, to encourage them in their boycott, total or partial, of America, Europe and Japan and to guarantee them against

of course think twice if they had to face determined Western opposition. But Europe had made it clear by its policy during the crisis that this risk was small: torn by internal strife, militarily impotent, dissociating itself from the senior partner in N A T O, it was in no position to offer effective resistance.

These in short are the likely long-term consequences of European policy. It would be fascinating to search in European history for a similar mixture of foolishness and pusillanimity, lack of foresight and self-deception on the part of its leaders. Probably one would have to go far back to find suitable parallels. As Samuel Johnson once said, 'It must have taken them a great deal of pains to become what they are, for such an excess of stupidity, Sir, is not natural.'

How likely is it that out of the ruins of this policy a more effective common approach will one day emerge? The obvious precondition for any effective Western counter-action is of course unity. This effectively rules out collaboration with Japan, which has made it clear on many past occasions that it will on no account participate in any concerted attempt to resist the demands of the Arab oil-producers. But within Europe, and between Europe and the United States such co-operation is not unthinkable, at least in theory. The next precondition is to reduce demand during the critical years ahead; there is considerable scope for saving fuel all over the world, particularly in the United States with its overheated offices and apartments and its enormous cars.* But there are limits to saving, nor does this by itself provide an answer to the problem. The search

---

Western military action. This would have certain disadvantages from the Soviet point of view for a Western economic slump would adversely affect economic ties between the Soviet Union and the industrialized nations. But against this drawback there is the hope that, if the slump in the West should continue for a long time, the position of the Soviet Union in the Middle East would become much stronger, and it could force Europe and Japan to extend economic support to the Soviet Union which, through its good offices, would ensure a limited supply of Arab oil.

* The United States in 1973 imported one million barrels of oil a day from North Africa and the Middle East – including countries which did not participate in the boycott. Yet turning down American thermostats by a mere three degrees could save 550,000 barrels a day and an all-out conservation programme during the winter would conserve 3.3 million barrels daily. (*Wall Street Journal*, October 25th, 1973)

for oil and gas will be intensified outside the area dominated by the Arab oil-producers; with much effort and a little luck Europe could be largely independent of oil imports some time in the 1980s simply by exploiting the resources in the North Sea and other European waters.[28] Work on other sources of energy such as coal, fission and fusion reactors, geothermal and hydroelectrical power, tar and oil sands, solar power, perhaps even wind-driven generators will be intensified. While oil was cheap these potential resources were neglected; but as oil became so much costlier, their exploitation will be economically viable. But even so there may be ten or more lean years ahead during which a few rich monarchs and dictators will have an effective stranglehold on Western industrial societies unless there is a political, and, if necessary, military answer to their challenge. In a less enlightened age a declaration of economic warfare would have been countered by similar measures and, if the threat was sufficiently serious, by military action. There are many ways of bringing pressure on the Arab oil-producers, such as seizing their financial holdings in the West, but in the last resort only the threat of military action will deter those who have proclaimed their intention 'to ruin Europe'.

This was understood in some Western quarters early on during the crisis. Senator Fulbright, not a superhawk, told the Arab nations that they were militarily insignificant, 'gazelles in a world of lions', and that they should take account of the pressures and temptations to which the powerful industrial nations would be subjected if their economies were threatened by severe and protracted energy crises. The weakness of this argument was of course that of the industrially powerful nations of the West only one was also militarily powerful, and that the oil-producers could turn to the Soviet Union for assistance. Such a policy would be suicidal from their point of view; nor is it altogether unthinkable that the Soviet Union (which also faces a long-term energy problem) might be persuaded to participate together with India and other third-world countries in the internationalization of the world's oil resources. It would not mean, after all, the subjugation of masses of down-trodden colonial people, but the expropriation of a few super-rich monopolists and their retainers for the benefit not of a few oil companies but of the rest of mankind – the reverse of the classical imperialist and colonial situation.

Egypt may be encouraged to take over the Libyan oilfields; Qadafi's antics have become as irritating to Egypt as to the West, and Egypt, in contrast to Libya, desperately needs the oil royalties. The internationalization of the Persian Gulf oil resources could be the major test for détente; in a bygone age Russia and Britain divided part of the Middle East into spheres of influence, and Churchill and Stalin did the same with regard to Europe. In the 'seventies, it is not the fate of large countries and peoples that is at stake, but of sparsely populated sheikhdoms. Such a policy would involve dangers, but the obstacles may not be impossible to overcome, provided, of course, there is the political will of which Europe has shown so little for so long.

The outbreak of the oil war, unlike the fourth Arab-Israeli war, was not a surprise. October 6th, 1973, was merely the beginning of a new stage in a long-drawn-out struggle with a momentum of its own, quite separate from the Arab-Israeli conflict.* The armistice did not affect it, nor would a peace treaty; there will be lulls in the war and temporary agreements, threats and promises. But the basic problem will continue to exist, the prosperity and the security of most Western industrialized nations will be in permanent danger as long as their very existence depends on the mood and ambitions of a few desert monarchs and dictators.

* Douglas-Home and Jobert were firmly convinced for many weeks after the outbreak of the war in the Middle East that it was pointless to deal with the oil problem as such but that the 'political core' should be tackled. They must have been among the last people in Europe to realize that the real danger was not a political embargo but financial extortion and that in this context the Arab-Israel conflict was quite immaterial. When at long last this dawned on them France, followed by Britain, opted with unerring instinct for the wrong approach to cope with the problem: auctioning oil against arms and political independence instead of acting in unison.

Conclusions

On November 11th, 1973, at 3 p.m. local time a six-point agreement was signed by Israeli and Egyptian representatives at the 101 kilometre mark on the Cairo-Suez road. The same day it was announced in Jerusalem that a thorough enquiry would be launched to investigate the alleged lack of preparation at the outbreak of the war and the way it had been conducted. Such enquiries are always welcome to historians but the terms of reference of this enquiry were, to put it mildly, somewhat selective. It was apparently taken for granted that greater Israeli vigilance in early October would have decisively affected the political outcome of the war, and that it would have been over more quickly, despite the fact that Israel no longer had complete mastery of the air over the field of battle. True, there would have been fewer casualties if Israel had been ready on October 6th, 1973. But with the outbreak of the war there would still have been massive political intervention on behalf of Cairo and Damascus from the Soviet Union, and the Arab oil-producing countries would have made cuts and declared a boycott. These, after all, were the vital factors, not the Egyptian and Syrian war machines, which no one expected to win a decisive victory.

Israeli military leaders had under-rated the potential of the adversary, and misread his intentions, a costly but not fatal mistake. In the final analysis Israeli failure was political not military in character, and an enquiry limiting itself to the issue of military preparedness can only arrive at part of the truth, and the smaller part at that. It is impossible to assert even in retrospect that Israel could have won the political as well as the military campaign had it pursued a different line of action. It faced great odds and it might have failed even if it had displayed greater political wisdom and foresight.* What can be safely said is that the settlement likely to

* 'It is no good to be small and alone,' Mrs Meir told the members of the executive of the Socialist International meeting in London in early November. Whereupon Mr Seewoosagur Ramgoolam, prime minister of Mauritius, reportedly advised her that his country too was small but had no problem with her neighbours. He forgot to mention that for a thousand miles there was no neighbour.

emerge after the fourth war will be of the kind that the Israeli Government could have obtained without undue difficulty after the Six Day War. It would have done so with its image unimpaired and without the sacrifices involved in a fourth war. Such a settlement would not have provided a guarantee against a new war but it would have made it less likely. Between the two wars Israel pursued a policy which in the long run was beyond its strength to sustain. Israeli strategy was dictated by considerations of national security in the narrow, military sense, to the detriment of political and economic factors; but even the bravest soldiers cannot fight without ammunition. Mrs Meir's government practised a policy of *immobilisme*; it had no concept for relations with the Arab world, the foreign ministry could take no important initiatives whatsoever. The government ignored developments on the international scene, such as the growing importance of the oil weapon, and Israel's increasing isolation. The 'national opposition' in contrast to the government did have a concept; its only drawback was that it was far more likely to bring about Israel's destruction than its survival. Those trying to get at the historical truth concerning the outbreak of the war in October 1973 and its outcome will be far more interested in the responsibility of the politicians than of the military leaders.

Militarily, Israel was a medium power, but its demographic, political and economic basis was that of a small country; it was not sufficiently aware of its dependence on the United States in an emergency. There were some Israeli leaders who saw the great risks involved in this basic discrepancy but they did not carry enough weight in the inner counsels of the government.

The outcome of the fourth Arab-Israeli war resulted in a field day for Israel's many critics, who interpreted it as a just punishment for Israel's many misdeeds. If the governments of nations were punished for their transgressions the world would have to manage without rulers. In the court of historical justice there is not one law for all; if Israel had been a major oil-producing country, or if it had two dozen submarines with mirved nuclear weapons, it would have been an honoured member of the community of nations. African states would not have broken off diplomatic relations, it would have been wooed by Heath and Pompidou and even the

Soviet Union might have treated it with due respect. These facts are unlikely to detract from the pathos of the moralists, just as some Israeli diehards will no doubt continue to argue that their country suffered a set-back merely because its policy was not aggressive enough. Lunacy, like Proteus, assumes many forms and shapes.

Certain options that were open to Israel before the Six Day War may no longer exist. On the other hand, it seems likely that détente will continue for a decade or two – unless the Soviet Union gains a free hand on its eastern flank and is thus able to pursue a more aggressive policy in Europe and the Middle East. While détente lasts, the understanding between the two super-powers will probably prevent another major Middle-Eastern war. As Israel takes a lower profile, as the 'Israeli danger' recedes and no longer overshadows every other issue in the Middle East, the centrifugal tendencies in the Arab world will reassert themselves. The many unresolved conflicts between 'conservatives' and 'radicals' in the Arab world (and between radicals and radicals) will again come to the fore and the struggle for power in the oil-producing mini-states may well bring about a realignment of forces.

Israel's political failure cannot be explained by reference to any specific mistakes committed by individual leaders. True, there was too much talk during the war, too many promises and boasts – the 'we-shall-break-their-bones' speech of the chief of staff, some of the declarations of Moshe Dayan, and of Mrs Meir. But it is pointless to criticize personalities, to dwell upon Mrs Meir's personal intransigence and lack of imagination when in fact a whole conception had failed. Politics is a cruel business, nowhere is the distance so small between *hosanna* and *crucifige*, between the Capitol and the Tarpeian rock where inefficient leaders were executed in ancient Rome. As the result of the earthquake in Israel yesterday's idols became controversial figures almost overnight: Mrs Meir, whose leadership had been almost undisputed, was found wanting in many respects, Dayan was regarded as a failure by those in the know, and there were recriminations all round. Of the members of the government only Yigal Allon, deputy prime minister, and Pinhas Sapir, minister of finance, emerged with their prestige enhanced. But Allon was in indifferent health, and Sapir, a capable politician, lacked the charisma of a national leader. These two had warned against complacency at a time when it had been unpopular to do so; they had realized well before October 6th, 1973, that the *status quo* could not and should not continue. But even they had not spoken out as loudly and as insistently as they should have done, and their warnings had been ignored. A great deal of self-criticism was needed, a pitiless re-examination of a policy that had been accepted as the collective wisdom for far too long. This was difficult enough for the political establishment to accept; the man in the street was not even fully aware to what extent Israel's freedom of action was limited. The discrepancy between the extreme demands voiced by public opinion and what could be done in reality became a major problem in Israeli domestic politics. The 'national opposition', Mr Begin and his friends, like the Bourbons, had learned and forgotten nothing; they were still living in that dream world in which everything seemed possible, provided only American Jewry would help and the government would show inflexible resolution and would not give up a single inch of territory. Thus, at the end of the war there were in Israel all the ingredients for a major crisis; it was not clear whether the country would emerge from this test stronger than before or whether it would soon be engulfed in a fratricidal struggle such as had once before in history caused the destruction of the Jewish State.

The fourth war would have ended with an Israeli military victory had it lasted a few days longer. But quite apart from the fact that the super-powers effectively prevented it, such a victory would have changed little as far as the political results are concerned. Egyptian political strategy was sound: the only way to regain the lost territories, or at any rate most of them, was through a new war, even though militarily the Egyptians certainly could not win it. It could be taken for granted that the Soviet Union, since its prestige was so deeply involved, would support the Arabs, and that a conflict which had been half forgotten would suddenly re-emerge as a major threat to world peace. It was the only way to induce the U.S. Government to regard the conflict with a greater measure of urgency and to bring pressure on Israel. True, there was the danger that a confrontation between the super-powers would bring about a dictated settlement, but in the circumstances this was bound to be more in Egypt's favour than the *status quo*. Had war not broken out, the

Arab oil-producers might not have made such effective use of the oil weapon; in the general climate engendered by the *jihad* they could do no less. Lastly, the war was likely to show the full extent of Israel's political isolation, even though it had not been the aggressor. The Egyptians and the Syrians kept the secret of the attack well, something which had been thought unlikely by friend and foe alike. They fought well, particularly in the early stages of the war; the Egyptian Army, once the butt of many jokes, regained its self-confidence to a large degree. But it was also true that the Arabs were saved from major defeat only owing to massive Soviet help. Since such help is seldom, if ever, in politics totally disinterested, it was clear that they would have to pay for it and not only in money.

On the morning after there was as much disappointment in Egypt and Syria as in Israel. The Arabs had been led to believe that victory was around the corner and that the ceasefire had saved Israel from final defeat. It was therefore with shock and disbelief that they realized when the war was over that the Israelis were in fact nearer Cairo and Damascus than before October 6th, 1973. There was talk of a fifth round and a sixth. But there was also the uncomfortable prospect that a future war might be fought with even more destructive weapons, and in such a war Egypt would be at least as vulnerable as Israel. Much depended now on Israel's willingness to reach a settlement with Egypt – and Egypt's ability to accept and keep it, irrespective of the bellicose non-combatants in the Arab world willing to continue the war to total victory and the last Egyptian soldier. There was as much bitter mutual recrimination in the Arab world as in Israel. The Iraqis withdrew their forces from Syria because they rejected the armistice; the Syrians complained that the Egyptians had not come to their help when they were under attack on the Golan; everyone was angry with King Husain who (they claimed) had not done enough for the common cause; and Colonel Qadafi, who had never heard a shot fired in anger, airily dismissed it all as an 'operetta war'. Israel had managed to unite the quarrelsome Arab world instead of trying to reach a settlement with Egypt. But would this new unity last?

Arab propaganda was on the whole more restrained than in 1967, but only while the going was good on the field of battle. Sadat frequently referred to the Israelis as the 'heirs of Hitlerism' which was apparently not meant as a compliment despite the fact that the Egyptian president had been an enthusiastic Axis collaborator during the Second World War, which led to his arrest by the long-suffering British authorities. Egypt emphasized that its intention was not to destroy Israel but simply to regain the lost territories. It also demanded justice for the Palestinian Arabs, which was fair enough; unfortunately, it was not at all certain whether the spokesmen of the Palestinians were ready to accept the very existence of the State of Israel. Even Syria kept silent in the beginning as far as its war aims were concerned; shortly before the outbreak of war it even announced its acceptance of Resolution 242, which it had rejected for the six previous years. But again, there were narrow limits to Syria's restraint and on October 15th, 1973, President Asad proclaimed that Syria's target was not just to regain the Golan Heights but a 'war of total liberation'. Soviet diplomatic envoys tried to persuade the Syrians that it was unwise to make public declarations of this kind, but they were not too successful.

The Soviet leaders had reason to be satisfied with the outcome of the fourth Arab-Israeli war; whether they acted wisely inasmuch as their long-term interests were concerned only the future will tell. That Egypt and Syria launched their attack with Soviet knowledge and connivance goes without saying. The Soviet leaders probably did not actually encourage the Arabs to go to war, though they could have prevented the war as on previous occasions by withholding fresh supplies of war material. But in this case they would have lost face and political influence; having to choose between this risk and the danger of a temporary strain in relations with the United States, they opted for what appeared to be the lesser evil. The Soviet Union has no vested interest in the restoration of peace in the Middle East and it will view with disfavour any move towards peace in the Middle East that does not strengthen its own position in the area. Its clients did better militarily than before and they made political gains. But the cost for the Soviet Union was considerable, both financially and politically. The Soviet Union demonstrated the excellence of some of its weapons, but at heavy cost; for this demonstration was bound to result in a new round of the arms race; the military lessons would not pass unnoticed in the West. Détente, for which the Soviet leaders had worked for years, suffered a set-back. True, the danger of nuclear war did not increase, but the Soviet leaders had hoped for massive loans and other forms of assistance from the United States. The big Western industrial concerns and banks were only too willing to oblige, but they could not do so without State support and guarantees, and these became more difficult to obtain. It is interesting and politically significant that support for close co-operation with the Soviet Union in the United States is strongest among big business and weakest among the trade unions and there is not much enthusiasm left of centre.

It is difficult to assess Soviet gains: its clients in the Middle East were no more reliable and grateful than before the war; the Arabs had expected even more help than the Kremlin could provide. The war was bound to produce new recriminations and suspicions, and an attempt to lessen Arab military dependence on the Soviet Union. The Soviet Union regards the Middle East as an area in which Soviet influence should be predominant and it has a specific interest in gaining control of the Persian Gulf. At the end of the war it was not much nearer to realizing this aim than before. The greatest Soviet achievement was indirect and perhaps unexpected: the rift in the Atlantic Alliance. Everyone knew about Europe's weakness – everyone but the Americans, who had exaggerated notions about the strength and the reliability of its allies. In October 1973 this fiction was destroyed, a painful but salutary lesson for American policy-makers. The same goes for détente in general. In the Middle-East crisis the Soviet Union had followed a fairly aggressive strategy, trying at one and the same time to reap the benefits of détente and to gain advantages over its adversary contrary to the letter and the spirit of its understanding with the United States. That it would act in this way few students of Soviet policy had ever doubted, but among the general public there had been widespread misconceptions which Soviet policy during the crisis helped to dispel to some extent. True, détente in one form or another is likely to continue, just as the Atlantic Alliance will somehow be patched up, but after the immediate crisis had passed Americans had a much clearer idea of what to expect of friend and foe.

The crisis in N A T O had been brewing for a long time, but a moment of truth was needed to show America that the governments of Europe would run for cover the moment their assistance was requested. Having to choose between assuring their oil supply and solidarity with the senior partner in the alliance, the answer given by the European capitals was unambiguous. As a result serious doubts were bound to arise in American minds. Would the Europeans not react the same way facing any pressure from outside? Would they fight if attacked? Did Europe still have the will to resist or would it always choose the line of least resistance?

Some critics of American foreign policy argued that the U.S. had not acted in its own best interests in giving support to Israel. But the moment the Soviet leaders made it clear that they would give all-out support to Egypt and Syria, the United States, despite certain misgivings, could not stay aloof. Its interests in the Middle East, needless to say, were not restricted to the existence of Israel, and these interests were bound to be affected, as the expropriation of certain oil installations and the oil embargo were to show. But the oil companies' holdings would have been expropriated anyway, perhaps a year or two later. At the end of the war America found itself in the unaccustomed position of being wooed by the leading Arab countries, who had realized that effective pressure could be brought to bear on Israel only by Washington. During the war and its aftermath there were no frantic attacks against America as in 1967; on the contrary, the general tenor of Sadat's speeches was friendly, and leading Egyptian diplomats began to appear in Washington almost the moment the war ended. Kissinger's visit to Cairo was another signal pointing to an actual improvement in U.S.-Arab relations. America has shown firmness during the crisis; as a result it was not any better loved by the Arabs, but unlike the Europeans it had earned their respect. Kissinger's policy in the crisis was based on shrewd judgment and good timing. He certainly did not want a decisive Israeli victory which would only have made the task of peace-making more difficult, and he regarded the crisis, as did others in Washington, as a major nuisance, for it threatened the whole détente edifice in which he had invested so much effort. He announced that the Soviet Union was acting responsibly, not because it was, but because he hoped that a further deterioration in relations with the Russians could be prevented. He tried to placate and to find common ground; having given vital support to Israel during the crisis, it was obvious that America would lean heavily on Israel to force it to make major concessions. The result, as in Vietnam and in other contexts, was likely to be a postponement of the day of reckoning.

For Britain, France, West Germany, Italy and the smaller countries, the Middle-East crisis was the hour of truth after more than a decade of indecision, weakness and the erosion of political will. Broadly speaking, two courses of action had been open to West Europe in the post-war period: they could have regarded the Atlantic Alliance as the main anchor of their security, giving due consideration to the military, political and economic interests of the senior partner in the alliance. Alternatively, Europe could have pursued a third-force policy, independent of the two super-powers; De Gaulle and his successors, who were the leading advocates of such a line of action, were also the main stumbling block on the road to European unity. For a truly independent European policy was possible only on the basis of both a credible defence effort and a far larger measure of political unity. There were frequent meetings between European leaders but there was no concerted policy: in a crisis every country would always put its own economic and political interests first. A third-force policy of this kind was of uncertain value, because there was nothing to replace the American nuclear umbrella. Thus the Europeans neither tried to make a serious effort to join forces and to pursue an independent policy nor were they willing to draw the obvious conclusions from their dependence on America. The Atlantic Alliance as far as they were concerned was a more or less one-sided undertaking on America's part; the United States was obliged to defend Europe, whereas Western Europe had few, if any, obligations vis-à-vis the senior partner in the alliance. Such a policy was bound to lead to a breakdown sooner or later; the Atlanticists in America had been fighting an uphill struggle even before the war of 1973, and Europe's behaviour during the crisis undermined American support for NATO even further. The majority of West Europeans – as a British weekly put it – could not see the connection between their own precarious situation (being unable to defend themselves against the Soviet Union) and what was happening across the Mediterranean: 'They would not help the United States to do for someone else what they wanted it to do for them.'[1] Europe was so fearful of the immediate problem facing it that it failed to take into account the far more serious long-range dangers.

Thus at a time of crisis Europe was reduced to the role of a passive onlooker. There was much indignation in view of the fact that it had not been consulted and there were futile gestures. America, it was said, would in future have to take the interests of its allies into account; the Europeans would get together and co-ordinate their policy. But such announcements failed to carry any conviction; when Europe had found it almost impossible to agree on the price of butter and sugar, the idea that it would be able to collaborate on far-reaching issues of foreign and defence policy seemed altogether fanciful.

The basic assumption underlying European behaviour during the crisis was that it would be possible to safeguard a normal supply of oil and that America, sooner or later, would have second thoughts about the wisdom of its policy and would again give Europe full backing. As a result of this miscalculation, the European leaders found themselves in the uncomfortable and slightly ridiculous position of being seated between two stools: on the one hand they had clearly over-rated American patience, and, on the other hand, they had failed to realize that, even if they succeeded in averting the immediate oil crisis, European industry and its security now depended on the goodwill of the oil sheikhs and whoever would succeed them. The way to resist the pressure of the oil sheikhs and colonels, politically, or, if necessary, by military force, was, of course, through concerted action together with the United States. Given the internal weakness of the countries of Europe and the lack of unity the prospects for such action could not be rated high.

Thus the crisis of 1973, far from acting as a spur to European unity, hastened the process of disintegration. In the past there had been a balance of power in Europe and it did not greatly matter whether one or two of the smaller countries, such as Sweden, used the opportunity to get a free ride as far as the defence of Europe was concerned. Western Europe as a whole cannot opt for neutrality because but for the alliance with the United States there is no equilibrium of forces and thus no freedom of manoeuvre and no room for neutrality. In this constellation the Soviet Union emerges as the dominant force on the Continent; the road leads not to independence and neutrality but to the Soviet sphere of influence. It is sad to watch the progressive degradation of a Continent which was once the political, cultural and economic centre of mankind. But if this is going to be Europe's fate, it will not be undeserved: 'Little people become their little fate.' (Horace)

The coming of the fourth Arab-Israeli war could be foreseen. Concluding my *The Road to War*, dealing with the origins and the aftermath of the Arab-Israeli conflict 1967-8, I wrote:

An air of fatality broods over the Middle East in which a fourth round seems likely in the not-too-distant future. If it comes it will be fought with more destructive weapons than last time, and the escalation into a conflict between the super-powers can never be quite ruled out ... The Soviet Union according to all that is known, does not want a nuclear confrontation with the United States, but its policy in the Middle East also shows that it is now willing to take higher risks in pursuing its aims, and this in an area where it probably cannot prevent escalation. This greater willingness to take calculated risks may have to do with the fear of losing influence in the third world, or being outmanoeuvred by China. There is a real anger with the Jews and a genuine resurgence of anti-semitism in high quarters in Russia, as traditional communist international ideology gives way to a new nationalism ... At this juncture the historian may be excused for discarding his customary caution and detachment: Cassandra takes over from Clio. Since the war Israel has not displayed a high order of political wisdom: military operations were obviously far better planned than post-war policy. There, as elsewhere, politicians and military leaders have many immediate pre-occupations; little time and energy are left for the quiet consideration of long term perspectives. Bigger and more fortunate countries may be able to afford this, for in the end they will somehow muddle through. In the case of Israel such neglect may have fatal consequences. However unlikely an agreement with the Arabs may at present be, approaches have to be made with an eye to the more distant future; Israeli policy vis-à-vis the Arab governments has to be based on the philosophy of the 'as if'. There are enormous risks involved and there is no guarantee whatever of success. The Israelis will have to talk to the Palestinian Arabs and the refugee organizations. The refugee problem remains a festering sore, yet, since the war, no constructive programme for its treatment has been prepared by the Israeli government ... The Arabs should be told that their present policy will lead them to further disasters. The existence of Israel may be a crying injustice in their eyes and their defeats a terrible blow to their national self-esteem. But they cannot hope to achieve more than a honourable settlement which would include Israeli concessions and a solution of the refugee question. The idea that with more effective weapons, a new war will bring a decision is even more dangerous; at the most the Arabs could destroy Israel at the price of their own suicide. In the unreal world in which they live, it seems not to have occurred to them that, if faced with the destruction of their state and the annihilation of their people, the Israelis, like Samson, would probably prefer to die with the Philistines, bringing down with them more than the 'ten millions' which some of the Arab Maoists are willing to sacrifice. Today these are apocalyptic visions, fairly soon they may be reality.[2]

Five years and one war later there is little to add to these lines.

Notes

CHAPTER ONE

1. Speech at Cairo University, April 25th, 1968, quoted in R. Stephens, *Nasser* (Allen Lane, London, 1971), p. 510.

2. Lawrence C. Whetten, 'June 1967 to June 1971' in *New Middle East*, June 1971.

3. *Strategic Survey*, 1970, p. 46.

4. Edward Luttwak: 'The Military Balance' in *New Middle East*, September 1972, p. 15; see also Luttwak in *New Middle East*, December 1971, p. 10.

5. Dan Margalit, *Sheder mehabayit halavan* (Tel Aviv, 1971), p. 55.

6. Quoted in Stephens, op. cit., p. 541.

7. The testimony was published in the Beirut daily *Al Nahar* in September 1971. It has been summarized and analysed in a valuable article by P. H. Vatikiotis, 'Egypt's Politics of Conspiracy' in *Survey*, spring 1972, pp. 83-99.

8. *The Military Balance 1973/4* (I.I.S.S., London, 1973), p. 31.

9. M. Burrell, *The Persian Gulf*, Washington Papers 1, New York, 1972, p. 77.

10. Gideon Rafael, 'U.N. Resolution 242' in *New Middle East*, June 1973.

11. David Kimche and Dan Bawly, *The Sandstorm* (Secker and Warburg, London, 1968), p. 272.

12. The official record of the Jarring mission is in U.N. document S/10070 submitted to the Security Council on January 4th, 1971.

13. For an account of the events during spring and summer 1970 see Margaliti, *Strategic Survey*, 1970; Yair Evron, *The Middle East* (Elek Books, London, 1973), pp. 110, et seq.

14. R. Stephens, op. cit., pp. 527-8.

15. Evron, op. cit., p. 214.

16. *Jerusalem Post*, October 29th, 1967.

17. *Ha'aretz*, September 22nd, 1967; quoted in *Middle East Record, 1967* (Keter, Jerusalem, 1971), p. 376.

18. *Ha'aretz*, December 15th, 1967; quoted in *Middle East Record, 1967*, p. 377.

19. A. Eliav, *Eretz Hazvi* (Am Oved, Tel Aviv, 1972).

20. For a brief summary of Israeli attitudes see Y. Ben Porat in *New Middle East*, December 1972.

21. Prime Minister Eshkol in a statement in the Knesset, October 30th, 1967.

22. *Al Ahram*, February 21st, 1969; quoted in Y. Harkabi, *Arab Attitudes to Israel* (Israel Universities Press, Jerusalem, 1972), p. 473.

CHAPTER TWO

1. Cairo Radio, June 12th, 1973.
2. Interview with the Zagreb newspaper *Vjesnik*, May 28th, 1973.
3. *Al Ahram*, July 12th, 1973.
4. *Mena*, July 14th, 1973.
5. *Vjesnik*, op. cit.
6. Radio Tripoli, October 2nd, 1973.
7. *Al Ahram*, May 26th, 1973.
8. Radio Tripoli, August 17th, 1973.
9. Radio Tripoli, July 23rd, 1973.
10. Cairo Radio, August 13th, 1973.
11. *Al Balegh*, August 14th, 1973.
12. *Al Raj*, September 13th, 1973; *Al Dustur*, September 13th, 1973.
13. *Al Nahar*, September 23rd, 1973.
14. Voice of Palestine, September 30th, 1973.
15. *Al Ahram*, September 26th, 1973.
16. *Jerusalem Post*, August 10th, 1973.
17. Yoel Markus, *Ha'aretz*, October 4th, 1973.
18. *Jerusalem Post*, Weekly Overseas Edition, October 2nd, 1973.
19. *Yediot Ahronot*, August 16th, 1973.
20. Sh. Tevet, *Moshe Dayan* (Weidenfeld and Nicolson, London, 1972), p. 341.
21. Radio Algeria, October 9th, 1973.
22. Radio Kampala, October 10th, 1973.
23. *Le Monde*, October 13th, 1973.
24. *New York Times*, October 13th, 1973.
25. *Al Ahram*, October 5th, 1973; *Pravda*, October 6th, 1973; Iraqi News Agency, October 3rd, 1973.
26. Radio Damascus, October 4th, 1973.
27. Cairo Radio, September 28th, 1973.
28. *Ha'aretz*, October 4th, 1973.

CHAPTER THREE

1. *Yediot Ahronot*, November 10th, 1973.
2. *Ma'ariv*, November 2nd, 1973.
3. *Jerusalem Post*, October 8th, 1973.
4. *Jerusalem Post*, October 9th, 1973.
5. *Jerusalem Post*, October 9th, 1973.
6. *Jerusalem Post*, October 10th, 1973.
7. *The Times* (London), October 12th, 1973.
8. Radio Damascus, October 6th, 1973.
9. Cairo Radio, October 7th, 1973.
10. *Al Anwar*, October 11th, 1973.
11. *Al Ahram*, October 17th, 1973.
12. Radio Damascus, October 15th, 1973.
13. *Neue Zürcher Zeitung*, October 11th, 1973.
14. *Le Monde*, October 9th, 1973.

15. *Le Monde*, October 10th; *Figaro*, October 16th, 1973.

16. *Pravda*, October 14th, 1973.

17. *Frankfurter Allgemeine Zeitung*, October 16th 1973; *Corriere della Sera*, October 11th, 1973.

18. *Le Monde*, October 24th, 1973; *Figaro*, October 24th, 1973; *Corriere della Sera*, October 25th, 1973.

19. General Haim Bar Lev, 'The lesson of the war', *Ma'ariv*, November 9th, 1973.

20. *Bamahane*, October 31st, 1973.

CHAPTER FOUR

1. 'Central Issues of American Foreign Policy' in *Agenda for the Nation* (The Brookings Institution, 1968).

2. US-Soviet Commercial Relations: The Interplay of Economics, Technology, Transfer and Diplomacy, June 10th, 1973.

3. *Frankfurter Allgemeine Zeitung*, October 9th, 1973.

4. *Le Monde*, October 9th, 1973.

5. *New York Times*, October 7th, 1973; *Washington Post*, October 8th, 1973.

6. *Daily Telegraph*, October 8th, 1973.

7. *The Times* (London), October 10th, 1973.

8. *International Herald Tribune*, October 11th, 1973.

9. *New York Times*, October 15th, 1973.

10. *Daily Telegraph*, October 13th, 1973.

11. *International Herald Tribune*, October 13th/14th, 1973.

12. *Washington Post*, October 17th, 1973.

13. *Ma'ariv*, October 19th, 1973; *Sunday Times* (London), October 21st, 1973.

14. *Le Monde*, October 18th, 1973.

15. *Figaro*, October 16th, 1973; *Le Monde*, October 16th, 1973.

16. *Le Monde*, October 20th, 1973.

17. *International Herald Tribune*, October 20th/21st, 1973.

18. *New York Times*, October 18th; *Figaro*, October 19th, 1973.

19. *Jen Min Jih Pao*, quoted by Peking Radio, October 8th, 1973.

20. *Hsin hua*, October 8th, 1973.

21. *Keyhan*, October 9th, 1973.

22. Nairobi Radio, October 20th, 1973; *Neue Zürcher Zeitung*, October 24th, 1973.

23. Kampala Radio, October 24th, 1973.

24. Raymond Aron, *Figaro*, October 20th, 1973.

25. *Daily Telegraph*, October 19th, 1973.

26. *Frankfurter Allgemeine Zeitung*, October 26th, 1973.

27. *Daily Telegraph*, October 26th, 1973.

28. *New York Times*, October 27th, 1973.

29. A. Weinstein, *Frankfurter Allgemeine Zeitung*, October 20th, 1973.

30. Theo Sommer, *Newsweek*, October 27th, 1973.

1. *New York Times*, October 18th, 1973; M E N A, October 18th 1973; T A N J U G, October 18th, 1973.

2. *New York Times*, October 21st, 1973.

3. Tass, October 21st, 1973.

4. *Pravda*, August 20th, August 30th, 1973.

5. *Izvestia*, September 11th, 1973.

6. *S. Sh. A.*, July 1973 (Arbatov).

7. *Krasnaia Zvesda*, August 14th, 1973.

8. *Pravda*, September 5th, 1973.

9. *Pravda*, August 16th, 1973.

10. *Pravda*, August 16th, 1973.

11. *Literaturnaia Gazetta*, August 15th, 1973.

12. *Pravda*, October 4th, 1973.

13. B.T.A., October 3rd, 1973.

14. *Pravda*, October 7th, 1973.

15. *Pravda*, October 8th, 1973.

16. *Pravda*, October 16th, 1973.

17. Agence France Press, November 14th, 1973.

18. *Literaturnaia Gazetta*, October 17th, 1973; *Krasnaia Zvesda*, October 19th, 1973.

19. *Krasnaia Zvesda*, November 14th, 1973.

20. *Jerusalem Post*, October 22nd, 1973.

21. *Ma'ariv*, October 26th, 1973.

22. *Le Monde*, October 23rd, 1973.

23. *Washington Post*, October 26th, 1973.

24. *New York Times*, October 24th, 1973.

25. Radio Damascus, October 24th, 1973.

26. Radio Damascus, October 23rd, 1973.

27. Ibid.

28. *Jerusalem Post*, October 23rd, 1973.

29. *Daily Telegraph*, October 24th, 1973.

30. Tass, October 23rd, 1973.

31. M E N A, October 24th, 1973.

32. *International Herald Tribune*, October 25th, 1973.

33. Ibid.

34. *Washington Post*, October 26th, 1973.

35. *Aviation Week*, November 5th, 1973.

36. *New York Times*, October 26th, 1973.

37. Ibid.

38. *Washington Post*, October 26th, 1973.

39. *New York Times*, October 27th, 1973.

40. Ibid.

41. Michel Tatu, 'Que s'est-il passé le 25 octobre', *Le Monde*, November 3rd, 1973.

42. *Izvestia*, October 26th, 1973.

43. *Pravda*, October 27th, 1973.

44. *International Herald Tribune*, October 29th, 1973.

45. *New York Times*, October 27th, 1973.
46. *New York Times*, October 31st, 1973.
47. *The Times* (London), October 30th, 1973.
48. *The Economist*, November 3rd, 1973.
49. *The Times* (London), October 29th, 1973.
50. *Frankfurter Allgemeine Zeitung*, October 20th, 1973.
51. *Daily Telegraph*, November 7th, 1973.
52. *The Times* (London), November 7th, 1973.
53. *Neue Zürcher Zeitung*, November 11th, 1973.
54. *New York Times*, November 3rd, 1973.
55. *Washington Post*, November 9th, 1973.
56. *International Herald Tribune*, November 14th, 1973.
57. *Ma'ariv*, November 2nd, 1973.
58. *Jerusalem Post*, October 31st, 1973.
59. *Ma'ariv*, November 9th, 1973.
60. *Jerusalem Post*, November 12th, 1973.
61. *Al Ahram*, November 2nd, 1973.
62. *Al Ahram*, November 6th, 1973.
63. *Al Ahram*, November 6th, 1973; *Christian Science Monitor*, November 7th, 1973.
64. *New York Times*, November 8th, 1973.
65. Cairo Radio, November 7th, 1973.
66. *Jerusalem Post*, November 9th, 1973.
67. *Jerusalem Post*, November 11th, 1973.
68. *Al Nahar*, November 11th, 1973.
69. *New York Times*, November 14th, 1973; *Daily Telegraph*, November 14th, 1973.
70. C. Sulzberger, *An Age of Mediocrity*, Macmillan, New York 1973, p. 654.

CHAPTER SIX

1. *Washington Post*, November 14th, 1973.
2. *Petroleum Press Service*, October 1973.
3. Baghdad Radio, October 7th, 1973.
4. *Daily News* (Kuwait), October 8th, 1973.
5. *Al Thawra*, October 10th, 1973.
6. Kuwait Radio, October 9th, 1973.
7. Baghdad Radio, October 11th, 1973.
8. *Daily News* (Kuwait), October 18th, 1973.
9. Iraqi News Agency, October 18th, 1973.
10. *New York Times*, October 18th, 1973.
11. J. W. Anderson, *Washington Post*, October 18th, 1973.
12. *Christian Science Monitor*, October 12th, 1973.
13. *International Herald Tribune*, October 24th, 1973.
14. *Le Monde*, October 24th, 1973; *Osservatore della Domenica*, November 11th, 1973; *Die Welt*, November 16th, 1973.
15. *Der Spiegel*, November 12th, 1973.
16. *New York Times*, November 7th, 1973.

17. *Sunday Times* (London), November 4th, 1973.
18. *Daily Telegraph*, November 17th, 1973.
19. *Sunday Times*, November 14th, 1973.
20. *Die Zeit*, November 9th, 1973.
21. *Der Spiegel*, November 4th, 1973.
22. Andrew Shonfield, *The Times* (London), November 12th, 1973.
23. *The Economist*, November 10th, 1973.
24. *The Economist*, November 17th, 1973.
25. *Daily News* (Kuwait), November 11th, 1973.
26. *Petroleum Press Service*, November 1973.
27. *Pravda*, November 9th, 1973.
28. *The Economist*, November 10th, 1973.

CONCLUSIONS

1. *The Economist*, November 2nd, 1973.
2. Walter Laqueur, *The Road to War* (Weidenfeld and Nicolson, London, 1968).

Index

Hundred Hours, War of (1956), 78, 80, 82
Husain, King, 23, 26, 29, 42, 48-9, 50, 53, 142, 194, 226: suppresses Palestinian revolt, 49-50; proposes federation with West Bank, 50; at Cairo meeting, 51-2

INDIA, 13, 57, 152, 204, 213
Iran, 46, 54, 152, 218: as oil producer, 197-8 and n, 201-3, 217; economic and political stability of, 204-5; attitude to oil weapon, 210
Iraq, 24, 49, 54, 67, 194, 204, 226: hostile to Egypt, 9, 171; relations with Russia, 15, 18, 20; as oil producer, 20, 197 and n, 201, 207; attitude to oil weapon, 207-8
Ismail, Ahmed, 54, 106
Ismail, Hafez, 39, 41, 54
Israel: after Six Day War, 1, 31-2, 36; in subsequent fighting, 2-8; at United Nations (1967), 22-5; policy of conciliation (1970-71), 25-7; subsequent hardening of attitude, 28-9; relations with America, 28, 59, 143, 145, 147, 151, 171-3, 187-90; relations with Jordan, 29, 50; political views in, for and against annexation, 33-6, 37; hostility towards Syria, 53-4; social and political conditions on eve of Yom Kippur War, 54-8, 62-6, 74-6; reaction to Arab terrorism, 60-62; general military strategy, 78-87; during Yom Kippur War, 88 ff., 108-9, 112-16; conditions on home front, 103-5; at United Nations, 144-5; growing isolation of, 151 ff., 216; Russian attacks on, 164-5, 166-7, 168-9, 173; accepts first ceasefire, 171; accepts second ceasefire, 173, 192-193; oil weapon aimed against, 207-14; summing up of military strategy, 222-6, 232-3
Italy, 57, 157, 183, 210, 215

JACKSON, SENATOR HENRY, 175, 209

Jackson Amendment, 163
Japan, 139, 140, 164: as oil consumer, 47, 198-9, 207, 211, 219
Jarring, Gunnar, 24-8
Jerusalem, 15, 26, 29, 32, 35, 47, 65, 79, 152, 173
Jobert, Michel, 63, 153-4, 157, 182, 185
Jordan, 24, 30, 40, 42, 47, 51-2, 53, 114, 171, 205: civil war in, 9, 27, 49-50; policy of conciliation towards Israel, 22, 29, 50, 53; rapprochement with Egypt and Syria, 51, 54, 71; part in Yom Kippur War, 90, 98, 104, 148
Jordan, River, 33, 36, 52, 98, 104

KAMEL, AHMED, 10
Khartoum conference, 2, 36
Kilometre 101, 193, 222
Kissinger, Henry, 66-7, 69, 89, 119, 129, 131, 137, 139-40, 162, 179; relations with Russian leaders, 71 n, 74, 123, 126-7, 134, 137-8, 141, 147, 167, 170, 175, 176-7; and Vietnam settlement, 123-4; and SALT talks, 123, 124, 125; relations with China, 123, 128; with Europe, 129-31, 181, 185; during Yom Kippur War, 142-51, 160, 161; visits Moscow, 158, 159, 160, 169-70, 180; visits Tel Aviv, 161, 171-3; negotiates for Middle-East peace, 187-95, 230; character and aims, 119-22
Kosygin, Alexei, 13, 22, 23, 161, 163, 167: visits Cairo, 150, 159-60
Kreisky, Bruno, 61-2, 76
Kuddous, Ihsan Abdul, 41, 67
Kuwait, 51, 150, 152: as oil producer, 197 and n, 201-3, 217-18; vulnerability to attack, 205; support of oil weapon, 207-8

LABOUR ALIGNMENT, 34, 63, 65
Laird, Melvin, 147-8, 210
Levy, Walter J., 197-9, 202
Liberation, War of (1948-9), 79, 81
Libya, 9, 41-3, 51, 67, 147, 152-4, 171, 194: proposes unity with